Between Love and Hate

A Guide to Civilized Divorce

Lois Gold, M.S.W.

Plenum Press • New York and London

Library of Congress Cataloging-in-Publication Data

Gold, Lois.
    Between love and hate : a guide to civilized divorce / Lois Gold.
       p.   cm.
    Includes bibliographical references and index.
    ISBN 0-306-44132-2
    1. Divorce--United States--Handbooks, manuals, etc.
  2. Communication in divorce mediation--United States--Handbooks,
  manuals, etc. 3. Communication in marriage--United States-
  -Handbooks, manuals, etc.   I. Title.
  HQ834.G65 1992
  306.89--dc20
                                         91-46192
                                           CIP

This book is a guide to coping constructively with the complexities of divorce. It is not intended as a substitute for legal advice.

ISBN 0-306-44132-2

© 1992 Lois Gold
Plenum Press is a division of Plenum Publishing Corporation
233 Spring Street, New York, N.Y. 10013

Printed in the United States of America

To the memory of my parents,
Joseph and Jeanne Kane

Foreword

JOAN B. KELLY, Ph.D.

I was troubled by the recent movie *War of the Roses*—troubled because of the message that such hateful and destructive behavior was the American way for divorcing couples; troubled because the print media made much of this poisonous manner of ending a marriage; troubled because it is evident, from my own and others' research, and from my mediation and psychotherapy experience, that the majority of divorcing spouses do *not* act like the protagonists in this movie; troubled because mediation clients who are working hard at divorcing with some restraint and dignity despite their anger occasionally ask me, with bewilderment, if they are *abnormal* in their attempt to divorce with civility. What was most sad about *War of the Roses*, finally, was that it vividly expressed our society's continuing acceptance, if not outright encouragement, of the hostile divorce.

Between Love and Hate is a powerful antidote to that message. It appears at a perfect time. We have learned much in the past decade about men and women whose marriages ended in divorce. Research has not supported the common belief that all divorcing men and women have extreme conflict, want revenge, can't cooperate about their children, and wish the other dead. This extreme stereotype, perpetuated by attorneys, judges, and the media, applies to perhaps 20 to 25 percent of divorcing individuals. Because of their intense distress and repeated destructive behavior, this minority commands the lion's share of society's attention and a disproportionate amount of the courts' resources. It is self-defeating for our society to continue to view this group as the norm, because it deters needed change within the legal system, among family and friends, and within individuals.

More positive for the future of our families is evidence that the majority of separating parents *do* have some residual ability to communicate and cooperate about their children. They are moderately angry at their spouse but not consumed with hatred. And two years after the divorce the number of parents reporting cooperation about their children increases and the number of spouses reporting high levels of anger and difficulty in communicating declines.

What we have come to understand is that couples divorce for very different reasons. Not all of those reasons are associated with high anger levels, destructive conflict, and punitive behaviors. An increasingly large group of American men and women divorce because they have gradually grown apart, love and intimacy giving way over the years to indifference. They do not divorce with great anger but, more often, in sadness, and they do not wish the other spouse harm. They seek divorce agreements that seem fair and supportive of each other's and their children's needs.

Other men and women divorce for reasons of serious lifestyle and value differences or because of the mental illness or substance abuse of a spouse or because there has been emotional and/or physical abuse and violence. There is more anger and conflict in these divorces, and considerably less ability to communicate, but there is no common yardstick of anger and volatility that applies to these divorces either. Some are extremely combative, falling into that extreme group that will require continuing legal intervention; others are much less so.

Among all of these groups of divorcing men and women are those who seek to divorce with less rancor and wish for the skills, a different decision-making forum, and the family's or community's encouragement to divorce in a way that allows them to preserve some dignity and self-esteem and that protects their children from unnecessary risk and harm.

Between Love and Hate is a wonderful book. Immensely readable, very human, at times quite moving, it is packed with information that will help couples divorce in a more civilized way. It is an excellent resource as well for mediators, psychotherapists, and attorneys who assist divorcing couples. Lois Gold has managed the difficult task of integrating diverse fields of knowledge and expertise, including family systems theory and practice, communication skills, negotiation theory and mediation concepts and skills, research on divorcing adults and children, and clinical observation. This book could have been three books, each quite separate, focusing on the adult process of disengaging from marriage and moving toward healing, parenting during and after divorce, and preparing for and successfully mediating divorce agreements. It is extremely helpful for the reader experiencing the bewildering facets of divorce to have these difficult processes combined in a way that mirrors their reality.

Between Love and Hate stands out among a large number of books available for divorcing men and women. One of the things that distinguished it from others is the extent to which readers are given genuine help in learning about and beginning the process of separating their behavior from their strong feelings. A wide range of exercises and self-evaluation tools are provided for the reader to take multiple steps toward achieving a civilized divorce: checklists, written and visualization exercises, brief questionnaires, key pointers, practical advice, sample letters, and symbolic gestures and rituals—each is intended to promote more rational thinking, more effective action, more enlightened self-interest, and, ultimately, healing and a moving forward.

Between Love and Hate has charted the high road. The book invites divorcing spouses to consciously choose a better course of action, explains why it is in their self-interest to do so, and provides the tools necessary to achieve the goals of civility and dignity. The author continually acknowledges the powerful and normal feelings of anger, of wanting to hit back, of wanting to flee from interaction, of wanting to embroil the children in loyalty conflicts. The pain that divorce parties experience is never given short shrift, but that pain is set within a broader perspective of what the individual may gain in the longer term. Civilized divorces increase and preserve self-esteem, empower the participants, promote a healthier adjustment for children and adults, and enable parents to retain or improve their working partnership on behalf of the children.

It is instructive to talk to those youngsters whose parents are attempting to navigate a civilized divorce. While they express sadness that their parents are divorcing, they are spared the stress, anger, and depression from having to endure the multiple injurious behaviors of parents who have chosen to engage in divorce warfare. They have not been asked to choose between parents; they have been given tacit or open permission to talk about and express love for either parent in the presence of the other; they have not witnessed fights or overheard raging phone calls demeaning the other parent. They have had access to both parents in person and by phone. Their parents have cooperated to attempt to meet the children's needs, and schedules have been modified when necessary to accommodate a child's or parent's needs. What is touching is that these youngsters actually understand how their parents' behaviors are different from those of so many of their friends' divorcing parents. And they are deeply grateful. They feel cherished and loved. Although they wish the divorce didn't have to happen, it is not perceived as a deathknell to their own aspirations and happiness.

The contrast between these respected and protected children and those who remain at the center of continuing parental controversy and reciprocal punitive reactions is striking. The latter, timid of expressing any interest whatsoever in one parent in the presence of the other, careful to draw boxes around their activities with each parent, stressed by being caught in the middle and encouraged to report, distort, spy, and reject, grow wary and weary, distrustful, and ultimately cynical. While their parents may feel they won the battle, the children feel as though they have lost the war. They deserve much better.

The civilized divorce is possible. It is difficult. It takes resolve, conscious effort, learning, practice, and self-evaluation. The long-lasting outcomes for those participants who decide to divorce in a civilized manner are worth it.

Preface

There is a hunger for a more respectful way to end marriage. I see it in the couples I counsel who have reached the sad conclusion that their relationship is no longer viable. I see it in the mediation clients who have chosen to try to work together to resolve the conflicts the divorce raises. I even see it in the couples who have been referred by their attorneys because their disputes have spun out of control. Underneath the anger and blame is always the wish that it hadn't turned out this way. Even with those couples who seem to have no good words for each other, or whose animosity has become a way of life, when I ask the question "Is this how you want your relationship to be?" no one has ever answered yes.

We have no models beyond negative stereotypes for how divorcing couples should relate to each other. Dealing with one's spouse is one of the most stressful and least understood parts of the divorce process. The idea of collaboration instead of competition, joint decision making instead of an adversarial contest, is relatively new. Although mediation has opened the door to cooperation, it requires skills that divorcing couples haven't needed before. It requires behaviors that go against their very reflexes.

Between Love and Hate grew out of the realization that even the most highly motivated couples know very little about how to resolve and negotiate the issues of separation and divorce. It also grew out of my years working in family court services before the development of mediation, when I watched how disputing parents tore their families apart.

Learning to work *with* rather than against a spouse is central to a healthier divorce process. I am convinced there is no getting around that. If children are to be protected, if the future of our families is to be preserved, then each person facing divorce must be willing to temper destructive impulses and take the risk to cooperate in resolving the painful and often complex issues the decision to divorce raises.

I have been involved in mediation since its beginnings in the 1970s. As a single parent formerly married to an attorney, I know firsthand the hard work of maintaining reasonableness. This book is designed to meet the needs of the growing number of people interested in avoiding court and preserving a civilized relationship for the sanity and well-being of themselves and their children. Based on the philosophy and negotiation strategies of mediation, this is a hands-on practical guide to divorce showing you how to be joint problem solvers instead of legal adversaries. My purpose is to help you move away from rather than against a partner, heal yourself rather than hurt your mate, and work for the greatest good in even the most difficult of circumstances.

The first part of this book focuses on separation: coping with the anger and uncertainty, establishing mutually acceptable ground rules, and understanding the emotional stages of divorce, including the seven keys to keeping your divorce from becoming a battleground. The second part addresses the critical issues of helping your children cope with the divorce and how to develop custody and parenting plans. Using the workplace as a model, I will show you how to build a collaborative, "business-like" relationship as parents. The third part focuses on how to communicate more effectively with your ex and de-escalate the inevitable angry and provocative exchanges. The fourth part walks you through the fundamentals of win–win negotiating and for developing settlement proposals. Chapters on reducing the adversarial nature of the legal proceedings and on mediation are also included. The final part covers tough situations such as dealing with difficult and hostile spouses, understanding the nature of post-divorce conflict, and using rituals for healing and letting go.

The book can be used by couples who are trying to work out their own divorce agreements as well as by individuals who are dealing with a difficult and uncooperative partner. Even if your mate is angry and antagonistic, you can learn how to avoid further escalation and release yourself from the hold these frustrating behaviors have on you. If you are using mediation, the techniques described will enable you to get the most out of your mediation effort. The sections on negotiation, conflict resolution, and becoming emotionally divorced are equally applicable to problems after divorce. I've included a variety of exercises, questionnaires, and checklists designed to help you clarify your own feelings, gain important perspectives, and practice negotiation and conflict resolution skills. Keeping a notebook or journal to record the written assignments and exercises will prove helpful.

Although the emphasis is on collaboration with your partner wherever possible, the book's purpose is really to assist you in your own personal journey. You can't control your former mate; you can't make him or her more responsible or cooperative or less angry. The book asks the question, How do you want to run your own life, independent of the response you get from your former mate?

The road from a troubled marriage to a civilized divorce is not easy. The enmity unleashed when marital bonds break can be fierce, the pain unfathomable. Divorce comes in stages. You may not be able to be very constructive now. And that is okay. You may not be able to read the book in its entirety right now. There may be sections that you are simply not ready to deal with, and that is okay. The book is meant to be a resource to which you can return as you move through this difficult period.

Often while writing I would question whether what I was advising was possible. I would ask myself if it is too much to expect former lovers—people who have shared commitments at the deepest levels—to be reasonable and fair with each other once this relationship has ended. I have listened to friends and acquaintances say, "Being civilized is a good idea, but if a couple really loved each other, they couldn't do it" or "If my wife left me, I'd kill her." I thought that perhaps as a mediator, I see couples through a prism of reasonableness, since I see only those couples who put out the effort. I no longer work in the courts; I tend not to see the couples who do battle. But I do see couples who struggle, who disagree, who are in pain, and who have hateful and angry feelings toward each other, often wishing they would never have to lay eyes on each other again. These couples are in no less pain and no less turmoil than those who wait on a court docket for months and months for a judge to determine their future. They have simply made a choice about how they will handle their own pain and conflict.

I questioned myself about what I really meant by being constructive. Am I asking others to think and behave in ways that are not possible, in which I myself failed? I had to examine my own relationship with my former spouse over the 14 years since our divorce. I thought, Are we friends? No. Do I hate him? No. Do I like him? Today he's okay. Has our relationship interfered with my life? Sometimes. Do I try to keep communication open? *Always.* Has it broken down? Occasionally. Has our daughter benefited from our efforts? Unquestionably.

Being constructive is not necessarily liking each other or agreeing—it is both parents' lifetime commitment to "damage control." I don't know that my situation is typical. There are people who get along better and are friends with former spouses; there are those who are barely civil.

As I look back, I think my own divorce was the hardest thing I have ever done in my life. But like many others, I survived and grew from the experience, and so can you. As unwelcome as divorce may be, it is possible to part with dignity and respect and to work toward a resolution that will benefit the well-being of parents and children alike.

Acknowledgments

I want to thank my many friends and colleagues who read sections of the book and whose editorial comments and words of encouragement clarified my own thinking and cheered me on. I particularly want to thank Janet Neuman, Jim Melamed, and Herb Trubo for reading an earlier draft of the manuscript and Anita Lohman, Don Sapsonek, Ann Milne, Helen Tevlin, Albert Bernstein, Julie Mancini, Nancy Bragdon, Nora Lenhoff, Rick Pope, and Ernest Cassella for their helpful feedback on various chapters. Special appreciation goes to Richard Forester for his computer wizardry, "inner" thesaurus, and love and support, and to my sweet daughter Elana for her patience and understanding—and for leaving me without a car most of the time so I could finish the book.

Special thanks to Herb Trubo and Josh Kadish for their input on the chapter on the legal process and to Robert Benjamin, who expanded the chapter and collaborated in putting it in its final form. I am deeply grateful to Deanne Boose, who helped retype and restore sections of the manuscript after my hard drive crashed. Special thanks also to Francesca Stevenson, Joan Biggs, and Sonja Johnston for their gracious assistance in publicizing the book.

I also want to thank Linda Regan, Naomi Brier, and Herman Makler of Plenum Press for their expert editorial assistance and my agent Natasha Kern for her advice and support.

This book couldn't have been written without the many couples who shared their stories and took the risk to try mediation even before its time. To them, my deepest respect and admiration.

Contents

II. PARENTING AND CHILDREN

6. Helping Children   83

7. Parenting Plans: The Transition to an Unmarried Family   99

8. Parenting as a Lasting Partnership: The Working Relationship   129

IV. THE FUNDAMENTALS OF NEGOTIATING

12. Getting Ready to Negotiate   *195*

13. Win–Win Negotiating Strategies   *213*

14. Working Toward a Settlement   *229*

Exercises and Questionnaires

FACING THE CRISIS OF SEPARATION CONSTRUCTIVELY

Part I provides an overview of the divorce process and shows you how to handle the changing relationship with your spouse, understand the emotional stages of divorce, and learn the seven keys to keeping your divorce from becoming a battlefield. It describes how to structure and negotiate the terms of separation and find the strength to manage the pain whether you are the initiator or the still-loving partner. In the throes of crisis, we often lose sight of the big picture. The theme of this section is to help you focus on your immediate choices and then take a long-term view of this difficult life transition.

A New Way

Reality is not destiny, it is a challenge.
EDWARD GALEANO

The marriage had no heartbeat. We were quietly suffocating. I moved out. We agreed we would work things out with the kids and the money. Three months later the only people still speaking were our attorneys. I don't know how it happened. I was depressed and felt lost without the kids. I was tired of being the deep pocket, tired of trying to take care of everything. There she was, sitting pretty in the big house, with the good car, and, most importantly, the kids. I wanted her to go back to work. I wanted to be with the kids more. I tried, I really tried to talk to her. She said I was pushing. I couldn't make her understand money was tight, that I was close to the edge. She said she was owed. She was tired of reigning herself in, tired of putting everyone else first. We got into horrible fights every time we tried to discuss it. The fights got worse. We couldn't talk anymore. I started to panic. She was being unreasonable. I was afraid I was going to lose everything if I didn't do something. I really tried to work with her. She just wouldn't listen. I had to call my attorney. I feel very bad about how things went.

BILL, *divorced father*

I wanted to stay on friendly terms for the kids' sake. They needed both of us. He was angry that it was taking me so long to find a job. The truth of the matter was that I was terrified. I hadn't worked for 10 years. I wanted to ease back into it, go to school, build up my confidence. He couldn't understand. I tried to explain that I needed time. He said if I wanted to be on my own I had to learn to take care of myself. I couldn't have it both ways. Then he'd start to yell about all he had done for me and make these ridiculous demands. We couldn't talk about it anymore. He wasn't being fair. I helped him through school. My friends said I deserved spousal support. I felt my survival was at stake. I had no choice. I didn't think it would turn out like this. There's terrible tension between us now. It is not good for the children. Maybe in a few years we will get over it.

SUE, *divorced mother*

More and more couples today are striving to have a civilized divorce. They want to protect their children, reach a fair settlement, and still be able to talk to each other afterward. But many, like Bill and Sue, get caught in an inexorable web of failed communication, threats and accusations, and escalating legal positions. They get off the track and can't get back on. They simply don't have the skills to successfully navigate the treacherous legal and emotional terrain of a dissolving marriage.

Not very long ago the mention of divorce conjured up fantasies of private detectives, scandal, and moral failure. The idea of divorcing with decency is a relatively recent phenomenon which provides us with few road maps to follow. We may know what to avoid but not how to avoid it. We know what is destructive but not how to be more constructive. For 40 years our legal system has cast divorcing spouses as opponents rather than as joint decision makers. Everything was routinely handed over to lawyers. The individual may have "won," but the family usually lost. This legacy has left us few, if any, role models for collaboratively resolving the issues of divorce.

We are taught to take responsibility for the course of a marriage but not for the course of a divorce. When we marry, we understand the importance of commitment, compromise, and communication. A successful marriage doesn't always follow, but we do try hard. The consequences are understood; no one wants the marriage to fail. The consequences of a "bad" divorce are also understood: continuing hostilities and conflict, exorbitant legal fees, and children caught in the middle. But there are no more commitments between separated individuals. There are no more rules of conduct. In most divorces it is each spouse for himself. Many couples think that their responsibility for working anything out ends the day one of them walks out the door.

The fact of the matter is that a healthy divorce, like a healthy marriage, requires effort. Most of us are totally unprepared for the hard work and commitment involved in keeping a divorce civilized. Those couples who have remained on reasonable terms with each other worked very hard at it. This doesn't mean that the ex-spouses weren't angry at each other or that their marriage had lacked passion. They simply wanted to keep their divorce from becoming a war zone. You don't have to let the acrimony and anguish that comes from severing emotional bonds destroy your family or poison your future. You do have a choice.

This book will show you how to deal with your spouse without making a lifelong enemy of him or her. It will show you how to work through your pain without turning it into paralyzing rage. It will teach you how to get beyond placing blame and find solutions. It will show you how to manage and negotiate the conflicts you face instead of escalating them; how to be joint problem solvers instead of legal adversaries; and how to bridge the raging river of divorce instead of establishing armed camps on either side. You will see that it is possible to have a civilized divorce and why the hard work involved is worth the effort.

NEW DIVORCE RITUALS

The way we divorce in our culture dishonors the institution of marriage. Marriage is one of the most important relationships we form in life. Its beginning is endowed with ceremony, sanctity, and hope. Its ending is marked by professionally orchestrated ritualized combat which, more often than not, leaves in its wake a trail of bitterness and hostility that ruptures families forever. Look at the rituals to which we have become accustomed: finding the best attorney in town first, jockeying for legal advantage, closing bank accounts, staking claim to the family residence, and grabbing whatever you can get your hands on before your spouse does. The vindictiveness runs so deep that some spouses want to destroy each other, using the legal system as their weapon. Others act in underhanded ways out of fear of what their partner will do. In my 20 years of practice, most people I have met whose divorce was bitter and acrimonious wished it hadn't been that way. But they didn't know that other options existed.

In divorce we don't have the benefit of ceremony or ritual as we do with other life transitions. Rituals surrounding mating and death are well established: people band together in the celebration of a marriage; you are surrounded in your sorrow when a loved one dies. In divorce you are alone. Where do you turn when divorce comes into your life? You pay a lawyer a $2,000 retainer because you don't know what else to do. You start the clock on countdown for the marital spoils. This is rarely helpful in the long run. As one man said, "There ought to be a better way to let go of twenty years of your life than court."

Every culture has rituals and ceremonies to help people move through important life transitions. Rituals are symbolic enactments that honor what is being left behind, acknowledge the change a person is experiencing, and usher in the new life status. Nothing like the bridal showers, bachelor parties, and rehearsal dinners which surround the entry into marriage exists to help prepare the person leaving what at one time was a sanctified relationship. Imagine what it would be like if there were customs that recognized, respected, and supported the difficult transition of divorce. Imaging if there were a formal period of "disengagement" that recognized the painful preparation necessary for uncoupling, just as there was once a formal engagement period that marked the preparation for entry into marriage. Imagine if there were a parting ceremony in which a judge or justice of the peace blessed the couple for their efforts, asked them to forgive each other's mistakes, described their continuing responsibilities to the family they may have created, and released them to go forth and prosper. Imagine if there were uncoupling ceremonies that were respectful of the efforts and achievements in the marriage.[1]

DIVORCE VOWS

If there are children, perhaps what we need are "divorce vows," which would sanctify the commitments to the family that has been created, just as the marriage vows once sanctified the commitments a couple made to each other. You might consider writing your own vows and devising a ceremony in which to express them, perhaps over the breaking of bread with your children. The following are examples of vows:

- I vow to continue to provide for the children's financial and emotional welfare.
- I vow to place the children's emotional needs above my personal feelings about my former spouse.
- I vow to be fair and honest about the divorce settlement.
- I vow to support the children's relationship with their other parent and never to do anything that might compromise that relationship.
- I vow to deal with the issues in this divorce as constructively as I know how so that my family can heal and we can all go forward.

I look back on a powerful event in my own divorce many years ago. I flew with my husband to Seattle to obtain a Jewish divorce, called a "get." It was strange traveling together, sitting side by side in a proximity that was both familiar and alien. We were on our way to end our marriage. What do you say? There were no distractions and nothing to argue about. All dressed up together and going nowhere, for the last time.

We arrived at the synagogue and were ushered into a small library where several holy men were sitting around a large oak table. Ivan and I were seated next to each other. No one spoke. The men barely looked up from their prayer books. The solemnity of the occasion hung from everything in the room, from the dark mahogany paneling to the deliberateness of the rabbis' every movement. There was no escaping. The final reality of ending our life together stood starkly before us. As the elders began to chant the prayers, Hebrew words that I didn't understand, tears began to fall. Not the familiar tears of rage, frustration, or hurt but of a profound sorrow I had not known before. I looked over at Ivan. He was crying also—Ivan crying! I had never seen him like this. For the first time, I felt his pain and saw him in his humanity—vulnerable, imperfect, and struggling. His tears touched me deeply, evaporating my shield of anger. At that moment I couldn't hate him anymore for doing what he had to do. I was filled with sorrow. But it was a sorrow that contained no blame; it was deep and pure and cleansing.

The rabbi asked if we wanted to continue. Unable to speak, we both nodded yes. The long silence that followed was broken only by muffled sobs and Ivan's words, then mine: "I'm sorry, I'm so sorry." The words reverberated as if for the first time they were genuinely true. Again the rabbi asked if we were sure we wanted to have this divorce. Taking a deep breath, I raised my pen and signed the document. Even as I recount this today, the details dimmed by the passage of time, tears well up. We said goodbye that day. It was as simple as that. But so much more that was not said was understood. That is ritual.

We all have feelings about our marriages which transcend our anger. They are buried beneath the pain. When you have shared a profound part of your life with another person, you don't want to feel it is being erased just because it didn't last forever. Your relationship was once full of hope, potential, and dreams. There is no opportunity to acknowledge what was good or to express your sorrow at its loss because when emotional bonds rupture, all the disappointed hopes, unmet needs, and unexpressed resentments surface. Conflict and rage are necessary distractions. They dull the edges of pain and forestall the enveloping emptiness. There are no quiet places except maybe alone at night when you can't sleep or at the office of your therapist or sometimes with a friend. Where can you say your final good-bye, acknowledge what was good, and respectfully recognize the passage of an important part of your life? Perhaps the only place is in the privacy of your own solitude.

What really breaks your heart is how a relationship born of love, shared visions, and goodwill has to end with such a competitive struggle for recognition or retribution for lost dreams. When someone dies, we don't dwell exclusively on what was negative in order to separate emotionally. Relationships die as well and for a variety of reasons: benign neglect, wounds that were not healed, symptoms that were ignored, or infections that spread. A mourner honors the life that was lost through death by remembering what was most valued in the person. Similarly, there was once life in a relationship that has died; somewhere that life must be acknowledged in the parting. We all seek affirmation from those whose love we once sought. Even in the end we want to know that we mattered. Even if the union was a mistake—the person was not who you thought he was or who you wanted her to be—even if you feel great relief in becoming free of your marriage, you and your ex-spouse once shared a profound intimacy in joining a part of your lives together. You must bring this period into harmony with the rest of your life.

If you had children, you need to affirm what is probably your highest concern—a commitment to the family you created—and to determine how this nucleus, this living organism, will divide and form two separate, not only surviving but thriving, units.

DIVORCE AS A TRANSITION

Divorce is a legal event, but for the family it is a gradual process of reorganizing and redefining relationships and expectations. Families continue, but divorce changes them. While the marriage may be over, when there are children, a couple must have a lifelong relationship that needs to be positive if the children are to thrive. Just as a good marital relationship is the basis for the strength of the intact family, so the divorced parents' relationship is fundamental to the healthy adjustment of the children after divorce.

Most parents have come to recognize the importance of

children having both parents after divorce. The bitter custody battle of yesteryear is not the representative divorce of the 1990s. With fathers participating more in the care of children and more couples opting for joint legal custody, most children of divorce today are to varying degrees part of two households.

We cannot count on the experience of previous generations to guide us in how a family lives in today's world. Today's children have kinship circles we could not have imagined in our youth: four parents, eight grandparents, biological siblings, half siblings, stepsiblings, stepcousins, stepaunts and uncles, former step-parents and siblings, and so on. We don't even have the language for these new familial configurations. As this first generation of children of divorce grows up, the definition of the extended family is likely to take on new proportions. I am reminded of a young boy whose parents divorced when he was 3. Both parents remarried. The boy was close to his stepdad, and he also had a close relationship and regular contact with his biological father. When his mother divorced his stepdad after 10 years of marriage, the weekends of this 13-year-old, who lived with his mom and half sister, were carved up between his long-standing visits with his biological father and his family, visits with his stepdad and stepbrother, and visits with his grandparents on three sides.

With half of all marriages ending in divorce and over 50 percent of second marriages failing, we are entering an era of the part-time family. We have not even begun to think about how these relationships will work. But one thing is certain: the old practice of fighting over custody of children and everything else is disastrous for everyone involved.

WHAT IS DIVORCE MEDIATION: IS IT FOR YOU?

In the last ten years mediation has provided an alternative to the risks of adversarial posturing. Statutes for the mediation of custody disputes now exist in almost every jurisdiction in the United States and Canada. Many couples turn to mediation as the neutral forum in which to discuss and plan the transition of the family. In mediation a trained neutral party, usually an attorney or a mental health professional, helps you work out the terms of your separation or divorce settlement. A mediator will help negotiate an interim separation arrangement, including who will stay in the house, how your joint expenses will be handled, and when the children will be with each of you. The mediator will also help you work out the final divorce settlement, including support arrangements and the division of your assets as well as a plan for parenting that ensures each of you the opportunity for a continuing relationship with your children.

A divorcing couple has common as well as competing needs and interests. For instance, you may agree on the children's need for the stability of the family home but one spouse's personal needs for the equity in the house may conflict with that goal. Mediation is based on a win–win orientation dedicated to resolving these conflicts. The goal in mediation is to help you work together to recognize your interdependent interests and find creative solutions that maximize the gain for each party in negotiating your competing interests. Mediation provides an informal, supportive atmosphere and gives each of you a chance to identify what is really important to you in forming a settlement.

Most of the time mediation is voluntary. This means you will have to convince your spouse to try this new method. Later chapters will give suggestions on how to do this and on how to recognize when mediation may not be appropriate. In an increasing number of jurisdictions medication is mandatory for disputes about custody and visitation. You may be required to try to work out a parenting plan using either court-sponsored mediation services or the services of a private mediator before your case can go to court.

Mediation does not take the place of legal representation. A mediator is an impartial third party and does not represent either spouse. You will need an attorney to review the settlement reached in mediation and to file the decree with the court. Your attorney will also help you develop proposals and advise you about your

legal rights so that you can be an informed negotiator. Even with
attorney fees factored in, mediation costs about half as much as
traditional attorney negotiation and representation.[2]

Mediation is based on the following set of philosophical
principles that guide its practice:

1. The family is the client, not the individual husband or
   wife. The mediator does not champion one party's interests over the other's but focuses on solutions that address
   the needs of all family members.
2. The mediator's highest priority is to help the parents focus
   on the best interest of their children and develop parenting
   plans that ensure the children a relationship with both
   parents.
3. The parties retain full control over all decisions and agreements. The mediator helps develop options and explore
   the alternatives but does not impose decisions on the
   parties.
4. The mediator is an advocate of each person's well-being
   but remains neutral as to the settlement terms.
5. Mediation enables parties to learn the skills to resolve
   future disputes.
6. The goal of mediation is to produce equitable and workable settlements, not a winner and loser.

Mediation is not for everyone. Some people are intent on destroying, on punishing, on making the ex-spouse pay. In these circumstances you need legal protection. But studies show that almost 90
percent of those who have tried mediation recommend it, whether
or not they have been successful in reaching agreement on all of
the issues. A cooperative process is healing. The way a relationship is ended can be just as important as the settlement terms. If
you proceed with an aggressive adversarial approach, you may
extract more money but you will also create bitterness that in the
long run is more costly emotionally.

A NEW PATH

We have come a long way from the view of divorce as moral failing, but we still have a long way to go to ease the trauma of dissolving a family. The divorcing man or woman of today is a pioneer facing new paths, new choices, and new challenges. The rules are in transition—from how you will share the responsibility of raising the children to what you owe each other economically. Different lawyers will tell you different things. The courts are unpredictable. Cooperation is a new idea and cooperation in a legal system that supports competitive self-interests is not without its risks, because if the other person is not operating in good faith, you stand to lose.

As more and more people part humanely, the way is lit for others. You have an opportunity to be creative, to take the risk to initiate positive intentions with your spouse, and to talk not only about preventing the divorce from becoming a disaster but perhaps about how to affirm what was once good between you. Realize that change spells opportunity. The difficult part is leaving what was familiar for what is unfamiliar. The first couples who experimented with joint custody couldn't get a judge or attorney to listen to them. They knew they wanted something better than the weekend-carnival Dad syndrome. They were told it wouldn't work. "If you couldn't get along while you were married, how can you share raising children?" they were asked. They proved this thinking wrong and charted new territory, allowing others to follow.

We hang on to the old not necessarily because it works but because it is familiar, predictable, and safe. If divorce in our culture is ever going to become more constructive, divorcing families will need to take the risk and explore new territory, just like those first joint custody families. Begin with the intent to manage your divorce in the most constructive way possible. Even if your spouse is not ready or able to be constructive, *you* can still respond in a constructive way.

This is not easy but it is learnable. Our cultural training leaves most of us woefully unprepared to deal well with conflict. Most people are crippled during a divorce; when the potential for conflict exists in every decision that needs to be made. The new divorce requires a level of maturity, conflict-resolution skills, commitment, and self-discipline that few can summon internally without great effort. As a Russian poet said, "Life itself required the new thinking."

2

Separation

New Roles, New Rules

> The secret of change is to focus all of your energy,
> not on fighting the old, but on building the new.
>
> SOCRATES

The sound of the gavel. The ordeal was over. It was the worst three hours of her life. In a daze she walked through the doors of the mahogany-paneled courtroom that sealed her fate. She looked at the man with whom she bedded for 15 years, the man who fathered her children, the man who nursed her soul when she faltered, the man who loved another woman more. The man who stored all his little irritations in his breast pocket until they suffocated his heart. She hated him now. She wished he would die. She would pretend he didn't exist.

When you separate, the last thing you are thinking about is how to maintain a constructive relationship with your partner. You are thinking about how to make the pain go away, how you will survive, how to bring love back—not how to get along. The idea of cooperating with the one person who has caused this pain seems unthinkable.

Divorce is the antithesis of marriage, yet it too places demands on a relationship. Just as a strong marriage is the foundation for a healthy nuclear family, a cooperative working relationship between divorced parents is fundamental to the post-divorce family and the welfare of its children. All of the research on divorce indicates that the *quality of the relationship between the divorcing parents,* that is, their level of conflict or cooperation, *is central to their children's adjustment after divorce.* Parents who chronically fight have children with more problems. Parents who get along have children who adjust better. If children are going to be protected in the divorce process, which means divorce becomes more civilized, we must reexamine our expectations about the relationship between separated or divorced spouses. We can't rely on our old assumptions. Let's look at some common myths and try to paint a more realistic picture for today's families.

THE RELATIONSHIP BETWEEN DIVORCING SPOUSES: MYTHS AND REALITIES

Myth 1: When the marriage is over, the "relationship" between spouses is over (divorcing spouses don't have to work at a relationship).

Once the decision to separate or divorce has been made, most couples do not even think of themselves as still being part of a "relationship," particularly not one worth emotional investment or effort. Though the relationship as it once existed is over, there is a new relationship that can be as significant to your future as any relationship you will ever have. The stakes are different, but they are just as high: the welfare of your children, future hostilities versus peaceful co-existence, and economic rebuilding versus disastrous legal fees. You and your spouse remain interdependent on most major issues: money, children, home, and hearth.

It is ultimately self-destructive to stop caring about how you and your spouse get along and to let your anger take over. As hard as it is, the relationship with a spouse during separation and divorce requires extra care and handling, not less. You have to be more careful about what you say and how to say it. Couples in trouble fail to realize that they must treat their changing relationship like any other relationship they want to work well enough to serve their needs.

Myth 2: You have to be friends and like each other in order to work together.

The motivation to tend this relationship does not have to come from a heartfelt desire to befriend or cooperate, but rather from a realization of what can happen if you don't cooperate. Call it selfish altruism. You ultimately benefit. If you have a bad relationship, you might not get to see any more birthday cakes or Christmas mornings with the children or child support checks. The conflicts with a former spouse can seriously stress new relationships you might form. I'm sure you have heard of people whose relationships or even second marriages have broken up because of hassles with an ex-spouse.

The key is to separate how you feel about your spouse from how you act. Think about what you have to get done with this person, not who he or she is. *Being civilized is an act of will, not an act of the heart*. If you discipline yourself to be civil and cooperative, you stand to benefit. You are doing it for yourself. One client put it this way:

> I would never talk to my boss the way I talk to my ex-husband and I don't like him either.
>
> Sara, *divorced 3 months*

Myth 3: When you get divorced, your emotional entanglements end.

Divorce severs the legal bond of matrimony, changes the legal obligations, and alters the financial structure of the family, but it does not easily sever the intricate emotional connections between people who have shared lives and had children together.

Seeing a former mate is almost never a neutral event. Meaningful emotional attachments become embedded in our physical as well as psychological reflexes. We try to cut off all of the tendrils so we no longer feel. We try to slash a hole in the picture where the other stood. We try to put the other out of reach of hurting us. We want to make the ex-spouse go away. But we can't.

One of the pioneers of family therapy, Carl Whitaker, has said that, emotionally speaking, there is no such thing as divorce. He believes that just as it is not possible to end emotional involvement with the family you grew up in, it is not possible to end all emotional involvement with the family you created. In some ways, then, on an emotional level, divorce is a struggle to solve a problem that is insoluble.

There is a Zen paradox that recognizes that the only way to progress beyond a certain point is to accept "what is" rather than fight it. Perhaps it is best to acknowledge that on some level the skeleton of the emotional connection with your former spouse will *always* be there. It doesn't have life, but it also doesn't disappear. The presence of children is a continuous reminder that there will always be blood ties. A deep connection exists even as you create a healthy emotional distance, because no one else shares with you the depth of feeling for your children as does their other parent.

Mary who had been divorced for 10 years put it this way:

> I dreamt about my ex-husband frequently while we were getting ready for our daughter's wedding. Often, I'd wake up in a horrible sweat dreaming we were still married. When we walked into the store to order invitations, there was a familiarity that was eerie. It was like a time warp. But as we stood facing each other at the altar, it was as if something had come full circle. Our daughter was getting married. Each of us in our own way had been there for her and helped her grow into this lovely young woman standing before us. I felt purged of the hassles of the last ten years. We were both so full of pride. In some ways I felt like he was still family. Maybe we could be softer around the edges with each other now. After all, soon we could be grandparents.

Incorporating the notion of your "relatedness" to your former mate rather than fighting it may be the most effective way to get on with your life. Accepting the mix of emotions about your spouse, both positive and negative, and the connection you will have through your children as "what is" may actually prove to be a relief.

Many people who have been divorced for a number of years talk about their former spouse as a kind of extended family. After being divorced for 14 years, I have come to see my ex-husband, his wife, and their three children that way. The ups and downs of their lives affect my daughter and therefore affect me. Their children come into my house looking for borrowed things or to see the new kittens. I find my ex's tee shirt, which has been worn by my daughter, in my laundry bag. My ex's 5-year-old sat on my lap during my daughter's Bat Mitzvah as her half-sister and father read from the Torah. I sometimes just scratch my head at it all. At other times I am caught completely by surprise that our lives remain intertwined. Melinda Blau in an article in *New York Magazine* said that divorce is one of the great cosmic jokes, because if you have children, you *never* get the other person out of your life. I am even reminded of the scene in *Godfather III* where Michael Corleone is lying in a hospital bed surrounded by his grown children and a tearful ex-wife is standing at a distance.

Myth 4: You have to look out for yourself; you can't worry about the other person.

When you first separate and the future of the marriage is uncertain, you often try to be nice, even accommodating. You don't want to rock the boat; you don't want to hurt your chances of getting back together. But when the hopes of reconciliation have died and the divorce seems inevitable, your concern about the relationship and the well-being of your spouse abruptly diminishes. You begin to think more of your own interest, and rightly so.

> The day she filed, something in me snapped. I had been trying to help her, you know, be real supportive. I accommodated her schedule with the kids, gave her the money she asked for. Then I suddenly asked myself, why am I doing this? She doesn't want me anymore. What about me? I'm not getting what I want . . . my family . . . why should I be so nice to her!
>
> ALAN, *separated 5 months*

This is a dangerous turning point. You stop caring completely about your spouse's needs and concerns as you increasingly focus on your own. The other person doesn't matter anymore or at least matters a whole lot less. You may be angry because your kindness and generosity didn't get you what you really wanted: the continuation of the marriage. Healthy self-interest is important, but if you focus only on what you want and stop acknowledging your spouse's needs and concerns, things will go downhill fast. Selfishness, withholding, and unwillingness to compromise often follow. The relationship can become increasingly antagonistic. Agreements are broken, money and children—the commodities of divorce—are delivered late or not at all. You each see the other as the bad guy and feel absolutely justified in whatever you do. Once this cycle has begun, it becomes self-perpetuating, can escalate quickly, and is difficult to reverse. Take care of yourself, but always be willing to listen to and negotiate about your partner's concerns.

SETTING THE STAGE FOR COOPERATION

Most relationships operate on automatic pilot. We don't usually have conscious strategies for them unless we run into trouble. When you separate, your relationship with your spouse changes from intimacy to something else—neither the role of friend or enemy really fits. This terra incognita of your new status is filled with minefields. It can't simply be left to run its course. You need to take charge of redefining your expectations, establishing new ground rules, and limiting contact to what you can emotionally handle.

Accept the Inevitability of Your Relationship with Your Spouse

First, you need to come to terms with the fact that you have to deal reasonably with this person who, at times, you wish would make your life so much easier by just dropping off the face of the earth. If you have children, you and your spouse will have a lifelong.relationship. You have to accept its permanence and make the best of it. Here is an exercise that might help:

1. Write down three reasons why you don't want to cooperate with your spouse. Write down the first things that

come to mind; the reasons don't have to be rational or mature. In fact, the more immature the better. Give yourself permission to indulge your childish emotions.

1. _____

2. _____

3. _____

2. Write down three reasons why you would want to cooperate.

1. _____

2. _____

3. _____

3. List three long-term benefits of cooperation.

1. _____

2. _____

3. _____

4. List three long-term consequences of not cooperating.

1. _____

2. _____

3. _____

Save these notes and refer to them whenever you are upset and angry at your ex.

Redefine Your Relationship with Your Spouse

Write a short paragraph describing the kind of future relationship you would eventually like to have with your former mate. This is not necessarily what is possible at this point in time, but it's what you hope could evolve in the future. You may hope to be friends and be interested in what happens in each other's lives. You may want very little contact except as it relates to the children. If there are no children, you may not want any contact at all.

Check Your Reserves: Limit Contact with Your Spouse to What You Can Handle

Seeing a former lover is painful, especially in the beginning. Ask yourself how much contact with your spouse you can handle *at this time*. For instance, do you need to limit contact and telephone calls? Do you want to confine discussions to specific times or specific subjects? Do you need to postpone talking about certain issues until you feel you are more ready to handle them? Do you need to understand more about what happened in the marriage? Do you want to move forward with the settlement and have certain issues resolved within a specific period of time? Knowing where you stand and what you need will make you feel more empowered, because it allows you to be proactive instead of just reactive.

Pay attention to your level of stress in your interactions with your spouse. Learn to set limits. You can say, "No, I can't deal with that now" or "I have reached my limit in this conversation; we will have to continue another time." When you start to feel frazzled, stop and ask yourself there questions: (1) How do I feel about what is happening now? (2) What are my emotional needs? (3) What can I do to take care of myself?

What you feel you can handle changes from week to week, even day to day. If you keep tabs on your emotional reserves, you won't feel as overwhelmed or out of control. This will also reduce the opportunities for destructive interaction, because you are keeping yourself in a more resourceful state rather than allowing yourself to continue when you are exhausted and emotionally depleted. Be sure your spouse understands that your need to limit contact or think things over is not a hostile gesture. A spouse can easily misread your need to set limits as an unwillingness to cooperate or as exclusion from the parental role.

Make a Commitment to Yourself to Be Constructive

Make a pledge to yourself to exercise the self-discipline to behave in a nondestructive manner, regardless of whether your spouse is able to do so or not. Your goal is to act as responsibly in this situation as you would in any other business or personal matter in which courteous, rational behavior is expected. There will be times when every fiber in your body will scream: "I don't care. I don't need this, I don't want anything more to do with him." Slammed phones and murderous fantasies notwithstanding, you should make every effort to honor your commitment not to let your anger get the better of you. Refraining from striking back is one of the biggest emotional hurdles of divorce. It goes against one's reflexes. When you call back after a fight, put the children's needs before your own, remain rational when you are upset, make decisions that are based on what is right even when you feel that you have been treated unfairly, and whenever you take steps in a constructive direction, you deserve a reward.

There are bound to be periods of hostility when all communication breaks down. But things don't have to end up this way. Your personal commitment is what will enable you to veer back toward a constructive course. It is your built-in safety net. In marriage, commitment motivates problem solving; in divorce, it can do the same.

If you and your spouse are able to make a joint commitment not to let things deteriorate into an adversarial relationship, you will be able to ride the ups and downs much better. John and Mary, who had been together for 7 years, agreed that they would never go to court, even though Mary's affair created bitterness and mistrust. During their separation there were fights, slammed doors, and weeks without speaking. Yet each of them knew how far they would let it go before calling the other to resolve matters. No matter how bad it got, they knew that neither would resort to nuclear weapons.

A good strategy to avert all-out war is signing a "good faith" written commitment in which you both state how you want to handle the divorce; how you will deal with impasses; and what your expectations are of each other. It could resemble the terms of a treaty. You can call it your "Separation Accords." An example would be a statement like this:

> We, John and Mary Doe, agree in good faith to use every effort to resolve our differences through a cooperative, nonadversarial process. If we are unable to resolve our disputes privately, we agree to seek the help of a neutral third party and exhaust all such avenues before seeking recourse from the courts. Any attorneys that we retain will be instructed to negotiate for a fair and reasonable settlement. It is our hope and intention to maintain a constructive divorce process so that we can appreciate what was good between us, protect our children, heal from the wounds, and move forward with our lives.

Signed: _____
                                    (wife)

_____
                                    (husband)

While this is not a legal document, you should both sign the letter and use it as a "good faith" point of reference between you. If you are unable to get such an agreement from your spouse, you can still be "unconditionally constructive," a concept Roger Fisher and Scott Brown describe in their book *Getting Together: Building a Relationship That Gets to Yes*. This means that you do whatever is good for you and good for family relationships regardless of whether your spouse reciprocates. Do not expect the other to always follow your lead, and do not follow the other's lead if it is not positive. You can still honor the commitment to yourself to be as reasonable and positive as you can be.

HOW TO TELL YOUR SPOUSE YOU WANT A SEPARATION OR DIVORCE

By the time most people have picked up this book, they have already discussed separation. But painful subjects are difficult to process, and the more understanding you have about the reasons for the marital breakdown, the less bitter the separation is likely to be. The following are some guidelines that may help you keep these difficult discussions from becoming contentious:

- Speak in terms of your own experience rather than characterize and blame your spouse for his or her personal failures. Describe how the problems in the marriage have affected *you* and brought you to this point.
- Describe problems in terms of the relationship not working anymore, that is, in terms of your failure as a team to work together, meet each other's needs, communicate, or resolve your differences. Discuss how the unending arguments have eroded the love or how you have grown apart or changed in different ways.
- Even when a spouse has been abusive or alcoholic, discuss the marital breakdown in terms of *your* unwillingness to live under these circumstances anymore.
- Don't make a unilateral decision without informing your spouse. Even if something snaps and you feel you must get away, coming home to a note and an empty house is an insult not easily forgiven. Such an exit should only be done when there is the possibility of real physical danger.
- If your spouse believes the marriage is salvageable and opposes separation, acknowledge these feelings, accept the anger, and describe how you are at a different stage. Be willing to talk through your reasons for wanting to separate many times so that your spouse can understand and accept where you are.

WHAT IF WE HAVE TO STAY TOGETHER UNTIL WE CAN AFFORD TO SEPARATE?

It is difficult to live under the same roof for very long after you have decided to separate. When finances dictate delaying separation, be respectful of each other's pain. Try to confine conversation to practical matters. If you want to discuss the marriage, agree to set specific times for this. Don't let it creep into everyday conversations. As long as you have to remain in the same house, try not to rub salt on each other's wounds. Try to stay out of each other's way. Consider having different nights when you are each "on duty" as parents. Have time on the weekend when one of you stays with a friend. It is important to have time in which you are not exposed to the stress of each other's presence. Separation often comes as a relief, because you have both come to see how unworkable living together is.

CAN THE MARRIAGE BE HEALED?

One of the factors that affects the course of a trial separation is whether the partner who wants to continue the marriage can tolerate the uncertainty of it all enough to give the initiating partner the space needed. The spouse who wants the marriage to continue risks alienating a mate further, because the anxiety and helplessness of being in this situation are difficult to tolerate. Most people deal with these feelings by trying to persuade their mate to reconsider. The endless promises of reform, apologies for past mistakes, or attempts to woo your mate back only create pressure and tend to push your mate further away. If you are a still-loving partner, try very hard to give your spouse some space to sort out his or her feelings. Find a therapist to help you deal with your feelings about the marriage and your anxiety about your future. This is not the time for you to turn to your mate to meet your emotional needs. Everything has its own time. Perspective and distance may be what is needed. You may have to bide your time, with no guarantees.

There is no rule as to whether a marriage can be salvaged once a separation occurs. Sometimes it can; often it cannot. The problems that brought you to the brink of separation were serious. Much damage has already been done. Many people are afraid that once the step toward separation is taken, there is no turning back. This is not necessarily true. To some extent it depends on what the separation means to the initiating partner. It can be a desperate signal to get a spouse to recognize the seriousness of the problems. In this situation it is not divorce but changes in the relationship that are desired. Sometimes separation comes after a long period of therapy or soul-searching and represents a healthy choice, because the mate has not been willing to get help to change dysfunctional patterns or participate in a course of psychological growth. Sometimes separation comes after months or even years of hard work to create a viable relationship or to gain the strength to leave an abusive relationship.

Because the dynamics of marital collapse are so complex and because we understand so little of ourselves and our relationships, the best advice is to go slow—to see how you feel after you have been separated, to carefully weigh your decision, and to see a marriage counselor or therapist if you haven't already. Your perspective will be different and your feelings may change after a period of separation. Sometimes the shock of separation produces changes in a mate that couldn't be made before. Timing is a factor in all relationships. At a minimum, give yourself adequate time to reconsider your decision about divorce and to explore the possibilities of reconciliation. Divorce is not always the best solution. Rebuilding a life, getting back on your feet financially, coping with the enormous adjustments of stepfamilies should you remarry— each has its own set of stresses and problems. Over half of second marriages end in divorce, and divorce doesn't always bring the hoped-for changes in one's life.

SEPARATION GROUND RULES

Once you separate, the rules of marriage no longer apply. You cannot rely on the assumptions under which you operated in the past. Your spouse is now freer to act as an individual and make unilateral decisions. You have to decide just how unmarried you are, what your separation means, where you see it going, and what your new expectations of each other are. First be clear about how you are defining the separation:

1. *Time-Out*: Is the separation a period of time-out to gain perspective or a hiatus from the marriage in which you each explore yourselves and develop as individuals without specifically working on resolving the marital problems? Do you need time to see how you feel about each other? If so, work out temporary arrangements about money and children and decide how much contact you are going to have with each other, how frequently you will meet to talk things over, and when you will review the situation. Then give each other the space that is requested.

2. *Cooling-Off Period*: Is the separation a cool-down so that you can actively work on the marriage without the tension and conflict of living together? Clarify each person's expectations about how you will work on the relationship (i.e., individual or marital counseling). Will you "date" each other or have sexual contact? Make sure that each person's expectations are clearly presented.

3. *Divorce*: Has a decision to divorce been made? How much time does each person need to deal with it emotionally before facing all of the practical details of final settlement? Be cautious about cranking up the legal machinery if one partner is still very angry. Time is likely to temper emotions and make both partners more reasonable.

Regardless of whether the separation is a time-out or a real split, you will need to make new ground rules and explicit agreements about how things will be handled during this period of transition or uncertainty. You will need to discuss how you will handle your joint expenses, how you will divide your responsibilities as parents, whether you will date—each other or new people—and what you expect from each other in terms of other joint obligations like maintenance or repairs on the family residence. You may want to meet with a mediator to help you negotiate these decisions.

Here is a checklist of topics you will need to discuss:

CHECKLIST FOR SEPARATION DISCUSSION

1. Financial
   A. Divide checking account
   B. Divide joint bills and debts.
   C. Do budgets of expenses for maintaining each household; separate ongoing living expenses.
   D. Agree on how the family income will be divided to cover the costs of two households. Will there still be a joint account and what expense are to be covered from it?
   E. Separate credit cards.
   F. Freeze or divide liquid assets.

2. Children
   A. Where will the children live during the separation?
   B. What is the schedule of time for being with each parent?
   C. How will responsibilities be divided for their routine care?
   D. How will decisions about them be made?
   E. What information needs to be exchanged (e.g., school and sports schedules, behavioral problems, minor illness), and how will this information be communicated—phone, weekly meetings, notes?

3. Your Relationship with Each Other
   A. How much personal contact or communication do you want?
   B. How much privacy or autonomy do you want?
   C. What practical areas do you feel you still need to be involved with each other about (e.g., house repair or maintenance)?
   D. What are the ground rules for using the family residence?
   E. Will you date other people?

Sandra and David: A Case History

Sandra and David's situation presented all of the classic problems that could have led them to a courtroom battle when David said he wanted to end the marriage. Even though their relationship deteriorated rapidly after they separated, they sought the help of a mediator. The mediator helped them manage the changes that separation brings.

When David said he didn't think he was in love anymore, Sandra was devastated. She knew they hadn't been close, but she didn't think their problems were serious. David hadn't been able to talk about the things that bothered him about Sandra. He didn't want to rock the boat and thought it was better not to let the little things bother him. He poured himself into his work, taking on new projects and increasing his traveling. He wasn't even aware that he was withdrawing from the marriage. When he and Sandra got ready to purchase a new house, he was overcome with a queasiness that wouldn't go away. He realized the children had become the sole focus of his marriage. He felt empty inside and began to think that the gulf between Sandra and him was too wide to bridge. For the first time, he started thinking about separation. Then "she" came along. The affair awakened feelings in David that had been cut off for a long time. As he felt life returning again, his rage mounted. He was mad at himself and mad at Sandra. He couldn't go on the same way anymore. Something snapped. He wanted out. There was no turning back.

Sandra was a graphics designer who hoped someday to write children's books. Her career was demanding and it was hard juggling her work, the family, and David's traveling. The babies were colicky and she was often tired and cranky because David wasn't there to help. She knew for years that a wall had been developing between them, but she didn't know what to do about it. She pretended it wasn't there and threw herself into activities. As long as she was busy, she felt no pain. They didn't fight, were cordial, had friends, and an active social life. From all outward appearance, they seemed like a happily married couple. It was easy for Sandra to think that there was nothing wrong, that she and David were just overextended. When she learned about the affair, her world collapsed. David was talking about divorce, wanting the children every other week and even about selling the house. Sandra was in a tailspin.

David felt an urgency about moving on. Every time he tried to talk about the divorce, he and Sandra would get into a shouting match. All of the rage about past disappointments that were never talked about at the time came pouring out. Nothing was ever resolved. Sandra felt betrayed and furious about the affair. As far as she was concerned, David could drop dead. If he wanted a divorce he could have it, but she wasn't going to cooperate. She wouldn't abide having his girlfriend anywhere near the children, nor would she discuss selling the house.

When David realized the extent of his financial demands, he started to panic about money. He kept putting pressure on Sandra, and she kept resisting. The arguments escalated. After a while, they couldn't talk at all anymore. David just wanted it over with. He felt he had to look out for himself. He called a lawyer, who encouraged them to see a mediator because they had young children. Sandra was reluctant at first. After much reassurance that David didn't want to hurt her or the children anymore, and that he wanted to act properly given their years of marriage, she finally agreed.

In mediation, David and Sandra were able to see that they still had a relationship to maintain as parents and that they had to keep their angry feelings in check or they wouldn't be able to function as parents. Sandra realized, and David came to understand, that she needed time to sort things out and heal before she could discuss the future rationally. They agreed to use mediation as the settlement process but decided that for 3 months David would put no pressure on Sandra to make decisions about the future. They also agreed to see a therapist since they really hadn't been able to talk about why the marriage fell apart. Sandra came to understand why David was panicking about money and said she would live within a budget for the household. They agreed that they would have limited contact and that nothing would be discussed except the children's schedule. They also agreed that if a discussion became unproductive, they would not let it deteriorate into open warfare but would continue it another time or table it for mediation.

David and Sandra left the mediation session with some feeling of hope that as time passed they would be able to communicate, even though they couldn't now, and would eventually be able to have a working relationship as parents, even though Sandra couldn't deal with David or his lover at the time.

The rest of the separation and divorce settlement was not easy. But Sandra and David did not destroy their family with their pain and conflict. Their story is typical. The difference is what they chose to do at a critical turning point. Their forethought and courage prevented their divorce from turning into a nightmare for everyone.

3

Timing

The Emotions of Ending a Marriage

Wait for the wisest of all counselors. Time.
PERICLES

With time hurts heal, perspectives shift, and feelings change. Divorce takes time. In the intensity of momentary feelings, the concept of time gets lost. Crisis focuses our attention on an ever-demanding present. There is only the now: today's bleakness means bleakness forever; bitterness is bitterness forever; loss is loss forever. Your survival becomes all-consuming. The future is an elusive image barely perceptible through the narrow lens of the painful present. The past, all that you shared together, the rich-ness of what you *did* create, seems to disintegrate and fall away. Divorce leaves you stranded in time. You block out memories in order to dull the edges of pain. You take one day at a time, because that is all you can handle. Swept up in the turmoil of intense emotions, you forget that you are a time traveler and that time is your ally. Look toward the tomorrows, and don't forget the impor-tant yesterdays.

Divorce is a passage. Try to see it in the wider context of your life. We don't have the benefit of the perspective of time until it has already passed. Your anger at being left with young children or at

33

seeing them only once a week is what you may be experiencing now. However, that is not necessarily how you will interpret these events in the months ahead. The humiliation of being rejected may turn into an appreciation of your spouse's courage for releasing you from a unhealthy or mismatched alliance. You may actually grow closer to the children as you spend time with them away from the influence of your spouse. The terror of being alone may turn into pride at being able to make it on your own. Being forced back into the workplace may be very positive in the long run. You can't know now what you will learn from your divorce as time goes on.

> I swore I would never speak to the woman who spent weekends with my children and husband while I was alone in my big, empty house. A year has gone by now. My house is filled with friends and activities. I feel content. I didn't realize how much the marriage drained me. I bear no malice toward her now.
>
> SONIA, *married 15 years*

> When we first split up I was consumed with rage. She betrayed the family. She rejected everything I valued, everything I gave. That was all I could see. I wasn't going to let her take one more inch. We fought over every detail. Looking back, I'm embarrassed at how I behaved. I don't see it the same way now. I never realized how dominating I could be. I didn't give her room to breathe. I made mistakes.
>
> PETE, *married 13 years*

You may notice how your feelings and outlook have changed since you first began to confront the collapse of your marriage. Perhaps you initially experienced a feeling of relief that you finally had the courage to separate; perhaps it was the alternating terror, denial, and shock that this couldn't really be happening to you. You may remember the first night you and your partner did not sleep under the same roof, the sleeplessness, numbness, loss of appetite. Then there was the gradual acclimation to being apart as the acute anxiety subsided into a dull but manageable ache and you settled into a new routine.

Separation is like an emotional roller coaster. You don't have control of your feelings and can't anticipate what will throw you back for another ride. An invitation to a great party lifts your spirits; then your spouse calls to tell you about papers the lawyer needs, and you're depressed. A reasonable exchange renews your optimism about reconciling and makes your day; a terrible fight douses your hope and sends you reeling. There are times when you feel rational and in charge of your life and other times when you are a wreck.

This is the normal emotional current of divorce. Everyone goes through stages. Rarely do spouses go through them at the same time because divorces are usually not mutual. The person who wants out has the advantage of having had more time to prepare emotionally and mentally; the still-loving partner may be in shock. You don't enter the stream at the same time. One of you has planned for the trip, has gear ready, and has acclimated to the water while the other may have been thrown in fully clothed. One of you may already be downstream and ready to turn the bend; the other can barely keep his head above water. You must take these differences into account.

Divorce is a process that occurs over time. It is not just an event that surrounds the legal document. It can take anywhere from several months to several years to actually get divorced—and even longer to recover. There are many points along the way for you to make conscious choices for hurting your spouse or healing yourself. Each stage of the divorce process presents opportunities for constructive responses as well as a seemingly endless array of obstacles and risks. The following section describes these stages and how to handle constructively the issues that arise.

THE EMOTIONAL STAGES OF DIVORCE[1]

Stage 1: Facing the Failing Marriage

The erosion of satisfaction in a relationship often begins innocently, imperceptibly. It starts when the glow of romantic illusion wears off and the couple fail to negotiate a more realistic union. It starts out when you give a part of yourself up to become who your partner wants you to be. It starts out when unexpressed feelings become the first stones in the wall between you.

Marriages are full of illusions, quid pro quos, and unconscious contracts about how the union will complete you, save you, or take care of you. The person who is to fulfill all of your expectations may step off the pedestal into everyday life and turn out not to be what you needed him or her to be. He is too domineering or too passive, insensitive or smothering, talks too much or too little, doesn't like to go out or is never home, ignores the children or indulges them, is selfish, spends too much money, drinks too much or any other characteristic that was not apparent earlier and that now seems incompatible with your needs.

The troubled marriage lives on deceptions and strategies to protect partners from facing or resolving what seems to be unresolvable. There is often a collusion to pretend that serious dissatisfaction isn't there. There is a periodic struggle, sometimes private and sometimes very loud, about what to do, who is to blame, just how serious the problems are, or whether one partner ought to go and get "fixed." These struggles can go on for a long time, above or below ground. Eventually, the couple begins to pull apart. They may avoid each other, pursuing independent interests. They may put a flurry of activity between them so they don't have to deal with each other. They may fight over every little thing because they can't resolve the real issue. They may withhold affection, not giving unless they first receive the love, attention, or acknowledgment they want from the other. The emphasis is on getting, not giving. Both spouses feel that they are not getting enough and find it easy to justify seeking comfort elsewhere.

A marriage may be salvageable at this stage because the spouses are still engaged with each other and fighting for something they want to recapture. But if help is not sought and things do not improve the emotional distance, conflict, or withholding of love becomes habitual. Sooner or later one partner will give up and become emotionally detached. This shift often goes unnoticed by the other partner.

Once detachment has occurred, the prognosis for rekindling the marriage is very poor. It is like a series of little emotional deaths. The pain can neither be tolerated nor denied any longer. A person stops caring. He has made what hurts not matter anymore, and has given up the emotional investment in the other. Fighting may subside into a cool coexistence. The detached person begins to think about the future without the marriage. He may fantasize about being single, where he will live, how he will survive, what kind of relationship he can have with his children. She rehearses the separation within the security of the marriage; she may even take concrete steps like going back to school or getting a job. The other spouse often has not understood the depth of the initiating partner's despair or detachment when the request for separation finally comes. How frequently I have heard a client say, "I knew there were problems, I just never thought it was this serious. I never thought she would file for divorce." Sometimes it is like being hit on the head with a two-by-four. The earlier signals were missed or denied, and now there is a desperate pleading to save the marriage. If a prolonged emotional detachment has occurred, the love has usually died and the marriage cannot be revived.

Risks During the Preseparation Stage

1. The emotional shock of actually facing separation can leave you panicked, overwhelmed, and confused about what to do. Be careful about impulsive decisions; give yourself some time to get your feet on the ground. Make changes slowly to allow each person enough time to process and integrate what is about to happen.

2. Often when a couple separates, there is a rush to gain a legal advantage. This is often the first step to what can become an increasingly adversarial relationship. If you can't discuss the terms of the separation with each other, particularly who will move out of the house and where the children will be, try to see a mediator.

3. If there is no communication, you don't know what the other's intentions are. This increases the need for legal protection

and creates mistrust. Sit down and try to rationally talk about how to handle the separation, as described in the last chapter.

4. Do not try to get the children to sympathize with your side of the story. Do not make the other parent the bad guy for needing to separate.

Ways to Be Constructive

1. *Recognize that you are both wounded.* Keep in mind that you are in this crisis together. The emotional injuries of facing a ruptured relationship need to be respected just as a physical injury is respected. Think about how you would relate to each other if you have been in a serious automobile accident together and were each limping away from the wreck.

2. *Agree to a cease-fire for a few weeks or longer.* You know each other's buttons; don't push them. Don't do or say things that you know will hurt or antagonize your spouse. If there has been a lot of conflict in the marriage, what you need right now is distance from the intensity of the conflict to assess the situation rationally.

3. *Try to see both sides of every issue.* In an ailing relationship, it is hard to see beyond your own pain and disappointment. You know very well what your partner has not given you, how he has fallen short, and what she has done to you. Most people have become habituated to seeing the marriage from their own perspective. Go out of your way to learn about how your partner sees things and how she has also been deeply hurt and disappointed. If you are the kind of person who has a tendency toward self-blame, then you will have to focus on understanding how your partner's failings contributed to the marital breakdown.

4. *Try to see beyond your feelings of personal rejection.* Consider the perspective the *relationship* is not working anymore; for example, the damage is too extensive to repair, the two of you together generated unhealthy patterns, or you have grown in different

directions. Write down the reasons the relationship didn't work and then list how you each contributed to the problem.

5. *Don't preclude the possibility of rebuilding the marriage.* Your feelings may change after you have been apart, especially if this is a first separation. The shock of separation can sometimes produce desired changes in the other person and as well as in yourself.

6. *Consider divorce counseling or individual psychotherapy*, if only to help you develop a broader perspective on what happened to the marriage and to help you separate more constructively. Anything that increases understanding will reduce feelings of abandonment and prevent the spiral of escalating hostilities they generate.

7. *Look at the separation as a crisis in your family.* Protect the children and make decisions based on what is best for them. Make this sacred. Wherever possible, sit down together and plan the separation by deciding how money and care of the children and the family residence will be handled.

Stage 2: Physical Separation

Two people rarely agree about the need for a separation or divorce. The more open communication there is about the decision to separate and the more each person comes to understand his contribution to the problems in the marriage, the less antagonism there is going to be about all the practical matters that need to be negotiated.[2] I cannot emphasize this point enough. When one person can't accept the separation or feels replaced by a new lover, things are going to be tougher. A divorce precipitated by an affair is a more difficult divorce. This must be understood by both parties. The abandoned spouse, in addition to being hurt, feels a sense of moral outrage. He has to deal not only with the rejection and loss of the relationship but also with the jealousy in witnessing someone else enjoy what he has lost or perhaps never had. The partner has moved on without giving proper respect or sense of closure to the marriage. The spouse with the new relationship has to take responsibility for the increased distress an affair brings to a divorce and handle the new relationship delicately. This may mean making reasonable accommodations to the spouse's ability to cope with the affair, especially where the children are concerned.

> There was no way I was going to support her if she continued to sleep with him in my house, in my bed, or entertain him with my money. She finally agreed to wait until we reached a settlement and every last bit of my stuff was out of the house before he would stay over. That helped.
>
> RICHARD, *married 11 years*

The act of separating joined lives is painful even for the initiator. Physical separation is only the first in a series of hard adjustments. It can be like a nightmare that doesn't end when you are awake. There is no way out but to simply plough through each day. You are in a state of crisis the first several weeks, with anxiety, panic, sleeplessness, loss of appetite, lack of concentration, numbness, and depression. Sometimes you can barely make it through the day. You have lost the familiar structure of your life and perhaps your surroundings, emotional support, and strongest family tie.

The Psychological Tasks of Uncoupling

Psychologically, the separation period is marked by several issues. First, you have to deal with what being alone represents, starting from Can I survive alone? to Who am I without this marriage? Even an unsatisfactory marriage provides some security. It is difficult to relinquish this attachment without believing in your ability to survive without it. The anxiety and panic that accompany the loss of attachment can keep you holding on to alliances that are no longer satisfying or healthy. Many people get involved in affairs, shifting their need for attachment to another relationship in order to be able to leave their marriage. They have not learned how to be alone and don't think they could survive it.

Second, you must cope with the enormous emotional up-heaval of this initial period. You are hit between the eyes with feelings you have probably never experienced before in your life. You can't think, you rage, you despair, you explode easily because you can't contain the storm within. You feel as if your life is going crazy. This is a normal reaction and has been variously described as temporary insanity or being "off the wall." It is a time when your emotional lid can come off. In addition to not caring anymore if you hurt your partner or not, you may find yourself having other unfamiliar feelings and acting in ways you never imagined you could: slamming phones, kicking doors, driving by and spying, screaming obscenities, name-calling, or aligning children against the enemy. This is a dangerous juncture in maintaining a construc-tive process because you are in an emotional, rather than rational, frame of mind. You will need to draw on your internal resources so that you don't inflict irrevocable damage. It is a time to honor your feelings about your losses so that you do less damage to yourself by being so angry.

A third psychological task is learning new ways of meeting a host of emotional needs that were once met, however unsatisfac-torily, in "coupledom." Loneliness will force you to reach out and try new things, meet new people, and take risks that you might not otherwise have been willing to take. Loneliness is one of the most painful parts of separation, but is also creates opportunities for growth if you see it as a challenge and are able to get beyond the stage of feeling sorry for yourself.

A fourth issue relates to the self-evaluation that comes when familiar roles change. The person you were in this marriage—what you did to please your spouse and how you acted in response to an unaffirming or deadening relationship—may not really be all that you are, were in the past, or can now become. When you lose the structure that helped define you, you are, as Robert Weiss in *Marital Separation* puts is, "between selves." Separation gives you a chance to experiment with new interests and people and provides an opportunity to develop a richer, renewed sense of self. We have all heard about how certain people changed once they got divorced—how he lost weight, how she got a permanent, how he started running, and so on. This is a stereotype but represents the kind of psychological sorting and experimentation that is as significant as what occurs during adolescence. In fact, this period is often referred to as a second adolescence. In time, a more evolved, mature you emerges, sometimes, ironically, becoming for the new partner what the first partner really wanted.

Another psychological task has been described as the review process. You try to put the pieces together by reviewing what you could have said, should have said, or should have done. If you did not see the breakup coming, sorting out your confusion may become a preoccupation. There is a compelling need to make sense of what happened and why. While reviewing the past is part of your own grieving, it is also important to keep on talking with each other about what happened. Sometimes you have to go over and over what seems like the same ground. Highly charged subjects are hard to absorb; things don't sink in at first. Every time you talk about the marriage, you will see it a little differently, speak of it a little differently, or hear about it a little differently. *Don't underestimate the value of continued dialogue.* Couples who have been able to talk about the seriousness of the problems leading up to their separation or who can talk about it once their anger subsides will be able to move beyond blame and develop some objectivity about the reasons for the failure of the relationship. This communication will help them deal with each other more fairly throughout the rest of the divorce, learn from it, and go on with their lives.

Finally, there is the expected ambivalence that characterizes any breakup. The decision to divorce is rarely firm at the time of separation, even for the initiator. You may find yourself alternately torn between repudiating your spouse and yearning for him. As you move through the separation you constantly test the decision you have made about your marriage. On some level you are always observing and evaluating your interactions with your partner.

When they go well you may feel that the marriage could work, but when they go badly you feel more resolute about the divorce. You may attempt reconciliations: little ones in your mind's eye, or actually dating or living together again. You will continue to do this mental tallying until your decision becomes clearer one way or the other.

Risks during the Initial Separation

1. The initial separation ushers in a highly emotional period; you are prone to mood swings, irrationality, and poor judgment. This is not a time to be making major decisions that could affect your future.

2. Avoid expressing your anger and feelings of rejection through the legal system. Do not withhold money or access to children when you feel rejected. Get emotional support to help you deal with your painful feelings.

3. There is a temptation to use the children as go-betweens or to pump them for information about what your spouse is doing. Even subtle questioning about the other household can make children feel disloyal or like they are spying.

4. There is a tendency to see a spouse who has hurt or betrayed you as unilaterally untrustworthy. Rarely is a person unreliable and untrustworthy in all areas. Try to differentiate between what you can and cannot trust about your partner. Were there lies about everything or just the affair? Has there been honesty about the children or money in the past? The risk lies in assuming the worst about your spouse and taking legal steps to protect yourself, which requires your spouse in turn to take even more aggressive steps against you.

Ways to Be Constructive

1. *Concentrate on self-care.* You have been hurt and you need to heal. Don't expect to function at your full capacity. *Do not underestimate the stress of divorce.* It affects your concentration at work, your driving, your patience with the children, and your health. Make

allowances for this and take care of yourself physically with proper rest, exercise, and good nutrition. Do nurturing things for yourself.

2. *Have a sounding board*. Seek out friends you can talk to objectively or find yourself a therapist or support group. If alcoholism, abuse, or addictive disease were factors in your divorce, support groups can be extremely important in your own healing.

3. *Limit contact with your spouse to reduce the stress this creates*. Stay away from each other for agreed periods of no contact. Limit phone calls and, if necessary, communicate in writing.

4. *Find an outlet to release strong emotions safely*. For example, sports, exercise, throwing darts at a photo of your spouse, tearing a picture of your spouse into shreds, attaching a photo of him or her to the bottom of your shoe and stomping around for 10 minutes a day.

5. *Concentrate on getting better instead of getting even*. Work on healing yourself instead of hurting or hating your spouse.

6. *Recognize both sides of yourself, the rational and the emotional*. Strong contradictory feelings coexist within you, and you can flip-flop suddenly. Nurture the emotional side, but try to make decisions with your rational side.

7. *Know when to get help*. If things deteriorate, try to get your spouse to see a mediator or a family therapist to keep things from going downhill even further.

8. *Get legal advice if you are concerned, but continue to try to work with your spouse*. Choose an attorney with a cooperative orientation who sees the value in negotiating and mediating.

9. *Don't push for a legal settlement if your spouse is still very angry or fighting the divorce*. A friend whose wife filed for divorce right after they had separated said to me, "I'm going to nail her; she

can't do this to me." Five months later, he was the one urging mediation.

Stage 3: Mourning, Grieving, and Emotional Regrouping

> I was crushed, like a part of me had died. For months I couldn't do anything but think about Susan, trying to get her to see we could work things out. I still don't think I am over her, but I am trying to move on.
>
> JIM, *divorced 1 year*

> I knew I was going to die if I didn't get out of this marriage. We couldn't talk. We buried our feelings until there was nothing between us except the shell of a life. I was depressed for a long time before I got the courage to leave. I think I must have been grieving for years. It was so sad. He is not a bad person.
>
> DONNA, *divorced 2 years*

Regardless of how the separation began, each of you in your own way will have to go through the process of grieving. Your relationship has died and this loss must be mourned.

Elizabeth Kübler-Ross, in her work on death and dying, has described five stages in the grief and mourning process. These stages are applicable to divorce as well. You do not necessarily go through the stages in sequence, nor are you and your spouse likely to be dealing with the same stage at the same time. Often it seems as if your spouse isn't really suffering the way you are. He or she may have begun mourning the loss of the relationship long before the actual physical separation, may be hiding or denying grief, or may not grieve until sometime later.

The Stages of Mourning

1. *Shock and denial.* There is an overwhelming anxiety and panic at the threat of the loss of a loved one, and the initial response is often to deny that it is really true: "She doesn't really mean it"; "He'll come to his senses after he has been away." Your denial may have started years before the separation, when you refused to admit that the relationship was seriously ailing.

2. *Anger*. When you can no longer deny the reality of your loss, there is anger and rage in response to the pain: "How can you do this to me?" You may direct your rage at your spouse or at no one in particular or be full of self-blame for the mistakes you made that can no longer be corrected.

3. *Bargaining and recapitulation*. You try to do whatever you can to regain the lost relationship by pleading for another chance or stating that you will make all the changes your partner has been requesting. You experience a feeling of regret, thinking "If only I had done XY or Z."

4. *Sadness*. You face your feelings of loss and allow yourself to be sad. You experience the painful feelings you have been avoiding. You think about the good times, you forgive yourself for the bad, and you cry and mourn the loss of the parts of your former life that you will miss. You embrace all of these feelings, even in small segments, instead of pushing them aside.

5. *Acceptance*. Finally, you reach a point at which you recognize that the situation will not change and that you must accept responsibility for your part, begin to make peace with yourself, and try to move ahead. You have already cried, felt sorry for yourself, and been angry. You have needed these feelings. You now realize that it is time to let go of the past and all of your hurt and angry feelings and look toward the future. The pain only becomes greater when you try to cling to something that no longer exists.

The mourning process is a crucial part of healing. It can take months or years. May people try to avoid it. They rush into a new relationship, a whirlwind of activity, or litigation. Or they cling to the past and hang on to their anger. They get stuck in one part of the grief process and don't experience the parts that would allow them to complete the cycle and move on. It is not uncommon to remain depressed and never experience the anger or to remain angry and not experience the grief. Mourning will pass but it cannot be omitted. Paradoxically, you have to probe deeper into your feelings in order to come out freer and healthier on the other side.

Risks during the Mourning Process

1. Some people get caught up in the anger phase and use the legal system to express their feelings of loss, rejection, or injured pride When you concentrate on battle, you are diverted from the pain of your loss but ultimately undermine your own healing.

2. Some people have a tendency to fixate on their role as the victim. By focusing on their suffering and misfortune they are able to elicit the sympathy of friends but are not able to move on with their lives. This is a stage, but you can move through it to better self-esteem if you acknowledge how much you were hurt and how helpless you felt, and begin little by little to see the actions you can take in your own behalf.

3. There is a risk of becoming absorbed by your anger because it feels so justifiable. The hostility generated by focusing on anger may block out pain, but it also creates a vicious cycle of retaliation. This fighting keeps you emotionally involved with your former spouse.

4. Many people avoid the mourning process because they are afraid their feelings will be overwhelming or that they will not be able to get themselves back together. Allowing yourself to experience your grief in small doses, seeing a therapist to help you work through your losses, and finding a supportive friend to talk to are ways to begin moving through the mourning you may have been avoiding.

How to Be Constructive

1. *Give yourself permission to grieve.* Lower your usual performance expectations. Allow yourself periods of time just to feel sad and to reflect. Remember what was good.

2. *If you haven't already, allow yourself to be angry that the marriage didn't work and that you are now facing all sorts of losses.* This is a different kind of anger than blaming your spouse or blaming yourself. As Virginia Satir, a well-known family therapist, has said, "If you have to throw shit, just don't aim it at anyone."

3. *Consider grieving rituals.* When you are ready, consider a grieving ritual where you symbolically enact a burial of the relationship. You could gather the things that remind you of your ex and bury them, store them in a sealed box, or even burn them one by one. You could do the same thing for the resentments you are still carrying around: write them down on separate pieces of paper, store them in a box, read them every day for a week, and then burn them. You could put a large photo of your spouse above your dresser and talk to it each day for 10 minutes, saying all the things you never said; at the end of a week say good-bye and bury it. You could write all the things you are sorry for or wished you have done differently on pieces of paper. Each day for a week put one of these written regrets on your bathroom mirror, reading it aloud in the morning and again in the evening. At the end of the week take the pieces of paper off the mirror one by one, saying out loud that you forgive yourself for whatever is written on each one. These rituals are designed to be cathartic, to let you get the deeper feelings of pain and grief out of your system. You could design a ritual of your own as a way of letting go of some aspect of the marriage. Let yourself cry and feel the emotions that come up, but have a time limit and do something nurturing for yourself afterward. Men especially are programmed not to cry or express pain, and they often have trouble permitting themselves to grieve. A ritual might help. (There is a more detailed discussion of rituals in chapter 17).

4. *Try to begin to forgive yourself as well as your spouse.* You did the best you could at the time. You can honor that. Clinging to your anger and resentment only hurts *yourself*.

5. *Let go of the relationship as a source of security, approval, or validation*. Let go of caring about what your spouse thinks. Learn to do the things that you formerly depended on your spouse to handle, like car repairs or cooking. Review the ways you have learned to depend on yourself, and try to do things yourself that you thought you could never do. Give yourself a goal of one new risk each week, and reward yourself somehow, even if it is just by acknowledging that you did it. This can be a slow process. Take your time. You can do it.

Stage 4: Rebuilding

The rebuilding stage is the period when you can finally think of yourself as a single person. If you have children, you can envision the prospect of having a new family with them apart from the family of your marriage. Even though you have the normal flashbacks, you are no longer dwelling on the past. You are experimenting with a renewed sense of self, have begun to social-ize and make new friends, and are clearly looking forward and making future plans. Although the practical realities of being a single parent or not having your children can be a struggle and although you still have disagreements with your ex, the divorce is no longer the central focus of your life.

Risks at the Rebuilding Stage

1. Failing to get an emotional divorce. You are tied to the past through continued hostilities and conflict with your former mate or by a prolonged separation without movement toward divorce.

2. Not getting on your life and not taking responsibility for rebuilding and going forward.

3. Continuing to see yourself as a victim of your situation. This will create self-fulfilling prophesies If you do not allow yourself to expect good things to happen, you will not take adequate steps in positive directions.

Ways to Be Constructive

1. *Create new family rituals and traditions.* Celebrate special occasions in new ways or think of special ways to brighten ordinary occasions (e.g., Sunday brunch, first Thursday of the month family dinners, or red food on Valentine's Day). These can become the basis of new traditions and special times for the post-divorce family and will increase the feeling of still being a family.

2. *Develop new circles of friends besides the ones you had as a couple.* Reach out and take one social risk a month.

3. *Date and seek out new relationships.* Become involved in new activities or rediscover past interests. Join recreational groups or community organizations that will enable you to meet new people.

4. *Maintain a respectful, business-like relationship with the children's other parent and keep the channels of communication open.*

5. *Encourage your children to feel comfortable and have a place of their own in each household.*

6. *When you have flashbacks of anger at your ex, use the energy to do something positive for yourself.*

RESOLVING BLAME AND GUILT: AN EXERCISE

Here is a sentence completion exercise that can help you come to terms with the breakdown of your marriage and perhaps help you begin to let go. Answer each question with the first thing that comes to mind, without editing your responses. Then go through the questions again and take your time. Write down all of your responses and save them. You may want to repeat the exercise in 6 months and compare your responses.

You may choose to ask your spouse to answer the same questions. If you choose to share this information with your spouse, I strongly recommend that it be done in writing so that each is free to explore his or her own feelings honestly, without feeling defensive. So much communication and information between troubled spouses is based on defensiveness rather than honest self-reflection. This sentence completion exercise is an opportunity to explore your feelings honestly and, if you choose, to tell each other what has really been in your heart.

1. I am angry at you for _____

_____

2. I am angry at myself for _____

_____

3. I should have _____

_____

4. You should have _____

_____

5. I wish we could have _____

_____

6. I am sorry for _____

_____

7. I want you to acknowledge _____

_____

8. I feel you owe me _____

_____

9. I feel I owe you _____

_____

10. I need to forgive myself for _____

_____

11. I need to forgive you for _____

_____

12. I learned from you and by knowing you gained in the following ways _____

_____

13. I enriched you in the following ways _____

_____

14. I wish _____

_____

15. I wish _____

_____

In this chapter we have explored some of the emotional territory of splintered relationships. I have tried to help you understand the stages you will go through, the importance of the perspective of time, and the importance of thinking ahead and taking the long-term view.

There is no easy way through the anguish and pain. All divorce is hard. The difference is in how you expend your energy. The divorce process will take its toll on you in one way or another, that is, in the high costs of continuing conflict and hostility or in the hard work of remaining reasonable and constructive. There is no escaping the pain, but you always have a choice in how you use your energy.

4

The Seven Keys to a Constructive Divorce

> No man in doing a difficult thing, and doing it very well ever loses self-respect.
>
> GEORGE BERNARD SHAW

You may be asking yourself how it is possible for two people who were not able to get along well enough to remain married to cooperate and work together on their divorce. Many a skeptical judge has said, "If they could get along so well, they would still be married." This is a myth.

Paradoxically, separation can bring a freedom of expression that didn't exist during the marriage. You can talk about how you really feel because there is nothing more to lose. The worst fear has been confronted. There are no more reasons to hide the things that couldn't be discussed. There are no more reasons to deny how bad things were. Many couples report that when they faced the reality of separating, they could finally have an honest dialogue, often for the first time. As one client said, "We talked more in three days than we had in three years. Then he moved out."

As time goes on, it becomes possible to communicate with each other differently because the relationship is no longer based on the dynamics of intimacy. The motivating rules and expectations that govern marriage no longer apply. As the elaborate dance of love ends, the emotional commerce of marriage—the desire for attention, approval, and support—becomes less important. Things that once mattered no longer do. As you let go, your reaction to the things your partner does or doesn't do, says or doesn't say, will be different. This change, which takes time to occur, presents opportunities to move beyond your habitual patterns and perhaps relate to each other in ways you couldn't in the past. Ironically, the trauma of divorce can provide the motivation to change what you couldn't change before.

> I always went along with what she wanted. I didn't want to upset her. I almost never said what I thought. Our whole marriage was like that. It got me an ulcer and a divorce. Now I speak my mind. I don't care if she disagrees. I don't have to kiss her good night anymore.
>
> JOHN, *separated 6 months*

> Right up to the end I fought the divorce. Finally, I had to accept that I couldn't make him love me. I stopped jumping through hoops to get his approval. I had done that for eleven years. I started taking care of myself instead of him. For the first time I felt strong, like an equal. He looks at me differently now. He doesn't push.
>
> LINDA, *separated 1 year*

THE DIVORCE HONEYMOON

Many couples go through a period when they first separate of being able to talk honestly and openly, when they are introspective rather than defensive, when they try to understand what went wrong. This is the time when the motivation to work out the divorce issues and keep things from turning into a battleground is strongest. Working through the details of the settlement later on may result in serious conflict, which can tear apart this feeling of wanting to cooperate. Talk to your partner about making an agreement to try to work things out cooperatively while you are still able to talk to each other reasonably—before new lovers, friends, or family get in the middle. If you can *commit* to trying to keep your divorce civilized and to use nonadversarial professional assistance, you will have a safety net when the going gets rough.

THE SEVEN KEYS

The principles on page 56 are the cornerstones for building a future that is not torn apart by the past. As obvious as they are, the elements of a constructive divorce become obstructed from view by the emotional intensity of the experience. It is all too easy to stop caring about what happens and start justifying destructive behavior. It is easy to get trapped in spiraling hostilities. *Photocopy this and paste it on your mirror.*

1. Take Responsibility for Regulating Your Own Behavior Regardless of What Your Spouse Does

Make a commitment to yourself not to escalate the conflict or damage your working relationship with your spouse *in the long term*. Keep that commitment whether or not your spouse reciprocates. Do not use his or her bad behavior to justify your own. Do not resort to a tit for a tat way of relating. Have some sense of just how far you will let a situation deteriorate before you try to improve it. Just as married couples reach a point at which a fight goes too far and they make up, if you let things go too far in divorce-fighting, you can end up in court.

There is a point where the level of tension, conflict, or open hostility crosses an invisible line, a point at which something snaps and one person gives up trying to cooperate and turns everything over to a lawyer. Restraining orders can then be imposed. Communication and compromise virtually disappear. I have seen individuals even in mediation make one too many nasty comments or attack a weak spot so hard that the spouse simply walks out of mediation, saying, "That's it, I won't be treated this way anymore. You can deal with my lawyer." When you continu-

1. TAKE RESPONSIBILITY FOR REGULATING YOUR OWN BEHAVIOR REGARDLESS OF WHAT YOUR SPOUSE DOES. Don't let your emotions completely dictate your behavior even if your spouse can't do the same.

2. SEPARATE YOUR EMOTIONS FROM THE DECISION MAKING PROCESS. Apply a standard of enlightened self-interest and reasonableness to the conflicts with your spouse.

3. SEPARATE YOUR JOB AS A PARENT FROM THE CONFLICTS WITH YOUR SPOUSE. Protect the children from the need you and your spouse may have to hurt each other.

4. ACCEPT RESPONSIBILITY FOR YOUR CONTRIBUTION TO THE DIVORCE. Don't get stuck in blaming your partner, because it will prevent you from learning and growing from your experience.

5. LEARN TO UNDERSTAND YOUR SPOUSE'S VIEWPOINT. Make an effort to see both sides because it will improve your chances of getting what you want and allow you to diffuse your anger and resentment.

6. BE WILLING TO NEGOTIATE, COMPROMISE, AND CO-OPERATE IN RESOLVING YOUR DIFFERENCES. Divorce is a long-term relationship when children are involved; the more you can learn about negotiating your differences now, the more you will be able to avoid serious problems later.

7. MAKE A COMMITMENT TO AN EQUITABLE AND NON-ADVERSARIAL SETTLEMENT PROCESS. Use the court only as a last resort; you will benefit more if you spend your money on counselors and mediators rather than on litigation.

ally act out your angry emotions, you risk crossing over into this "destructive zone" with each negative interchange that leaves one of you frustrated, upset, or angry. The escalation of hostility and the complete breakdown of trust are very hard to reverse. Since you don't know each other's breaking point, the best course is prevention, by limiting your own contribution to this kind of volatility.

At times this will feel like you are going against all of your natural reflexes. You will hate your spouse and won't care what happens. You will want to act out angry emotions. You will want to compensate for the way decisions were made in the past. You will want to prove that you are "right," and show your spouse how bad, wrong, or unworthy he or she is. You will want to get even, and nothing else will matter. Everyone going through a divorce feels these things and acts on them *some of the time*.

When you want to have a reasonable discussion or talk about a sensitive issue you will have to exercise an enormous amount of self-control. You will have to rehearse what you want to say and how you are going to respond to your spouse's provocations. You will need a method of calming yourself down. It will feel stilted and unnatural to communicate with a former intimate with formality and forethought. But because so many hot issues can flare up, it is important to learn mechanisms for relating differently so that the old buttons aren't always pushed and you can cool down if things escalate.

> Every time I called John to ask something about the kids or finances, I had to literally brace myself to stay level-headed and stick to the subject. I had to watch every word I said because his excuses would enrage me. I mean I have to take deep breaths, count to ten, the whole bit. It made me mad I had to work so hard at being calm especially when he wasn't. At least we didn't get into the same old screaming matches.
>
> JAN, *separated 6 months*

We'd have civilized discussions for about four minutes, then the whole thing would break down. We're trying to decide whether to sell the house, and she starts in about how I never cared about what she needed, how I was a lousy lover. What did that have to do with it? I'm tired of her harangues. She can go to hell.

Jim, separated 3 months

Here are three techniques that will help you stay more level headed and manage your emotional reactions better whenever you want to have a reasonable discussion with your spouse:

Model on a Successful Relationship

Talk to your spouse the way you would talk to a colleague you respect at work. Think of an acquaintance, business associate, or colleague with whom you get along well. Close your eyes and visualize yourself discussing a problem with this person. Notice your behavior, your attitude, and your language. Now imagine talking to your spouse as if you were talking to this person. How would you ask for a favor, how would you express a difference of opinion, and how would you negotiate a joint responsibility? How would you stay calm in a business setting if the other person became upset? As an exercise, visualize yourself talking through an issue that is coming up with your spouse the way you would talk to your colleague or "model." Take a few minutes to practice this exercise.

Get into this mind-set before you have an encounter or discussion with your spouse. Act as if you were speaking to your colleague regardless of how your spouse talks to you. Do not lose your cool just because your spouse does. If discussions get heated or you find yourself unable to think of what to say, take a deep breath and ask yourself what you would say or do if you were talking with your colleague at work. Use this as your standard. Or, as one of my divorced friends suggests, pretend you are a banker and your spouse is a customer requesting a loan; now discuss child support.

Mental imaging or visualization works because it allows you to utilize skills that are available to you in other situations. By programming yourself mentally to be in the other situation, a different set of automatic behaviors, which can override the difficulty you are currently encountering is activated. Another example of visualization is in this instruction from the *Inner Guide to Skiing*: "Imagine the mountain a big bowl of vanilla ice cream and you are hot fudge flowing down. Now ski." Your mind follows the image. It is focused on something other than your struggle. Similarly, you must focus on the image of your colleague, not your spouse. These techniques work, but you do have to prepare mentally.

Slow Down Your Reactions

When you are upset, don't just react. THINK. When our bodies tense up, breathing becomes shallow, limiting the flow of oxygen to already tight muscles. You literally forget to think. You forget how to calm yourself. A few deep breaths, in which you concentrate on the breathing, perhaps counting to five as you exhale, eases the tension in the body, allows you to regain control, and gives you time to think about what you want to say. Breathing is a relaxer. It can be used as the mediator between your upset feelings and your response. If you are the kind of person who always says whatever comes to mind, then the practice of slowing down and thinking before you speak can be helpful in many situations.

Too much emotion clouds anyone's judgment. When we are angry, upset, or depressed, we tend to lose perspective and the controversial issues appear pervasive. The picture looks darker than it really is. An argument over child support can turn into "that untrustworthy bastard; I can't depend on him for anything." The trick is to recognize this kind of reaction as a reaction and not make decisions based on these feelings. Whenever you find yourself overgeneralizing (saying, "She always . . ." or "He never . . ."), chances are you are upset and it is best to stop talking or thinking about the issue and come back to it later.

Use Deescalating Procedures

Every encounter with your partner has the potential to escalate out of control. Learn to pay attention to the rise in temperature and devise a predetermined way of cooling down. If possible, agree jointly on what your deescalating procedures will be. You can cool down by taking a time-out to collect your thoughts, counting to ten, walking around the block, or ending a discussion. In the following paragraphs are some other ways to deescalate.

- Pay attention to the early warning signs of an unproductive discussion and intercede *before* it turns into a bad fight. A discussion headed for trouble is characterized by any of the following elements: talking but not listening; being closed-minded, defensive, or inflexible; repeating the same things over and over again; arguing over the past; resorting to power struggles; or having a growing sense of frustration and a feeling of going around in circles. You get caught up in these patterns without realizing it. From the inside, you can't see when you are the one who is being closed-minded or defensive or is not listening. It is easier to notice these behaviors in your partner or have them pointed out to you by a third party. Increase your sensitivity to these "getting nowhere" patterns so that you will be able to recognize them early on.
- State that the discussion doesn't seem productive as soon as you first begin to observe *any* of these elements. Sometimes just acknowledging an unproductive discussion is sufficient to put it back on track. Try to refocus on the issue being discussed, and listen more openly to find out what is really concerning the other person instead of defending yourself. "John, we seem to be going in circles and criticizing each other's parenting. I thought we were trying to figure out how to make sure the kids have enough clothes at both houses. What do you see as the problem with the clothes, and do you have any suggestions?" If this kind of refocusing doesn't help, it is better to calmly and honestly end a discussion rather than angrily continue it.
- Another technique is to take a heated issue under advise-

ment, like a judge. Say to your spouse that you are having a strong emotional reaction to this issue and you need time to calm down and reflect. It is easier to think once your emotions have quieted down and you are not feeling defensive or under attack.

• You can use a code word, like *erase*, as a deescalator. Say it when you have said something that you want to take back or when a discussion gets way off track. In a way, this serves as an apology except that it is easier and faster to say. If both participants have agreed to use a code word, there is more freedom to quickly undo a destructive comment without lengthy explanation or discussion. It is particularly useful when one of you has hit below the belt and inflamed your partner, for instance, by name-calling. When you use *erase*, it must be treated like the cancel key on a computer: that is the end of it. Don't go back and discuss what was "erased" or whose fault it was. It is understood that the comment was a mistake and is taken back. For example, if your spouse says, "You are not a good parent, you don't really care about the children, you just want the time to go to bars to pick up men," and your counterresponse is, "Look who's talking; you were off having an affair while I was home with the kids, you never did. . .," one of you just says, "Erase," you take a deep breath, put your attack aside, and go back to what you were discussing, like who is going to pay for soccer camp.

In summary, when emotions get too heated, you can take a time-out, count to ten, take a few deep breaths, take the issue under advisement, "erase," or apologize if you acted in an inappropriate manner. Flare-ups are bound to occur; but if you practice these damage control procedures, you may be able to continue a discussion without letting it skyrocket out of control. And remember that when you do remove yourself from a volatile or unproductive discussion and give yourself time to think, you are taking care of yourself.

2. Separating Emotions from Decision Making

Don't make decisions when you are upset, and don't make major decisions based on your anger, guilt, or pain. The emotional overload of divorce seriously weakens your capacity to think rationally. Your perceptions are colored by the intensity of your feelings, and you feel absolutely justified in actions and decisions that you might normally question. It is easy to be driven by emotions that are untempered by reason. It is only later that you can look back and realize how immature and irrational you were. While you are living through a divorce, you may simply not see or care about the possible repercussions of your actions. You may do what satisfies your immediate feelings.

I had a client who took his wife off his health insurance policy without telling her because he felt that if she really wanted her independence, she could take care of herself. The wife in turn refused to let the children go to a special event with their father. In the long run both jeopardized their own interests, because the husband was liable for his wife's medical costs while they were still legally married and the wife invited her children's resentment for denying them an opportunity for fun with their father.

Everyone acts out emotions some of the time. But in divorce you can get into trouble when you allow your emotional side to dominate. When you are functioning at your best, problem solving and emotions work together. In the throes of divorce, your rational abilities are impaired because of the overload on your emotions. Recognize this impairment *as if it were a physical handicap*, and get help to strengthen your objectivity and improve your problem-solving abilities. See a therapist, go to a mediator, or talk to a friend who understands both sides.

Try to view difficult situations or decisions through both the emotional and logical parts of your brain. As an exercise in control, you can say to yourself, "My emotional side wants to kill, maim, or mutilate." Acknowledge how you feel, even if it is irrational. Let yourself feel it. Give yourself permission to have the feelings— but not to act upon them. For example, the emotional side might say, "If he brings that slut around the children, he can forget about joint custody. I hope he drops off the face of the earth. I am not going to cooperate with that selfish bastard, he doesn't deserve to be a father. . . ." Then take a few deep breaths, calm down, and get in touch with your rational side. Try to look at the situation objectively: How does your spouse view the situation? What are your real needs in this situation? What can you realistically affect, and are there any other options? What can you offer your spouse to get him or her to agree to what you want? In this example, the wife's rational side might say, "I feel hurt by his involvement with another woman. He has the right to date, but I am not ready to handle the children being around her. I don't think it is good for them to see him with another woman so soon either. I can ask him not to have her around the children for the next three months."

This exercise may seem like a lot of extra work, but think of all of the damage that has to be undone when you act irrationally. I have seen couples who have already worked out agreements in mediation come to a session and threaten to call the whole deal off in retaliation for hurtful things that were said during the week. The solution is not to ignore your intense emotions. You need some safe venue for their expression. You can fantasize whatever evils you want to befall your spouse. Have some outlet in the privacy of your own home where you can drain off some of your hostility; as suggested earlier, try throwing darts at a photo of your mate or taping a photo to the sole of your shoe.

Divorce becomes destructive when spouses lose access to their rational side and when they can't use reason to temper their emotions. Most people have to work very hard at maintaining reasonableness. Strengthen your rational capacities by using the previously described exercise just as you would strengthen any weakened muscle by exercising to bring its function back. You can use the chart on page 64 to help you think something through whenever you experience an especially strong emotional reaction to an issue. After you have sorted out your feelings and looked at the situation more objectively, develop a plan based on a balance

Emotional side	Rational side	Reasonable position
I want to make her suffer the way I have. I'll take the things I know she wants from the house.	She has also suffered.	I'll decide what I want most out of the house.
I gave 16 years of my life so *he* could do whatever he wants. Now I'll do whatever *I* want.	He also worked hard to provide for the family. He does care about the kids.	I will only make accommodations that are convenient for me. I don't have to change my plans for him.
She only cares about what she wants, so she can go to hell. I'll fight for whatever I think is fair.	She thinks she has made concessions, but I think I have made far more.	I'll make a list of the major concessions we have each made for future reference.

between how you feel, what you need, and what is reasonable. Get what you need rather than getting even.

3. Separating the Job of Parenting from the Conflicts of Divorce

Couples who have handled their divorces constructively have learned to separate their relationship as parents from their relationship as a couple. They are willing to put the children's well-being above their own needs to control or hurt each other. Protecting the children from their conflict is sacred; the children become a demilitarized zone.

> After my wife's affair, I didn't trust her at all. I felt betrayed and humiliated. He was a mutual friend. I thought if she could disregard my feelings this way, she could be as insensitive and selfish to the children. I hated her. I wanted to think of her as a bad parent, but I knew in my heart of hearts she had always been an excellent mother. The kids came before anything. I had to admit she was rejecting me, not the family. I forced myself to be civil and respectful to her as a parent. It was the hardest thing I had to do. I did it for the kids.
>
> RALPH, *separated 6 months*

Children create profound and lasting ties between adults, even if those adults no longer love each other. After separating, a couple with children are still thrown together in awkward and unfamiliar ways. What seemed natural, being a parent, becomes uncertain, tentative, and in jeopardy. What was automatic and natural, a given, now needs to be explicit and negotiated. Being a parent is suddenly cast in a new light. Successful parents approach this challenge creatively. They do not work against each other. They respect the children's relationship with the other parent. They share. They develop agreements about how the details will be handled. They learn to separate their feelings about each other from their relationship as parents. Most of all, they are willing to exercise enormous self-discipline to carry this out.

Most of the problems divorced parents have occur because they have been unwilling, or have not yet learned how, to separate the conflicts that existed in their marriage from how they relate as parents. They continue the marital fight, power struggle, and retaliation through the children. To be successful parents after divorce, you must isolate the parental role functionally and emotionally. You must pull apart the strands of the fabric of the family, keeping the colors and patterns of the fibers representing you as parents but eliminating the strands that represent you as lovers, intimates, and mates. You must gently unravel activities, responsibilities, dreams, and feelings that were once part of a whole and divide them into parts. You begin to see and relate to this person—who was once your children's mother or father and your wife or husband, lover, and friend—as only mother or father.

In the beginning it helps to think consciously about and concentrate on being a parent when you have to talk to your ex about children. *Remind yourself that you are talking to the children's parent, not to your spouse.* In a sense it is like wearing two hats, one for the role of parent and one for the role of spouse. Put on this metaphorical parental hat whenever you have to discuss the children with your ex. We all wear different hats for our different roles in life—at work, at home, or with friends. We act in distinct ways with different people in each of these situations. The parent persona is now another role that you have to consciously assume when dealing with the person who is no longer your spouse. In time, it will become automatic.

When communicating with your ex, you can test yourself with the following question: How am I responding now, as the parent or as the spouse? Am I John the husband who has felt dominated and is going to take a stand or John the father who is looking at what is practical under the circumstances? Am I Mary the rejected spouse who is resisting overnight visits or Mary the mother who knows Jimmy misses his Dad? Sometimes you may not want to admit the answer. The biggest obstacle is your own hurt and desire to hurt your spouse.

If it is difficult for you to separate these roles when you need to interact as parents, try the mental imaging technique described earlier in this chapter. Close your eyes and do a brief visualization in which you see yourself performing parenting tasks and then visualize your spouse doing things with the children.

4. Accepting Responsibility for Your Contribution to the Divorce

My anger held me together for a long time. I blamed her and made the divorce difficult. I don't think I really understood why she left until the day we signed the decree in the lawyer's office. She looked different in that light—she could do what she wanted. I guess I never understood that she wasn't doing what she wanted, that I wasn't giving her what she needed. She told me, but I thought she was just upset and would get over it.

DON, *divorced 1 year*

It can be years before you understand what really happened to your marriage. It is like a puzzle with missing pieces that fall into place as the years go by. You hardly know where it comes from, but suddenly you have a perspective that was not there before. You see something about yourself that your spouse had been saying all along. You grasp things about your former mate that you never understood before. You realize how you may have "enabled" situations for which you blamed your partner. You realize how you blamed yourself for problems that were your spouse's. If you want to grow and heal from your divorce, it is essential that you look at yourself, try to understand your role in the collapse of your marriage, and not make blaming your partner the focus of your attention. *If you stay married to your blame, you are never really divorced.*

Anger is a medicinal balm. It dulls the ache in the gut. It restores self-esteem because the other one is at fault. It gives you something to cling to instead of emptiness. You need your anger, for a while. Many people hold on to their anger longer than they should. There comes a time when it is necessary to put aside anger. Eventually, you must forgive not only your partner but yourself. We do the best we can with what we know at the time. Believe that if you had known how to communicate effectively, understand each other more, and resolve conflicts better, you would have. You probably dealt with the marriage the best way you knew how *at the time*. So did your spouse. You both made mistakes.

5. Learning to Understand Your Spouse's Viewpoint

Make special efforts during the separation to see things from your partner's point of view. Failure to see the other person's side is frequently a blind spot in an ailing marriage that is carried over to divorce settlement discussions. You tend to concentrate on your own emotional reality since that view is closest and most familiar to you. You see your own losses and suffering, but not your spouse's. You see your budget constraints but think your spouse has plenty of money. You make assumptions and jump to conclusions without having all of the facts.

When you have been hurt, you don't want to see the other person's side. You don't want to see your mate's behavior in the context of your own. It is easier to think your spouse is acting with cruelty because he or she is evil and not because of being hurt, being self-protective, or reacting to something you said or did. Any relationship, even a divorce, is a system. You are always responding to what the other says, doesn't say, does, or doesn't do. Your spouse is reacting to you *just as much* as you are reacting to your spouse. Failure to understand this perpetuates your one-sided view.

6. Learning to Negotiate, Compromise, and Cooperate in Resolving Your Differences

Conflict is an inherent part of living with other people. In our culture it is imbued with all sorts of negative connotations. What matters is how conflict is handled. When differences are approached competitively—that is, in terms of who is right, at fault, or to blame—conflict will take a destructive course. It becomes a win/lose game based on asserting power and achieving your goals at the expense of the other. When disagreements are approached cooperatively, the focus is mutual problem solving. In this case conflict follows a constructive course since the goal is finding solutions that work for both. It is a win–win approach in which the integrity of the individuals and their ability to work with each other are preserved.

Conflict during divorce is unavoidable. The potential for disagreement exists in every decision that needs to be made, from who gets the china to the amount of child support. What is troublesome is that fights are not always about what you think they are about. The fight over the china may not really be about the china but about feeling owed. The more you have worked through your feelings about why the marriage fell apart, the less these feelings will extend into all of the practical matters and settlement negotiations. Then the disagreements over the china will have to do with how you really feel about the china, not about each other. Your conflicts are likely to be based on real differences in needs and interests rather than on who was more at fault in the divorce, thus creating an atmosphere more conducive to negotiation and problem solving.

Couples who successfully navigate the divorce minefield try to be problem solvers. Although it doesn't happen all at once, they stop competing over their differences and fighting about who was right. They accept the divorce as a reality for which they must find practical solutions. They accept the fact that they can't change each other or the past. They spend their energy on the question Where do we go from here? not Whose fault is it that we got here? They are willing to compromise, make trade-offs, and meet the other halfway to resolve the issues divorce raises.

7. Making a Commitment to an Equitable and Nonadversarial Settlement Process

Always strive toward a principle of fairness while recognizing that you may often disagree about what is fair. Make a commitment not to use the court to resolve impasses but instead turn to mediation, arbitration, or the various settlement conferences with judges that are now available. If you agree about how divisive and destructive litigation can be for your family and you make a commitment to exhaust mediation or other settlement procedures before seeking recourse from the courts, you will reduce one of the major threats in divorce. The threat of court can be either a motivator toward settlement or a club with which to beat each other. You cannot predict what the judge will decide; you cannot control the outcome. If you know you will be using court only as a last resort, you retain control over the final settlement. Your differences feel less dangerous. It will be safer to talk honestly and you can tolerate periods of conflict knowing that you have a way to deal with impasses. You have an enormous safety net in a commitment to use a neutral third party if you get stuck.

> Mediation was not easy. It was painful to sit there with him and be rational about how our lives would be split apart. I left each session drained and emotionally exhausted. There I was with a baby and a marriage that wasn't working. Nothing could make that feel O.K. Nothing could give me back my broken dreams. At times I just couldn't face him, and we had to postpone meetings. In the end, mediation was worth it. We solved problems. We had never been very good at that. We had never learned to work together as a team.

There were not great alternatives in our situation. We came up with something we can both live with. We can still talk. I can let him be a parent. We understand each other better.

MARGARET, *divorced 1 year*

Being constructive is easier said than done. It requires a generosity of spirit that may not have existed in the marriage. There are many obstacles, but intention and commitment are the first steps. Behavior is organized around intention. If your intention is to be constructive, then your behavior will be more constructive. You may even consider making your intention the seeking of the highest good for everyone—a lofty goal, unreachable for most, but worthy of consideration. Do what is in the direction of good, whether or not your spouse reciprocates. Eventually he or she might. Someone has to go first, always. Positive actions tend to breed positive responses. Consider making a positive overture when you feel ready. During your angry period this may be out of the question, but at least try to limit the damage by thinking about the future. Try to follow the seven keys. You will see how these principles are ultimately in your self-interest and contribute to your own healing. In the words of one client:

I failed at my marriage, I wasn't going to fail at my divorce.

KAREN, *divorced 1 year*

5

Healing

That which does not kill me, makes me strong.
FRIEDRICH NIETZSCHE

The loss of a love relationship arouses your most primitive instincts. It overloads your emotional circuits. It taxes the capacity for rational thought. It puts you face-to-face with pain you didn't know existed. However, with pain comes choices. What kind of survivor are you going to be? What path will you choose to make your way through this period? Whenever we face a crisis, we all have choices about whether to draw on the survivor or victim tendencies within ourselves, whether to put our energies into self-healing or hurting back. There are going to be times when you will feel sorry for yourself, times when you will blame your spouse for your misery, times when you will feel defeated by the weight of a lost dream, by how hard it all is, and by how alone you feel. But there can be no recovery if you succumb to the role of pure victim. Ultimately, you have to stop and ask yourself how you want to see this period of your life when you look back on it. Do you want to feel ashamed over your immature and destructive behavior? Do you want your children angry at you when they become adults for estranging them from the other parent? Or do you want to look back and say, "I handled this crisis with integrity."

A trauma like divorce is also a crisis of the spirit. Your faith in yourself, your dreams, and what you've come to expect from life is shaken. You question who you are, what you did to deserve this suffering, and whether you are making the right choices. Many people turn to spiritual paths for help during a crisis because we can't always answer the questions our suffering raises. Our lives are often profoundly changed after a crisis. As Ann Kaiser Stearns has stated in *Living through Personal Crisis*: "Losses shatter our virgin thinking. As we lose our innocence, we learn how vulnerable we are. We know we are capable of profound suffering. We know we can hurt in ways previously inconceivable. Afterwards we can never quite forget the fragility of our humanness no matter how courageously we survive."[1] Sometimes all you can do is try to heal yourself and go forward.

One way healing occurs is through connecting to a source of strength, whether it be a higher power, higher ideals, or a higher self. You heal yourself when you nurture and cultivate your higher instincts at each crossroads and prevent your anger, despair, self-pity, or desire for revenge from running rampant. Whenever you transcend your ego's need to strike back in retaliation for being hurt, whenever you are able to forgive those who have hurt you, and whenever you act for the benefit of others, you promote self-healing. The way we do things counts. Marsha Sinetar in her book *Elegant Choices, Healing Choices* talks about the part of us that watches how we do things. Whenever we make highly ethical decisions, act for the greater good of the whole, or respond with integrity, we feel good about ourselves. Choices in the direction of virtue are healthy choices because they influence us in the direction and quality of our choice.

This book provides numerous resources for dealing with the practical problems of getting through divorce as constructively as possible, but ultimately your *attitude* is what will carry you through this painful period. If you make self-healing, rather than hurting, one of your goals, you will gain mastery over some things you might have thought were beyond your control. There is a strength that comes from setting your sights on a higher plane.

She kept talking about not wanting to be with me. Finally I began to think this could happen. I realized we weren't going to grow old together. I think now we just have to work toward ending it and being decent about it. I want to dissolve this marriage in a fair, rational way. I want to fulfill my obligations, but not give away my future. It's as if I have been in a cave and now I see a point of light. I have to go find that light—a release from a whole series of stresses, demands, and unhappiness. I see in her a scared, unhappy person who sees in me a life preserver. She is not really loving me. All I can do now is keep moving toward that light.

ERIC, *separated 2 months*

The intention to heal—the state of mind that says I will conquer this—is what works the miracle of self-healing. This determination changes the chemistry of the brain and can produce amazing reversals of disease. Norman Cousins and Bernie Siegel have written extensively about the power of the mind to heal the body and the pivotal effect a patient's attitude can have on his recovery. They suggest that there are vast untapped resources within each of us that can bring about positive change and restore health.[2]

Healing is a natural occurrence. A surgeon merely sets a fracture; the bones mend themselves. What we have to do is to consciously align ourselves with these positive forces within us. Though Western medicine is just beginning to research the role of attitude and mental states in healing illness, this approach is fast becoming an important new frontier.

In a crisis like divorce, the desire to heal can be a very powerful force in your own recovery. If you make healing your goal it can direct you toward decisions and actions that are positive in the face of pain. It can give you strength when you feel helpless and defeated. Consider letting healing become your mantra. Begin each day with a short meditation or self-affirmation: "My goal is to heal myself and my family. I am not a failure because my marriage didn't endure. I can survive and in time create a new future." Say this every morning. When you feel your anger is driving your actions, ask yourself two questions: What response would be beneficial to my own well-being and healing? What is the most positive way I can respond to what is happening now? Another exercise would be to visualize yourself already healed from your wounds. In the evening before you go to sleep, close your eyes and visualize yourself with the weight of the divorce lifted. Even though this may be difficult to do, try to see yourself having more energy and looking forward to doing something you really enjoy. It is important to remember what it was like to feel good.

There are many excellent meditation tapes on the market for self-healing, building self-esteem, and respond to a crisis as a challenge rather than as a victim. They are not hocus-pocus but can really work to counteract negative self-talk by providing positive ideas and images for your conscious and unconscious mind to absorb.

YOUR HURTING AND HEALING SIDES

I have urged you to try to follow a positive path. But as much as you try to do this, there will be another part pulling at you: your hurting self, the one who has had sorrow in love, the one who wants to blame someone, the one who just wants to lash out and doesn't care what happens. This part of you is there; it would be foolish to deny its existence. It is a human response to threat. However, when you are emotionally agitated, you can't see beyond your fury. Reasonableness is obliterated. You forget that there is another part of you sometimes buried deep inside. It is that part of the psyche that Gerald Jampolsky, in his book *Teach Only Love*, says has a "preference for peace." This part of you has higher instincts; it recognizes your great loss, sorrow, and broken spirit and longs to be whole again. Make a conscious effort to nurture this "healing" side; otherwise, your anger and pain will blind you to its existence. When you can touch your higher instincts and listen to the preference for peace within, you will ease your own pain and find alternatives to behaving unfairly or destructively.

As you acknowledge both the destructive and constructive parts of yourself, you can temper your negative impulses by remembering your deepest desires for healing. Right now you may be too angry to want to draw on your healing self, but in time cultivating this side can become a real source of strength.

There is a technique from Gestalt therapy in which you have an inner dialogue between the two conflicting feelings or "parts" of yourself. When you find yourself struggling with your anger or with a difficult decision, have a dialogue in your head between your "hurting" and "healing" parts. Let one begin by saying what it feels and what it wants to do; then let the other part respond with what it feels and might want to do. Continue this dialogue until you have fully explored both sets of feelings and the choices that might follow from each side. For example, your spouse refuses to discuss something of importance and tells you to take a hike:

HURTING SIDE: I don't have to take this; she can't treat me like this. I'll show her that she can't push me around.

HEALING SIDE: Maybe she is stressed out. Maybe she thought we wouldn't be able to resolve it. Maybe she is punishing me for losing my temper the last time we tried to talk.

HURTING SIDE: Still, she has no right to refuse to discuss something relating to the children. If she is going to jerk my chain about time with the kids, I'll refuse to pay for her car insurance.

HEALING SIDE: That would just escalate things. How important is it really that she talk to me about this now? Maybe I should let it go this time, or write a letter. It is not healthy for me to get all worked up and strike back. It is better to let small things go. I'll work around her and make a different plan to take the children on an outing.

Another example: You have just heard that your former spouse has taken a new lover on a trip the two of you had always wanted to take together. Your hurting side feels jealous, betrayed, and even more rejected. It wants to devise a plan to make your ex-spouse suffer the way you are suffering. You think of flaunting something that would make your ex jealous and hurt. You think of destroying something he or she values, some object that is still in your possession. Your healing side says, "I must put my energy into making myself happy. I will talk to a friend for support; I will plan a trip of my own. I will go running, go to a movie, anything that can help me put my energy into something enjoyable or positive for me."

INNER GUIDANCE DIRECTS YOU TO YOUR HIGHER GOOD

Spiritual thinkers believe that everyone has an "inner wisdom" that can be used to help guide one's life. Calling upon your inner wisdom in times of difficulty can help you cope with something that seems overwhelming or unresolvable. The idea is that we know more than we think we do about what is best for us—if we would only take the time to tune into ourselves.

There are many ways to develop your inner guidance. Perhaps one of the simplest and most common ways is to do what Shakti Gawain in her book *Visualization* suggests:[3] Take a few minutes to close your eyes and breathe deeply. Focus on your breathing and *allow your mind to empty*. Imagine that you are moving into a very deep and quiet inner place where you have a certain wisdom and awareness of what is true for you. Believe that this place exists. Let yourself visualize a place that is quiet, safe, and serene. Listen, and feel what is there. Ask for an answer to a question or problem, and then trust that the reply that comes from this place of inner wisdom is true. Ask what decision is best for all; ask to be guided to a solution that will work for everyone's benefit. You can use this technique of seeking inner guidance to help you cope when you are confronted with obstacles, with mean or nasty behavior from your ex-spouse, or when you need help with hard decisions.

MAPPING YOUR FUTURE

In the throes of crisis, it's difficult to see beyond your immediate pain. Many people try to survive a crisis one day at a time. It is hard to even think about the future while you are in the midst of loss. But there is a point when you eventually turn a corner and begin to see the road around the bend. The clearer your vision of the future becomes, the more successful you will be in moving toward it. If you don't know where you want to go, you will never get there.

Right now, you may be thinking that it is impossible to imagine yourself in the future with a new life. It is hard to imagine yourself calmer, knowing where you stand economically, accustomed to a new routine with the children, having created a home that is yours, feeling attractive to the opposite sex, noticing them noticing you, and finished with the everyday hassles of your divorce. It is hard to see outside the center of a cyclone. Yet that is precisely what you must try to do. To achieve success in any area, you must first be able to visualize yourself succeeding. By making your positive intentions and desires more vivid, detailed, and real, you increase their ability to create the life you want.

Begin to think about the life you would hope to create once you have come to terms with the divorce. If you were the initiating partner, what was it you wanted for yourself by leaving your marriage? If you were the still-loving partner, start to think about what you want for yourself if you can't have your marriage. So often we know what we *don't* want, but we don't have a very clear image of what we *do* want. Write a short paragraph describing what you want in your life. Give yourself permission to express *all* of your desires. Picture yourself thriving, not just existing.

VISUALIZE SUCCESS: AN EXERCISE

Here is a visualization exercise to help you see beyond your current situation and bring your future goals into greater focus.

It is based on the work of Milton Erickson, a seminal figure in the field of hypnosis. Visualizing successful outcomes is now a well-known technique and is frequently utilized in peak performance training for professional athletes.

Sit comfortably and close you eyes. Think about some distant time in the future. It can be 5 years, 2 years, 6 months, or even 2 months from now. Think about what you want for yourself at that particular time. What are your goals? Once you have a sense of what you want to achieve, visualize yourself having succeeded in achieving these goals. What is your life like, what are you doing, how do you feel, what do you look like, how do you interact with the important people in your life? Spend about 10 minutes visualizing yourself in all kinds of situations, having succeeded in achieving your goal. Then go back and think about what you would have had to do in order to have achieved these goals. Think about all of the little steps you would have had to take and the changes you would have had to make to get there. When you have completed the visualization, you might want to write down the steps and changes that you have just imagined were necessary so that you will have them as a reference.

You can also use this technique to solve a specific problem, like how to have the kind of relationship you want with your children in the future or how to attain more financial security. See yourself at some point in the future with your problem solved. Choose a point in time and answer the same questions posed in the preceding paragraph. What would you have had to do to solve your problem? What little steps or changes would you have had to make to achieve your goal?

HOW DO YOU WANT TO LOOK BACK ON THIS DIVORCE?

Ask yourself how you want to look back on your divorce years from now. How many people have you heard say how differently they would act now if they could do it over again and how sorry they were for some of their actions? If you think about how you want to look back on this crisis in your life, you can better make the decisions that will create the outcome you desire. Take a few minutes now to close your eyes and ask yourself how you want to remember the way you and your spouse handled the ending of your life together. In your heart of hearts, how would you want your good-bye to be honored?

We all have the ability to find constructive energies within ourselves even in the face of great pain. If you want release from your anger, if you don't want to retaliate blindly in response to an attack, and if you want to find the inner strength to cope with hard decisions, you must develop your inner voice of reason to help you choose the healthiest alternatives. Finding this part of yourself can steer you closer to your own goals and away from focusing exclusively on your past with your former mate. It will help you move in the direction of health, in the direction of healing, and in the direction of your future.

PARENTING AND CHILDREN

Part II addresses the critical issues of helping children, developing plans for custody and parenting, and dealing with the emotional issues that create obstacles to being a good parent outside of marriage. Using the workplace as a model, you are shown how to build a collaborative "business-like" relationship as parents and keep your antagonisms from ruining your children's lives.

6

Helping Children

Children begin by loving their parents; as they grow older
they judge them; sometimes they forgive them.

OSCAR WILDE

After divorce, being a parent will never be the same again. Even as
you read this, you cannot possibly anticipate what it means. The
"take it for granteds" of parenthood dissolve in divorce. You might
miss the morning routine, the homework, the bedtime story, the
weekends, the summertime, Christmas morning, or the stolen
moments that come from just being together. You get fragments
that you try to make whole. You may spend weekends with
someone else's children while your heart aches for your own. You
may eventually live with another's children and not your own. The
other parent will be tucking your children in at night, hearing
about their day at school, or taking them on a fancy vacation. You
may come home to an empty house and miss them terribly. There
is not enough of them to go around. Both parents miss out. There
is a reason for everyone to be anxious. A precious commodity has
suddenly become scarce.

> My daughter has been with her father every other week since she
> was four. The first time she left I felt like I had lost my baby. I
> couldn't bear the thought that this was the way it was going to be
> from now on. We have been doing this for five years. I handle it

okay, but I have an ache when she is not with us that I don't think
will ever go away.

DOROTHY, *divorced 5 years*

Separation is a time of great anxiety and anguish for parents.
These feelings are often camouflaged by competition and power
struggles. You try to hold on to what you have left. You punish the
other parent for what you have lost. Everyone in the family feels
vulnerable.

Children are anxious about being abandoned and wonder
who will take care of them. They worry about whether the separation is their fault. They question how much the absent parent still
loves them. They wonder whether they will have to choose between their parents and what they can do to get their parents back
together. They think about what will happen to their room, their
friends, and their pets and whether there will be money for camp,
college, or the new bicycle they were promised. They grieve for the
loss of the family as they knew it; they miss the parent they are not
with. They are upset if their parents are fighting, and they are
angry about their pain. Often they keep all these feelings bottled
up inside.

Parents are anxious about losing precious time with their
children and worry that the other parent will undermine their
relationship with them. They are concerned about maintaining
their place in the children' affections and about not having the
same influence on them. They are often uncomfortable about the
other parent's influence. They will not have the same control over
what happens in their children's lives—how they are disciplined
or fed or what they are exposed to and taught in the other parent's
home. They worry most about the pain they are causing their
children.

These worries are justified. Everything is changing for everyone. But if you are willing to deal with change on the level of
shared anxieties rather than faulting and competing, you can
eventually bring harmony to these new family structures.

My mother never forgave my father. Throughout high school I had to listen to her chastise him. He stayed away as far as he could. My life changed. I missed out. I never really got to know him. He died last year.

BONNIE, *age 18*

WHAT THE RESEARCH TELLS US

Adults have a natural instinct to protect their young. When threatened with their own survival, they can lose sight of the needs of their offspring. Some children react by becoming invisible; others misbehave, do poorly in school, or become aggressive with their peers. Some talk to you about their feelings, others don't. I have never met parents in the midst of separation or divorce who weren't concerned about their children. And they should be.

Poorly handled divorces have a long-term impact on children. In the recent book *Second Changes*, which is based on a study of 60 divorcing families spanning 15 years, Judith Wallerstein describes some sobering findings.[1] Only one-third of the children were clearly doing well 5 years after divorce. Thirty-seven percent were troubled, depressed, and having difficulty at school, and nearly that percent were still witnessing intense parental hostility. When she went back and interviewed these families 10 years after divorce, 41 percent were doing poorly, "entering adulthood as worried, underachieving, self-depreciating, and sometimes angry young men and women." Many girls who seemed to have adjusted well initially suffered from what she termed the "sleeper effect": they struggled with significant anxieties about betrayal, abandonment, and rejection, anxieties that emerged as they entered adulthood and became involved in relationships of their own. Other children were thrown into the role of parent in relation to an adult who was depressed and unable to function well. These children took on excessive responsibilities for managing the family and in some ways were robbed of their childhoods.

This landmark study began in 1971 in collaboration with psychologist Joan Kelly, before legislation requiring the mediation of custody disputes was enacted.[2] While the findings are based on a relatively small sample with no control group, they should serve to warn us. The children who did well after divorce had parents who had recovered enough to put their energy into being a parent, who were able to put their conflicts aside, and who allowed the children to have a close relationship with the other parent.

Perhaps we are not making children enough of a priority in divorce. Perhaps we are not disciplining ourselves enough to protect them from our conflicts and pain. Most parents don't intentionally hurt or deprive their children. Caught up in their own struggles, they just don't see the impact of their behavior on their children. They don't see how denigrating the other parent wounds a child. *Many children emerge from divorce thriving, but this is the result of the hard work and efforts of their parents who were willing to take the long-term view.*

Divorce is not just an event. It is a chain of events, a process of change in the life of the family that can last for years. Most children can successfully cope with the short-term crisis. Study after study in the last decade concurs with the findings of the Wallerstein and Kelly study in that the longer-term adjustment of children is related to the quality of life in the restructured households. The amount of parental cooperation or conflict, the amount of contact with the nonresidential parent, the physical and emotional availability of the primary parent, and the ability of the parents to deal well with the stresses and adjustments in rebuilding their own lives all combine to affect the children's quality of life. The recovery of children to some extent, then, is dependent on the recovery of the parents. Children's psychological energies are diverted from their own growth and development by the chronic and cumulative stresses of dealing with divorced parents who fight, don't pay support, visit erratically, use them as weapons, or make messengers out of them.

The evidence suggests that when the destructive factors are minimized (e.g., parental hostility or lack of adequate contact with a parent, particularly a father), the behavioral measures show very little difference between children of divorce and children from intact nuclear families. Most of the research describing children in divorced families as having a greater number of social, academic, and psychological adjustment problems as compared to children in intact nuclear families is based on the traditional arrangements where the mothers retained custody and the fathers visited on alternate weekends.[3] It is a widely accepted finding that a more positive adjustment and better academic performance in boys is associated with greater contact with the father.

"Let me stress one point," concluded Judith Wallerstein, in a recent keynote address,

> it is the continuity of the relationship between the children and two relatively intact parents accompanied by the capacity and willingness to cooperate in raising them that is the winning combination for children in the post divorce years.[4]

THE CPR OF HELPING CHILDREN: CONTINUITY, PROTECTION, REASSURANCE

Cardiopulmonary resuscitation, better known as CPR, has become standard emergency procedure to help save heart attack and drowning victims. On the basis of what the research suggests, let's look at the CPR for helping your children survive the trauma of their fractured family: Continuity, Protection, Reassurance.

Continuity

Try to maintain as much of the regular routine and familiar surroundings as possible. Introduce changes gradually. Keep the children in the same house and the same school as long as possible. Use the same babysitters and child-care providers. Continue to be involved in the same activities with them—scouts, soccer, little league, and so on. As much as possible, try to maintain the same caretaking patterns that existed when the family was together. This means that if childrearing responsibilities were shared, try to formulate a schedule that allows the children to continue to feel cared for by both of you. If you had a family in which the mother was the primary caretaker, the children look to her for their needs; she should continue to have primary responsibility, with the father's involvement increased gradually, if so desired. Traditional custody determinations were based on the concept of preserving primary attachments. Respect your children's attachment to both parents.

A sense of stability comes from continuity and predictability in the environment. Have regularly scheduled times for the children to be with the out-of-home parent that they know they can count on. This reduces the fear of abandonment. It is not a good idea to rely solely on a "drop by" arrangement. Try to approximate or even increase the access to *each* parent that existed prior to the separation. Be creative in designing a schedule that maximizes the time with each parent instead of using babysitters. Consider having the children be with the other parent if you have a class or a meeting in the evening, even though it's not part of the schedule. Children benefit from quality time with both parents, and while the disruption of daily contact may give a parent less time, it can be turned into quality time.

Protection

Most of all you must protect the children from your conflicts. All of the research points to parental conflict as the single most significant factor associated with poor adjustment in children of divorce. Protect your children from your hatred and anger at your ex-spouse. Don't put them in the middle of your disagreements, don't ask them to be messengers because you can't talk to each other, and don't pump them for information about the other parent's household. Don't confuse your feelings toward each other with the children's feelings for each parent. Children need to preserve their relationship with both parents; their developing sense of self derives from identifying with their parents, and it hurts a child to hear a parent denigrated. Be civil for your child's sake.

Reassurance

Reassure your children that they are loved and wanted by both of you. Tell them that the divorce is not their fault, that they will not be abandoned, and that they will continue to have both a mother and a father. Young children especially need repeated reassurances. Also reassure them that as parents you are still in charge and will manage the affairs of the family even though you cannot live together as husband and wife.

Explaining Separation to Children

1. *Assure your children that as parents you are still in control, capable of making decisions and exercising authority.* Separation can shake the foundation of a child's world. Your children will feel more secure if they can see that their parents are still capable of making decisions for the family. If communication with your spouse has broken down, consider using a mediator or family therapist to help the two of you get back on track as parents. Tell your children that you will be getting help to try to resolve matters.

2. *Explain clearly what will happen when you separate*—what will change and what will remain the same. Reassure them about the important things that will remain the same—from favorite blankets, which can go back and forth between households, to soccer games and college plans.

3. *Use neutral language that blames neither parent.* Choose your words very carefully when explaining why you are separating or divorcing. It is better if both parents sit down together with the

children. While adapting the explanation to their age, and not going into personal detail, use language that describes the mutual problems you and your spouse are having: love being lost, being very different people, not being interested in the same things anymore, not being able to get along, or not being able to make each other happy anymore. Explain that both of you have worked on the marriage but one or both of you feels there has been too much damage to be repaired; express how sad you are that this is the solution for now. It is tempting to want the children to side with you if you feel that the other parent is in the wrong. If you make the other parent the bad guy for wanting to separate, you put the children in the middle. This creates antagonism, conflict, and disloyalty toward the other parent, whose love and approval they also need. Be careful not to blame the other parent for "leaving us" when you discuss the separation with your children. You can say that you each feel differently about the need to separate, thus respecting your spouse's right to have different feelings and different needs.

4. *Give your children permission to express their feelings.* Children need to feel confident that they will not lose your love or approval if they express their longing for the other parent or their anger at you. The parent who remains in the house tends to get the brunt of the children's anger. It is often risky for children to be angry at a parent who has already left because they fear alienating and losing that parent altogether. The out-of-home parent too should let the children know that he or she accepts and can handle their anger. Tell them that it is okay to feel sad, hurt, worried, and angry at *you*. Let them know that you are sorry for the hurt you are causing and that you still love them and know they love you. Remember that you have been struggling with the problems in the marriage and the decision to separate for a long time, but it is new for your children, even though they may have sensed or feared it. Try to think about the feelings and fears you had when you first contemplated separation. This will enable you to put yourself in your children's shoes.

5. *Reassure your children that they are not responsible for the marital problems.* Children often blame themselves for their parents' divorce. Explain that divorce is adult business, that they can't fix it, that it is not their responsibility. Preschoolers, in particular, need repeated reassurance that they did not cause the divorce. They reason egocentrically, don't understand cause and effect, and are likely to believe that their bad thoughts or behaviors caused the breakup. School-age children also often worry that their misbehavior contributed to the parents' problems that resulted in the breakup. Reassuring them that they are loved and wanted and that they were in no way responsible will help alleviate these feelings.

6. *Give your children permission to have a relationship with the another parent.* Children worry about being disloyal by loving two people who don't like each other. They worry about alienating you or hurting your feelings by liking and wanting to be with the other parent. It helps to give them permission, if not your blessing, to have a close relationship with the other parent. Tell them explicitly that they have a right to their own feelings and their own relationship with the other parent and that this is okay with you. It may take enormous internal fortitude to say this, but it is especially important if there is a lot of animosity between you and your ex-spouse. Allow your children to miss the parent they are not with and to talk about the other parent in your home. Be careful that you are not asking them to take sides about *anything*.

7. *Tell the children the schedule or tentative plans for spending time with each parent when you have agreed on what it will be.* It will give them a sense of security and relief to know that they will not be asked to choose. While you should not ask them to make choices between the two of you, you can ask for various kinds of input, depending on their age. Young children need a regular and consistent routine that parents direct. With school-age children, for example, you can say, "We are going to try this schedule for two months and then we will talk about how it might work

better." You can have periodic reviews in which you ask the children if they are seeing enough of the out-of-home parent, if they are going back and forth too frequently, or if they would like longer or shorter blocks of time in each parent's home. But don't make them choose one parent over the other (e.g., don't ask whether they would like to go with you or with their mother on Friday).

8. *Make sure your children feel that they have an established place in each parent's home.* They need to feel they are included in the life of both parents, especially the parent with whom they don't share a primary residence. Communicate to them that they have a home in both houses, even though they may not be spending the same amount of time in each house. Encourage them to participate in the decoration of the second residence, especially a sleeping area that they can claim as their own space. Have them bring over some of their own special things, favorite posters, stuffed animals, and toys. Creating their own niche will help them feel a part of the second residence and have a sense of security.

9. *Keep the children abreast of major developments and plans for the future.* Assure them that major changes will not be sprung on them unexpectedly. Tell them in advance about plans to move and change schools, as well as the effect major financial changes will have on their lifestyle.

SIGNS OF STRESS IN CHILDREN

If there is conflict, tension, and competition over the children, they are going to react with distress. Parents who are angry and don't trust each other often misread this distress as something the other parent is causing, when in reality it is the hostile relationship and the tension the children feel in the transitions between households that is causing the distress. Children sometimes react by becoming anxious about visiting the other parent's house, or they may return home from these visits moody, aggressive, or withdrawn.

Children can also become quite manipulative in the face of competing parents. When parents don't agree, children will go to the parent from whom they get the best deal. When parents are not in contact, the children can exaggerate the differences to their own advantage. They may also echo your complaints about the other parent, quoting things out of context, and telling you what you want to hear in order to assure you of their loyalty to you. They will also play on the insecurities of each parent: "Mommy lets me do XYZ," or "Daddy is taking us to Y." Pretty soon the children have control of two anxious, insecure parents, who are too busy competing with each other to see the situation they've created.

Children may also regress under stress, reverting to earlier behaviors. The 3-year-old may wet his pants, the 2-year-old may demand a bottle, the 11-year-old may whine and cry and refuse to do things she knows how to do. Thumb sucking may come up again. In most cases these things pass as the tension in the family eases. Some children, however, develop serious behavior problems or become discipline problems in school; it is as if they are trying to get their parents' attention diverted onto themselves and away from the parental fight. Sometimes children fantasize that if they have serious enough problems, they may be able to reunite the parents.

You can be sure that your children will show signs of distress as long as you fight and compete over them. Sometimes a cycle develops where the children's symptomatic behavior is used as rationale by one parent to limit visits with the other parent. This may actually increase your child's emotional stress because it deprives him of contact with the other parent. Behavioral acting out is quite common at transitions. Even if both households are good, going from one to the other is still a change your child has to cope with. Every child deals with change differently. Get professional help if you see continuing behavioral disturbances in your children or if you are not able to curb the hostility and competition between you and your ex.

PSYCHOLOGICAL TASKS OF DIVORCE FOR CHILDREN

In addition to the normal developmental tasks a child must master in the progression toward becoming an adult, the child of divorce has to master the divorce. Just as you progress through various stages in coping with divorce, so do your children. Judith Wallerstein has identified six psychological tasks children of divorce face.[5] You may be able to facilitate your children's struggle with these issues by helping them talk about their feelings and understand their experience.

Task 1: Understanding and Accepting the Realities of the Divorce

The first task for your children in coping with divorce is to have a realistic understanding of the changes the separation or divorce will bring. Young children especially have fears and fantasies about what is going to happen. They need the reassurance of what life will be like, what routines will be maintained, and what will change. Children need help accepting and coming to terms with the changes in their life as a result of the divorce.

Task 2: Strategic Withdrawal

Children need permission to distance themselves from adult issues and help in finding ways to protect themselves from their parents' conflict. If the divorce becomes a preoccupation, it will drain their psychological energy from normal developmental challenges and interests. Encourage the children to be involved in activities they enjoy. As a 10-year-old boy said about a recent separation, "When I'm playing soccer, I don't think about it."

Help your children understand that divorce is adult business and that it is not their responsibility to fix it or to help Mommy and Daddy resolve their conflicts. Suggest ways they can protect themselves from being pulled into an adult conflict. A 3-year-old whose mother screamed obscenities about the father's girlfriend learned to put her hands over her ears whenever her mother did this. A 9-year-old said, "Please don't say bad things about Mom in front of me." Where parental conflicts are very intense, it might be beneficial to seek additional resources for the child such as a therapist or support group for children.

Task 3: Dealing with the Loss

Everyone, including the children, must mourn and accept the loss of the family as they knew it. Children have to overcome feelings of rejection, powerlessness, and not feeling lovable that are related to the departure of the parent who no longer lives in the home. They have to be helped to understand that the loss of contact or involvement of the nonresidential parent is not a reflection of their own worth or that parent's lack of love. The feelings of rejection are obviously reduced if both parents remain actively involved in the children's lives after divorce. The involvement also lessens the children's feeling that they are being divorced along with the parents.

Task 4: Dealing with Anger and Self-Blame

Children, like adults, must learn to resolve anger through understanding and forgiveness. As children mature, they should come to understand why relationships fail and to see that no one person is to blame for a divorce. With maturity comes the ability to see both parents as fallible human beings capable of mistakes. When children forgive their parents, they can put the divorce behind them if their parents have. But if children are continually pulled into the parents' disagreements or asked to take sides, their unresolved feelings about the divorce or anger toward a parent will remain strong.

Task 5: Accepting the Permanence of the Divorce

All children harbor hopes that their parents will reconcile. For a period of time, the wishes for reconciliation can be a preoccupation. Some children actively devise strategies to bring their parents back together. Many cling to these wishes long after divorce or even after remarriage. Acknowledge your children's wishes for reconciliation, while gently helping them accept that it is not going to happen.

Task 6: Taking a Chance on Love

Despite the failure of a parent's marriage, young adults need to believe that long-lasting love is possible. Only then will they be willing to take the risks of being open and vulnerable to intimate relationships. Children who witness a terrible marriage and destructive divorce may renounce marriage altogether. As they mature, talk to your children about your marriage and divorce, about the mistakes you made, about what you learned, and about what it takes to make relationships work.

REASSESSING YOUR GOALS AS A PARENT

Divorce is a crisis that calls for all sorts of reexamination. The way you will carry out your parental duties changes dramatically. Your time with the children will be your own and will not be influenced by the presence of your spouse. This changes the dynamics of your relationship with your children. Separation or divorce is a good opportunity to take stock of yourself as a parent, review your goals and priorities, and see if there are any changes you want to make in the way you relate to your children. As we've noted, parents dealing with separation are so immersed in their own problems that it is easy to lose sight of the children's experience and feelings. The following questions will help clarify your thinking as a parent. It is helpful to write out your answers so you will have them for future reference.

PARENTING REVIEW QUESTIONNAIRE

1. What do you believe are the most important qualities in a parent–child relationship? _____

   _____

2. What basic values do you want to impart to your children? _

   _____

   _____

3. Is there any way you want to change your relationship with any of your children? _____

   _____

4. What are some of the ways you want to improve as a parent?

   _____

   _____

5. What do you want to give your children that you did not receive from your parents? _____

   _____

6. What do your children need to help them adjust well to the separation or divorce? _____

   _____

7. If your parents were divorced when you were a child, how is your children's experience of divorce different from your own? How can you help them in ways that you weren't helped? __

   _____

   _____

8. When your children are adults and look back on the divorce, how do you want them to remember your handling of the divorce? _____

_____

_____

Divorce doesn't have to damage children. Most children are resilient and will adjust if the parents handle the divorce constructively. Make sure you and your ex-spouse cooperate in your parenting efforts and support the children's relationship with their other parent. The next chapter will help you formulate the details of your postdivorce parenting arrangements based on the unique circumstances of your family.

7

Parenting Plans

The Transition to an Unmarried Family

> Parents are teachers of human beings,
> not owners of human beings.
>
> VIRGINIA SATIR

> It is not the divorce per se, but the conditions and agreements the parents create during and after divorce that will determine the child's adjustment.[1]

The legal terms are *custody* and *visitation*. But the real issues are these: How will you continue to be effective parents in separate households? How will your family function after the divorce? If you are only asking the question, Who will have custody? you are solving a legal problem, not a family one. You and your ex-spouse brought your children into the world together, and divorce doesn't alter that fact. But it does require you to rethink how you will see them through. The family doesn't end at separation or divorce, it changes. In time, you will become two distinct families connected by common children. This transition from one household to two, from a nuclear family to what has been described by researcher Constance Ahrons[2] as a "bi-nuclear" family, takes time. Figuring out the details of when the children will be with each of you, how child care will be shared, who will be responsible for doctor and dentist appointments, how decisions will be made, or even who stays home with a sick child all takes negotiation, planning, and experimentation. If you get hung up on who gets custody, you will get locked into competing positions in which there are only two choices. Someone will be hurt because each of you has to make the other wrong in order to be right. When you are caught in this competitive process, you miss examining the significant ways in which you can both continue to be involved with your children. Once you have answered the fundamental question of *how* these children are going to be raised by parents who no longer live together, then you can add the legal label of custody.

Framing the issue in terms of how you will share your parental rights and responsibilities requires you to accept certain assumptions: (1) the children need both of you; (2) you each have a right to an active role in their development; (3) you are willing to share the tasks of parenthood in some as yet undetermined fashion; and (4) you both agree that conflict and competition over the children will hurt them. This approach does not assume there will be agreement as to how everything should be worked out, or that disagreements about childrearing won't exist, only that you respect or at least can tolerate the other parent's right to have a relationship with the children. It also assumes that you each see the other as an adequate parent, even though your parenting styles or strengths may be different.

If you do have reservations about your ex-spouse's parenting abilities and you want to limit the children's time with the other parent, it is a good idea to examine your reservations carefully, since motivations about these things are rarely pure. Make a list of the shortcomings your ex has as a parent and how these characteristics might negatively affect the children. Then analyze your list. Do the limitations you listed reflect differences in parenting styles or values? Will exposure to your ex really hurt or burden your children or just expose them to values you personally don't embrace? Is your spouse adequate but simply less skilled and experienced than you? Do your reservations stem from your anger or reluctance to share control because you don't trust your spouse?

Or is the issue perhaps really your unwillingness to be away from the children because it is hard and you will miss them?

If you believe that your ex-spouse has serious limitations as a parent that make him or her inadequate to care for the children except on a restricted basis, then you probably need to work with your attorney to arrange a custody or visitations study through the Family Conciliation Court Services of your local domestic relations court or through a private mental health professional. They will assist you in evaluating the problems and help you devise a plan that safeguards the children. Independent psychological evaluation is needed in situations where there have been allegations of sexual or physical abuse or untreated drug or alcohol abuse.

LEGAL CUSTODY: WHAT THE TERMS MEAN

Sole Custody

In sole custody, one parent has the major responsibility for the care of the children and the authority to make all decisions regarding them. The other parent has designated visitation rights. There may be informal negotiation over schedules or holidays, but if agreement can't be reached, the legal custodian has the right to make the final determination except in regard to the provisions in the decree. Traditional sole custody arrangements with alternate weekend visitation have become less and less satisfactory because they leave the custodial parent overburdened and subject the children to long absences and little quality time with the noncustodial parent, who is usually the father. Even when there is sole custody, the present trend is to include more extended weekends and midweek visits with the nonresidential parent.

Joint Legal Custody

Joint legal custody gives both parents equal authority to make major decisions in regard to the children's health, education, residence, and schedules or any other significant issue affecting their welfare. Joint legal custody does not necessarily mean the children spend 50 percent of their time in each home. Parents can agree to any schedule of time that works best for the family.

In joint legal custody, there can be a designation of either "joint" (or "shared") physical custody or "primary" physical custody. When one parent has primary physical custody—or primary "residential responsibility," as it is also called—that parent is the managerial parent, responsible for overseeing the children's routine care and activities; the children spend more time in that parent's home. In joint *physical* custody, the parents tend to share the time and responsibilities more equally. It doesn't work to try to force a fifty-fifty schedule if logistic constraints are a problem. What seems to be important about joint custody is the philosophical commitment to the concept that children need the continued involvement and active participation of both parents. That commitment and the legal right to joint decision making is what distinguishes joint custody from sole custody.

Split Custody

Split custody is the least common of any formal arrangement because it separates the children. Each parent is responsible for one or more of the children, whose primary residence is with that parent. A visitation schedule between the children and the nonresidential parent is set up according to the particular circumstances of the family. Each parent can be designated as sole custodian for the children in his or her household, or the parents can have joint legal custody of all the children with the designation of primary physical custodian of the children in their care.

Coparenting

Coparenting is the term used to describe sharing and coordinating the tasks of parenting. While it is not a legal term, it describes a form of joint legal custody in which physical custody is shared fairly equally and both parents remain actively involved in the day-to-day life of the children. Both parents do the driving, go to the teacher conferences and school activities, help with homework and lessons, make clothing purchases, take the children to the doctor, and so on. The children spend blocks of time ranging from 3 days to 2 weeks in each home. Some families rotate on a weekly, monthly, semiannual or annual basis. Whatever the rotation, even when it is not fifty-fifty, coparenting is a two-home arrangement. The children are not "visiting"; they live in both homes.

Coparenting and joint custody require more effort and expense than traditional sole custody arrangements. While joint custody has many benefits for children, these arrangements require a high degree of cooperation and commitment. They are not for every family. You should be prepared for the extra expense of maintaining two homes that can adequately accommodate your children and expect the extra work involved in coordinating your children's lives between those households. Remember there are many degrees of shared, cooperative parenting. Some couples communicate frequently to coordinate plans and share pertinent information. Others have divided their schedules and responsibilities more formally and prefer to function autonomously. Coparenting is on one end of the spectrum.

IS JOINT CUSTODY FOR YOU?

The idea of joint custody has challenged traditional beliefs about male and female parental roles and what children need to grow and thrive. It is hard to imagine that going back and forth between two homes is good for a child. We operate on the belief that stability comes from a central home base. However, for families in which both parents have always been and want to continue to be intimately involved in the care of the children, joint custody has benefits for everyone involved. Professionals know that it is possible for divorced parents to develop a civilized, cooperative relationship outside of a marriage and that children can receive a strong sense of stability from a consistent and predictable schedule, not just from having the same bed and toothbrush each night. Whether joint custody is good for your family depends primarily on you and your ex-spouse's ability to cooperate as parents and on how you see and value your former spouse as a parent.

The following questionnaire will help you evaluate yourselves compared to other couples who have been successful with joint custody. It is based on research identifying the attitudes, skills, and characteristics common to couples who have been able to share parenting satisfactorily.[3]

IS JOINT CUSTODY FOR YOU?

Yes/No

_____ 1. Can you communicate and negotiate fairly well about the children?

_____ 2. Do you basically respect your former spouse as a parent despite your marital disappointments and personal differences?

_____ 3. Can you put your disagreements and conflicts aside and concentrate on the children?

_____ 4. Can you share control and allow each other to parent in your own styles?

_____ 5. Are your fundamental childrearing values and practices similar?

_____ 6. Can you tolerate the differences without seeing them as detrimental to the children, and can you distinguish between the important and unimportant differences?

_____ 7. Do you value what the other parent has to offer your child?

_____ 8. Are you willing to tolerate the personal inconvenience and extra work in coordinating schedules?

_____ 9. Is your child able to handle transitions?

_____ 10. When you were married, were the childrearing tasks shared (not necessarily equally)? If not, is there a mutual commitment to increase sharing now?

While this survey is not a scientific instrument, you can use it as a guideline to evaluate whether you meet what seem to be the basic criteria for joint custody. If you have more than one or two negative answers, then you and your spouse are going to have to work to become comfortable with joint decision making and shared control.

FOUR TYPES OF PARENTING RELATIONSHIPS AFTER DIVORCE

Researcher Constance Ahrons identified four types of parenting relationships after divorce.[4] She characterized these relationships as Perfect Pals, Cooperative Colleagues, Angry Associates, and Fiery Foes. Fifty percent of the couples in their study fell into the first two categories and were able to relate in constructive and civilized ways.

The Perfect Pals, couples who basically remain friends, represent a very small percentage of the divorcing population. These couples respect each other as people and as parents. In most cases the decision to divorce was mutual, and neither person harbored feelings of abandonment or rejection. After the divorce these couples tend to consider themselves full partners in parenting and rely on each other for support. They collaborate on planning events and celebrations and in discussing problems. This type of relationship is not necessary for joint custody or shared parenting. Although some people do maintain close personal ties with a former mate, this does not represent the norm. It is very difficult for former lovers to be friends. Relating constructively and acting cooperatively does not require friendship.

Cooperative Colleagues, I believe, is a more realistic and achievable model. These couples do not feel that they have to like or accept each other. They put their standing differences aside to compromise and work together for the sake of the children. Their commitment to their children outweighs their negative feelings about each other because foremost in their minds is their desire to minimize the trauma of divorce for their children. They respect each other's rights as parents, divide the time spent parenting, and share in their children's activities and life events but not with the same camaraderies as in the first group. While they are able to negotiate disputes about money and schedules reasonably well, it always takes effort.

The Angry Associates, on the other hand, allow their bitter and resentful feelings to enter into all of their interactions with each other. They barely accept each other's right to parent. The children are often caught in the middle as the parents vie for their loyalty. Life after divorce is characterized by unpredictable blow-ups. Old antagonisms are easily aroused by everyday matters. These couples have not healed or forgiven each other, and their children suffer for it the most.

The Fiery Foes live in a war zone. These people cling to the wrongs, are unable to recall any of the good times, and view their former spouse as the enemy. Fights and legal battles continue to rage while there is very little respect for each other's rights as a parent. Sides are taken by family members and friends, and the struggle continues as a central element of their life even after divorce. Children caught in this struggle are often forced to choose sides and may end up losing a parent. It is not uncommon for visitation to decline over the years because the conflict surrounding it is so severe.

This research, I believe, accurately characterizes the types of relationships parents form after divorce. The key to success for the Perfect Pals and Cooperative Colleagues is the fact that both groups have learned to control their conflicts. They make compromises, accommodations, and trade-offs and try to find creative alternatives. They are willing to look for solutions and do not get hung up on fault finding.

What Is a Parenting Plan?

Since the importance of a cooperative relationship between parents after divorce has been increasingly recognized by lawyers and judges, terms that are more neutral and less divisive are being used to describe the various elements of the divorce process. In many areas *parenting plan* is being used instead of *custody* and *visitation* to describe postdivorce parenting arrangements. *Custody* and *visitation* may still be the legal terminology that will appear in the decree, but *parenting plan* implies that both parents have a mutual obligation to determine their postdivorce parental responsibilities and duties. Some states even require a specific parenting plan as apart of a custody order.

A parenting plan defines the rights and responsibilities of each parent and the specific arrangements and agreements about such issues as time spent by the children in each household, holiday schedules, how decisions will be made, and how costs will be allocated. The plan can be incorporated as a stipulated agreement into the divorce decree. You may also use a parenting plan as an informal agreement to describe your expectations of each other, your commitments to your children, and your intentions as parents in the future. While some of these provisions are not legally enforceable and may not be included in the final decree, they reflect your personal goals as parents and are an important ritual in the restructuring of family life.

What Are Your Needs in Formulating a Parenting Plan?

Even though you may have very strong feelings about what you want, it is important to approach discussions about your parenting plan with an open attitude and willingness to experiment. You may need to try out more than one time schedule before you find one that works best for your family. The schedule you agree upon when you first separate may not be what is needed when things settle down and everyone has become accustomed to the separation. Be flexible and willing to make changes as circumstances change. Don't view things that don't work as failures but, rather, as information that you can use to formulate a better plan.

Before you negotiate a parenting plan, it will be helpful for you and your ex-spouse to clarify your general goals and preferences. Ask yourselves the following questions:

- What level of involvement do you want to have with the children?
- Do you want to share routine caretaking responsibilities?
- Do you want to share decision making and how?
- How much time should the children spend in each household?
- How much contact, discussion, and interaction as parents do you want or are you able to handle?
- Do you want to change anything from the way your responsibilities for the children were handled or shared when you were married?
- What do you think the children would want?

Some people draft very detailed arrangements with specific times, dates, responsibilities, and procedures for making changes. Others have verbal agreements and work out the details as they go along. If you find yourselves in disagreement about legal custody, try to work out the details of the parenting plan, as discussed in the following pages, before trying to negotiate the legal custody. You may find that if you negotiate specific arrangements that satisfy both parties, it may be easier to work out an agreement on legal custody.

HOW TO DEVELOP A PARENTING PLAN: THE SEVEN BASIC COMPONENTS

What follows is a checklist of things to consider in developing a parenting plan, along with some examples of workable options. Consider submitting your ideas in writing to your ex-spouse. This will allow you time to think about each other's ideas instead of just reacting to them emotionally. It is important to remain open-minded and to think about your partner's concerns and desires and not just automatically reject them because you feel threatened or disagree on some point. Chapter 13, on win–win negotiating, shows you how to negotiate and resolve the areas in which there is disagreement. Mediation can also help you to learn to listen to each other better and negotiate your differences peacefully.

1. Residence

Will the children have one primary residence or two? When will they stay with each parent and for how long? Here are some of the common arrangements:

- One home base, with alternate weekends and one regular midweek contact with the other parent; the weekend may include Friday through Sunday, Monday, or Tuesday.
- Two primary residences, alternating weekly, semimonthly, monthly, or yearly; or divide the week in half, for example, Saturday through Tuesday and Wednesday through Saturday and alternate Saturday nights.
- Alternate primary residence between the school year and summer, with every other weekend and one midweek visit with the nonresidential parent.
- To the arrangement of one primary residence with alternate weekends and a midweek contact with the nonresidential parent you can add a weeklong visit each month or every other month to provide children with the opportunity for extended time with the nonresidential parent.

Basically, you can take a block of time (2 days to 1 week) and rotate it weekly, monthly, or semimonthly and also have shorter contacts (midweek dinner, weekend breakfast) in between so as to minimize shuttling and not create separations that are too long for young children. It helps to hang master calendars in each household. These can include the major holidays as well as monthly or even yearly schedules.

2. Holidays

How will the major holidays and summer vacation be shared? Make a list of the major holidays that matter to you. You can share holidays by (1) dividing them, with each parent getting the same holidays each year; (2) alternating major holidays annually; or (3) dividing the holiday in half when feasible; for example,

Christmas eve and Christmas day. Some ex-spouses simply work it out on a flexible basis from year to year. Others alternate the right to first choice for the time they prefer for the Christmas holiday, including the right to take the children out of town. Some even celebrate holidays together, such as Christmas dinner, birthdays, or Mother's or Father's Day.

3. Financial Support

How will each of you contribute to the financial support of the children? Traditionally, a flat payment is made to the primary residential parent by the nonresidential parent. Many states now have child support guidelines based on income, the needs of the child, and the ratio of time spent in each parent's home. These guidelines may be available through the state child support division or county court. You can use these schedules to help you compute a flat payment, or you can work with your attorney or mediator. The court approves the child support arrangement as well as other terms of your financial settlement when you divorce. Check with your attorneys about whether your private agreements meet the legal requirements in your state. When incomes and time in each household are similar, parents can (a) pay their own way and divide medical or other agreed major expenses equally or in proportion to income; (2) add up all of the expenses and divide them annually or quarterly; or (3) divide the financial responsibility for various costs (e.g., one parent pays for summer camp and music lessons while the other pays for orthodontia and soccer). Generally, arrangements that enable independent decisions work better than ongoing accounting and consulting over expenses.

4. Managing Routine Care

Who will be responsible for overseeing the children's routine needs, like medical/dental appointments, school activities, lessons, homework, transportation, and child-care arrangements?

Or will these be shared and, if so, how? With joint custody, each parent usually takes care of the routine arrangements when the children are with that parent. If you have joint custody, decide if one parent is going to be the "managing partner" or if duties will be divided. Many parents designate certain areas of responsibility (like medical, dental, lessons, or sports) to each parent. The parent responsible for that area does all the arranging and driving while keeping the other parent informed of major events or concerns. Regardless of your custody arrangement, you will need to clarify what kind of information about the children's activities, school functions, or health will be communicated to the other parent.

In sole custody, the custodial parent usually takes care of most of the children's needs. However, involvement with a child's extracurricular activities and sports is a good way to stay connected if you are a nonresidential parent. When the amount of time you spend with your child doesn't feel like enough, a richer experience can be maintained through participation in your child's organized activities, such as sports, Cub Scouts or Brownies, or even just providing the transportation to these activities.

5. Decision-Making Authority

How will decisions be handled? What areas require consultation and joint decisions, and which decisions can be handled independently by the residential parent? Make a list of the kinds of things that you think ought to be mutually discussed or that require notifying the other parent. Make a second list of the kinds of things that you think could be handled without consulting the other parent. Issues you might consider include day care, school performance, religious education, behavioral problems, summer camp, illness or medical treatment, out-of-state moves, discipline, participation in recreational activities, change of school or residence, dating, and curfews. Compare lists and negotiate a master list. Some of this may seem like common sense, but every divorced family is comfortable with different levels of collaboration.

The more clearly things are spelled out now, the less misunder-standing and conflict there will be later. One of the toughest issues to resolve is who will have the authority for determining the children's residence if a parent is planning to move out of state. If there is joint legal custody, do the children go or stay? In sole custody, the residential parent usually has the right to make a unilateral decision to move with the children. Whether you have sole or joint custody, you may want to consider incorporating specific relocation provisions into your parenting plan now.

6. Legal Custody

Will you have joint, split, or sole custody? After working out the details of your parenting plan, you will have to negotiate the legal status. Depending on how you have decided to share the routine care and decision making, you may agree to one of the following:

- Sole custody with one parent having final authority in all areas
- Sole custody with specific areas requiring joint decisions
- Joint legal custody with primary physical custody to one parent
- Joint legal and joint physical custody
- Split custody with each parent having sole custody of one or more of the children
- Split physical custody with both parents having joint legal custody of all the children

Joint custody statutes differ from state to state. These statutes affect what a court does when a dispute arises over joint custody and gives the parties different bargaining chips. In most states a judge will not grant joint custody over one parent's objections. Even though there is no legal presumption favoring women, most men don't in fact get joint custody unless their wives agree because it is a sociological reality that women typically assume the primary parenting role. I find that many women who resist or object to joint custody do not have a philosophical disagreement about supporting their husband's involvement with the children but have a great deal of anxiety about sharing control and decision making with a former spouse with whom they've had difficulty resolving differences. Also, many women who have been the primary parent are uncomfortable giving up that role or that control, especially when a child is young. Many do not think their husbands have had the experience necessary to take care of the children on an extended basis.

Disputes about joint custody are sensitive issues in today's climate of gender politics and changing social realities. It is easy to get caught up in arguments about parental rights. Try to address your partner's underlying fears and concerns rather than get caught up in the issue of equal rights to make decisions.

One way, however, to handle an impasse over joint legal custody is to have a provisional agreement, either for sole or joint custody, that is subject to mandatory review by the parties privately or in mediation after one year. Some attorneys or judges would say that this is simply putting off the decision, but I think it is a way of having the opportunity to see how things settle down after the divorce is final. In the chaos of a disintegrating marriage, it is hard to know how well you will ultimately be able to handle parenting together. Neither of you is functioning at your best right now. Many parents are willing to agree to terms when there is a mandatory review clause, which allows for future changes. Moreover, research indicates that within 2 years after divorce, conflict subsides and the level of cooperation between former spouses does increase.[5] In the meantime these issues can be negotiated with a mediator or discussed with your attorney.

7. Impasses

How will disagreements or major impasses be handled? Disagreements that can't be easily resolved are bound to occur. Even if you have made detailed agreements, not everything can be anticipated. There are going to be times when you have conflicting needs about things like changes in schedules or vacation plans. It is a good idea to have a method of dealing with impasses as part of your parenting plan. This is less of an issue in sole custody because the custodial parent has the authority to make all final decisions (even though this does not necessarily resolve these problems to everyone's satisfaction). If you opt for joint custody, there are several ways you can handle the more routine impasses: you can alternate the authority to break impasses; you can flip a coin; you can give each person the right of first choice on disputed issues on alternating years; you can do it one person's way this time and the other person's way next time; you can make a provisional plan trying it one person's way for a designated period of time; and you can give each parent designated areas of primary responsibility and final authority. For major impasses you may agree that you will use a mediator; you may even decide to have monthly or quarterly mediation at first to address problems and develop ground rules.

RESIDENTIAL SCHEDULES: WHAT THE RESEARCH CAN TELL US

Parents often ask me how much time children should spend in the nonresidential household or whether moving back and forth between two homes will be damaging to their children. They hear so much conflicting advice from attorneys, friends, family, and other professionals that it is hard to know what is best. Everyone has their own biases. The subject of two homes stirs impassioned controversy, especially where very young children are concerned, because it goes against traditional notions of what constitutes stability in a child's life.

While there is a consensus and clear evidence about the importance of interparental cooperation and the children's need for regular contact with both parents—particularly the nonresidential father—there is disagreement among authorities about the relative benefits of joint *physical* custody. Experts in divorce can't say with certainty what schedule is best because there is virtually no research that directly compares various schedules. Furthermore, the research comparing joint custody to sole custody is limited, with samples too small to draw definitive conclusions.[6] We don't know whether spending half a week in each household is preferable to alternating weeks; whether alternating weeks is better than alternating monthly or semimonthly; or even whether shared physical custody is preferable to one primary residence. So much depends on the individual circumstances of the family at any given time.

While the type of custody arrangement alone does not predict how a child will adjust, Kelly reports that there is some evidence that in sole custody arrangements children living with the same-sex parent do better than those living with the opposite-sex parent.[7] Since the situation in which the mother has custody has been the traditional arrangement, this may account for the fact that, in general, girls tend to be less adversely affected by divorce than boys. Interestingly, in examining why boys respond more negatively to divorce than girls, Zaslow found that boys fare more poorly if they live in the custody of *unremarried* mothers, while in postdivorce families involving a stepfather or if the father has custody, girls do worse than boys.[8] The issue is what forms of postdivorce life are stressful or act as buffers against stress for boys and girls. Better adjustment and higher academic performance in boys is tied to closer contact with their fathers, and studies indicate that school-age boys in joint custody or paternal custody have fewer problems than boys in maternal custody. In fact, in a review of the research presented at a recent meeting of the American Psychological Association, Joan Kelly, an authority on divorce, concluded:

> Traditional mother custody arrangements in which the father visits alternate weekends and four evenings a month leaves children feeling deprived. . . . the common arrangement of mother custody and father visitation is not what boys need.[9]

Particularly where young children are concerned, different child specialists in any community will probably make different recommendations. Many counsel against regular overnight visits for babies, while others advise close contact with both parents if both have shared the child's care. While it is agreed that infants and toddlers need stability in their environment as the major element in a parenting plan, not all authorities agree on what constitutes stability. Some experts define stability in terms of the same routine in the same environment, that is, the same bed and the same parental figure. Others define stability in terms of consistency and predictability in a child's routine and environment.[10] They argue, for example, that three days in each household, week in and week out, is a consistent and predictable routine that doesn't disrupt a child's sense of security or stability.

In one study of 25 families with preschoolers, Wallerstein and McKinnen found no evidence to suggest that joint custody was injurious or that the children in the study would have fared better in a sole custody arrangement.[11] In another study on joint custody, in which families were helped through mediation and support groups to develop parenting plans, Brotsky, Steinmann, and Zemmelman found no evidence that preschool-age children could not handle a joint custody situation.[12] In fact, Judith Wallerstein, at the 10-year follow-up of her study of 60 divorcing families, found evidence suggesting that children who were preschool age at the time of a divorce actually were considerably less burdened by the divorce in the long term because they didn't have the understanding and painful memories school-age and adolescent children had.[13]

The question is, With which parents and under what circumstances is joint custody or a dual-residence arrangement beneficial for a child? One must balance the value of maintaining closeness with the parent in the second home and the burden to the child of moving back and forth. What seems to account for success in this new form of family life as much as anything is the couple's level of commitment to coparenting, their respect for each other as parents, and their willingness to endure the inconvenience and put forth the effort to compromise and resolve differences cooperatively. In studies children living in joint custody situations described themselves as feeling loved by and close to both parents, in contrast to feeling close just to the primary parent. Generally, they did not mind making the extra effort of moving between homes since it enabled them to maintain a close relationship with both parents. Several studies found children of joint custody more satisfied with their arrangement than those in sole maternal custody. These joint custody youngsters had less of a sense of loss and deprivation that is characteristic of children in sole custody. Joint custody also provided the reassurance, especially important for boys, of the continuing commitment and involvement of their fathers.[14] Joint custody, however, is not recommended for families entrenched in custody and visitation disputes or where there is intense conflict. In their research, Janet Johnston and Linda Campbell found that the children in these families were being torn apart by the parental fighting and hostility that erupted at the transitions between households. Children from families in turmoil do better with more formalized visitation arrangements, which involve less frequent transitions.[15]

What is clear from all of the studies is that children do best when there is cooperation between parents, when they can maintain a close relationship with both parents, and when their parents are able to rebuild their own lives. Beyond that, the parenting plan and residential schedule depend on the particular circumstances of each family—the ages and sex of the children and the predivorce patterns of sharing parental duties. In the long run children are not going to remember whether they spent 4 more days a month at Mom's house or at Dad's. They are going to remember the overall atmosphere between their parents, whether there was conflict and competition over them or peaceful coexistence. They will never forget the horrible experience of court. Reaching a livable, working agreement on parenting and custody, regardless of whether it slightly favors one parent, has benefits to a child that are greater than the details of any particular plan.

PARENTING PLANS AND THE DEVELOPMENTAL NEEDS
OF YOUR CHILD

In developing a schedule of time in each home, the ages of the children and their developmental needs are essential considerations. The following paragraphs summarize the children's developmental needs from infancy to adolescence as they relate to parenting plans.

Infants and Toddlers: Birth to 3 Years

In order for babies to bond with both parents, they need to be cared for and played with by both parents. If you separate when your child is still an infant, contact with the nonresidential parent should be frequent but probably limited in the number of overnight visits unless the baby has been equally cared for by both parents and the parents want to continue this pattern. Some authorities would argue against regular overnights for infants because infants do best when their routine remains constant. But fathers who want to and know how to care for babies also need the opportunity to bond. Consistent routines are of paramount importance in formulating a plan for infants and toddlers. They learn that the world is a safe place through the predictability of their care and contact with loving caregivers. Feeding schedules, naps, and other routines need to be maintained between households. Use the same child-care provider. If there has been one primary caregiver, a schedule that includes one overnight a week and contact for a few hours three or four times a week with the other parent often works well. The overnights can be extended as the baby gets older. If the child is verbal, telephone contact can be used to help the child sustain the separations. A toddler can handle weekend visits with the nonresidential parent.

Preschoolers: 4–5 Years

Preschoolers test their independence, incorporate more adults and activities into their world, and begin to formulate their sexual identity. They can now handle longer separations from their primary parent. This is the oedipal period, when young children love the parent of the opposite sex and wish to have him or her all to themselves. Preschoolers need contact with the same-sex parent to reassure them that they haven't driven that parent away. Preschoolers also have fears of being abandoned. They need lots of reassurance and a predictable schedule of time with the out-of-home parent. Young children don't have a concept of time, and long separations can provoke anxiety. Having a master calendar in both houses with stickers representing Mommy and Daddy, which children themselves can affix, helps them understand when they will be with each parent and lets them feel as if they are participating in the scheduling process.

A preschooler can probably handle joint physical custody if (1) care has been provided by both parents prior to the separation; (2) there is a high level of cooperation between the parents; (3) the blocks of time are short so that the separations do not cause undue stress; (4) there is consistency of routine, schedule, and caregivers; and (5) the child is resilient and has the temperament to handle change.[16] The child whose parents have shared the primary caretaking could probably handle 3- or 4-day blocks of time with each parent. Families in this situation often divide the week in half on a Wednesday-though-Saturday schedule, alternating Saturday nights. Some 5- and 6-year-olds can handle a week in each house with a midweek visit with the other parent. Transitions between households are made easier by the presence of siblings.

A young child who has primarily been cared for by one parent needs the continuity of that base but can adjust to gradually increased periods of time with the other parent. A possible initial schedule might be one day and night of each weekend and one other midweek visit with the out-of-home parent. As time goes by, the schedule could be extended by alternating longer weekends (i.e., Friday through Monday, or even Thursday through Monday, with a regular midweek contact). Visits by the nonresidential parent to preschool or participation in school programs are other ways to increase contacts. Sometimes a nonresidential parent who leaves for work later than the residential parent can visit in the morning and drive the child to preschool.

School-Age: 6–12 Years

Children between the ages of 6 and 12 are engaged in the world of school, extracurricular activities, and friends. Maintaining continuity of school and friends is important in formulating any parenting plan. If parents are cooperative, it is a real plus to a child if both parents remain in the same neighborhood. Younger children (ages 6 to 8), especially boys, tend to experience intense sadness in reaction to the parental separation. They are unable to protect themselves as well as older boys, who may mask their real pain by a pretense of bravado or by throwing themselves into sports or other activities. As indicated earlier, studies show a boy this age is particularly vulnerable to the loss of contact with his father. A boy needs predictable and regular contact with his father if they no longer live in the same home.

Children this age have a heightened concern about what is fair and right. They are easily aligned with the more victimized parent and can be very angry at the parent who has violated their strong sense of fair play or whose fault they perceive the divorce to be. These children may also attempt to take on the responsibility for making things fair to both parents, making sure that neither feels slighted and that their time with each is equal. They can be quite vigilant about the details of what is equitable. Reassure them that it is not their responsibility to make things fair and that they do not have to take care of either of you.

School-age children are able to handle a dual residence if school and peer relationships are preserved. The value of close contact with both parents often outweighs the inconvenience of moving back and forth for the school-age child. Some children are good at managing the logistics while others are bewildered and confused—the soccer shoe, shin guard, or math book invariably tends to be at the other parent's house. It is important to appreciate your child's strengths or weaknesses and provide the supports needed.

Adolescents: 13–17 Years

Adolescents are striving for independence, formulating their own identity, and testing themselves against family values and limits. They need continued guidance from parents who can work together so that the adolescent has a safe harbor and isn't pushed into premature disengagement from a tottering family or from parents who are acting like adolescents themselves. Friends and activities are more important to the adolescent than the close contact with parents needed by younger children. The effort of living in two homes usually outweighs its advantages for the adolescent. It is common for children who have lived in a joint physical custody arrangement to return to a primary home base when they enter their teens.

Time with the adolescent's nonresidential parent needs to be arranged on a flexible basis, although some regularly scheduled contact each week is a good idea. Dinner once or twice a week, invitations for special events or activities, and the freedom to "drop in" seem to work for many families. As frequency of contact diminishes, the quality of the contact becomes more important. Getting quality time with a busy high schooler is a challenge for any parent, but the preferences of adolescents about where they would like to live and how they want to spend time with the nonresidential parent should be given every consideration. They also need the flexibility to be able to reschedule plans with their parents when necessary.

Adolescents are old enough to understand what is going on and make independent judgments about the divorce as well as about their parents' conduct. They lose respect when they see parents disintegrate into combatants or behave immaturely. As a result, parents who behave poorly make themselves undesirable as role models. Adolescents can become cynical about love relationships and marriage as they witness the painful and brutal ending of their parents' marriage.

Avoid the mistake of making a confidant out of an older child and revealing the conflicts you are having with your spouse. I have counseled many adults whose parents divorced when they were in high school and who still remember with bitterness how one parent denigrated the other. Teenagers need parents who continue to provide the structure of a family, who present a united front in terms of rules and expectations, and who are able to keep them out of their disputes.

The Goals of the Parenting Plan

You will want to formulate a parenting plan that gives children meaningful time with both parents, respects their ability to tolerate separations from each parent, minimizes the sense of loss they feel when one parent moves out of the home, and approximates the way you were each involved when the family was together. In summary, a good parenting plan should be based on the following considerations:

1. The developmental needs and ages of the children
2. The psychological attachments of the children
3. The way the childrearing tasks were shared in the married family
4. Preserving a close relationship with each parent
5. A consistent and predictable schedule that minimizes the transitions between households
6. The ability of the child to handle transitions
7. Maintaining the continuity of the home and school environment
8. Parents' career demands and work schedules
9. The need for periodic review of the plan, noting trouble signs and revising as your child's needs and circumstances change

Explaining the Parenting Plan to the Children

The children will feel more relaxed if they clearly understand how the family is going to be structured in the future. They need to understand the meaning of joint custody or shared parenting, not just the logistics of the arrangement. Explain what shared parenting implies—that they will continue to be loved and cared for by both of you and that as parents you will consult, as you always have, about what is best for them. They should understand that the parent with whom they are staying is the "on duty" parent, who is in charge of day-to-day decisions and permission, but that all major issues will be decided by both parents. Explain that they really have two homes (even if not for an equal amount of time), two places where they can feel safe and secure and to which they can retreat or bring their friends.

If one parent is to have primary responsibility, explain to the child that that parent is going to take care of him or her and explain how and when the other parent will be involved. Make sure that the child understands what the lines of authority will be. It may be helpful to review the plan each year so that, as they mature, the children's understanding of the parenting plan deepens and their questions are answered.

Drafting the Parenting Plan

The divorce decree usually will not contain all of the details of your arrangements as parents. A well-written parenting plan provides a clear record and reference for how things are going to work in the future. The following plan is a guideline with sample introductory language. It follows the checklist described earlier in this chapter. You can draft the specific details and language to fit your situation. This form is not intended to be comprehensive, but it will give you a basic outline or starting point. Developing your own parenting agreement is a good opportunity to think through your philosophy and put your commitments to the children in writing. You can make your parenting plan as detailed or general as you like.

SAMPLE PARENTING AGREEMENT GUIDELINE

This agreement represents our best efforts and thinking about how our family is going to work in the future. We believe our children need to have two parents who love and are involved with them. It is our intention to support each other's relationship to our child(ren) and share parental duties and responsibility as outlined below.

1. *Living arrangements*:

   a. The children will be with the mother from _____ and the father from _____ . They will be picked up at _____ o'clock and returned at _____ o'clock.

   b. In the summer, they will be with each parent on the following dates: mother _____; father _____ .

   c. Changes in the schedule will be accommodated wherever possible, and mutually acceptable substitute times will be arranged.

   d. If a parent cannot accommodate a request to change the schedule, it is the responsibility of the parent making the request to find alternate child care.

2. *Vacations and holidays will be shared as follows*:

   Labor Day weekend _____

   Thanksgiving _____

   Christmas vacation _____

   President's Day weekend _____

   Spring vacation _____

   Memorial Day weekend _____

   Fourth of July weekend _____

   Summer vacation schedule _____

   Birthdays _____

   Other _____

3. *Responsibilities for routine care*:

   a. The mother will be responsible for overseeing the following areas _____ (e.g., medical and dental appointments, lessons, school functions).

   b. The father will be responsible for the following areas _____

   _____ .

   c. Each parent will keep the other parent informed of major developments in the area that they oversee.

   d. Responsibilities in the summer are as follows:

   Mother _____

   Father _____

4. *Decision making*:

   a. Each parent will be responsible for the day-to-day decisions when the children are in that parent's home.

   b. Neither parent has the right to make a unilateral decision on the following major issues; these will be discussed jointly before decisions are made:
   Education
   Change of residence
   Child-care provider or center
   Medical treatment other than well care
   Schedule changes
   Other _____

   c. The (mother/father) will have final responsibility for the major decisions in regard to _____

   _____ .

d. In the event agreement cannot be reached, the following procedures will be used: _____

_____

_____ .

5. *Financial responsibility*:

a. The costs for the children will be shared as follows: _____ shall pay _____ a monthly sum in the amount of $_____ per child to cover routine costs.

b. Costs for _____ (child care, summer camp, school tuition, recreational equipment) will be shared as follows: mother _____ (%), father _____ (%); or each parent will pay the costs for the following activities: mother _____ _____; father _____ .

c. College expenses will be shared as follows: _____

_____

_____ .

d. The (mother/father) will provide health insurance. The (mother/father) will be responsible for unreimbursed medical and dental costs.

e. Orthodontia shall be financed as follows: _____

_____

_____ .

f. The tax exemptions for the children will be divided as follows: _____

_____

_____ .

g. Other arrangements: _____

_____ .

6. *Legal custody*:

   a. We agree that we will have joint legal custody subject to the terms and agreements outlined above.

   b. We agree that the (mother/father) will have primary legal custody subject to the terms and agreements outlined above.

8. *Miscellaneous agreements*:

   We agree in good faith to submit future disputes that we are unable to resolve privately to a mediator or mental health professional before we seek recourse from the courts.

8

Parenting as a Lasting Partnership

The Working Relationship

> Children sweeten labors, but they
> make misfortunes more bitter.
>
> FRANCIS BACON

I don't know how I am supposed to act. He starts to yell at me, telling me I am trying to control everything again. I end up bringing up the affair. I get off the phone really upset and realize we never even discussed which night he was going to pick up the kids for dinner. It's so stupid. It always ends up this way. I don't know how to change it. It feels like we're still married.

JANET, *divorced 1 year*

She calls again at the last minute and asks if I can take the kids this weekend because she has to work. My stomach gets in a knot. I swore I wouldn't accommodate her anymore. I did that for fourteen years. I'll be damned if I am going to make it easy for her one more time, but I don't want the kids to have to spend the day at the babysitters. I do it every time. I deserve a medal.

GEORGE, *separated 4 months*

Janet and George are struggling with the greatest demon for divorcing parents—their past relationship. It is where you have

129

lived emotionally for the past 2, 3, or 23 years. It is not easily set aside. It can suck you in like an undertow, and you won't even realize it. When you are relating to your former spouse as you did when you were a couple, you behave differently than you do with anyone else. It brings out the worst in you.

Part of the problem is not knowing how to relate to each other when your marriage ends. There are no cultural norms, or even adequate terminology, for the relationship between divorced parents. You are governed neither by the norms of marriage nor the norms of friendship. You are not casual acquaintances. In the groundbreaking book *Mom's House, Dad's House*, Isolina Ricci proposes that we think about the parenting relationship as a business partnership. She suggests that parents model their behavior and expectations on relationships in the world of business rather than in the world of intimacies. Many people find this idea useful. One of my clients said that all she could think of was being friendly or nasty and neither seemed appropriate. Being businesslike fell somewhere in between. What you are striving for is a working relationship based not on intimacy or friendship but on a respect for your common purpose.

You have a mutual concern—the raising of your children. Make a conscious decision that you want to create a successful partnership for this endeavor. Your common goal is to produce healthy, well-adjusted children. You are both invested in that outcome and have already put in considerable time and effort in "product development." Now you face corporate reorganization. Your enterprise will have two headquarters or one headquarters and a branch office or become two independent, autonomous corporations. You have to develop a reorganization plan. The controlling partners have to specify the responsibilities of each new office and decide how the parent company will finance the costs of establishing the second office, how the transition will be handled, how joint operations will be coordinated, and what the level of teamwork or autonomy will be in the new management structure.

When a company reorganizes, it must plan and negotiate. Everyone involved needs to know what the new rules, procedures, and lines of authority are, or the employees will be in turmoil. When expectations are not made explicit, there is room for misunderstanding, which can easily be taken for bad faith, especially if the two principals don't get along. Change will occur either through default or design, and the transition will be more successful if there is a preliminary design and careful planning.

HOW TO DEVELOP A WORKING RELATIONSHIP AS PARENTS

Step 1: Be Businesslike

1. Use business etiquette and protocol. Use the workplace as a model for your behavior. Make a conscious decision to relate to your former spouse as you would a colleague at work. Before having contact with your spouse, you can use the mental imaging technique, discussed in chapter 4, in which you visualize yourself talking to a respected colleague. You can also think about being businesslike as one of your gears or modes of operation. We shift gears all the time to make ourselves do things we don't want to do, from getting up in the morning to making phone calls we dread. Let the business mentality gear be your emotional overdrive whenever you have to deal with your former spouse about the children or financial matters. Put your foot on the metaphorical clutch, take a deep breath, and shift. If you can shift consciousness in this way and remain businesslike regardless of your spouse's behavior, you are less likely to have your old buttons pushed.

2. Adjust your expectations to model the workplace rather than personal relationships. Don't expect friendship, emotional support, or approval from your former spouse. The purpose of a business relationship is to transact business, not have emotional needs satisfied. Seek emotional fulfillment in your other personal relationships.

> I wanted to prove to her that I was a good father. I couldn't seem to ever do it "right." There was always some criticism—I should make them finish their dinner, say thank-you, check their homework

more carefully, not leave their shoes by the front door. It never ended. I couldn't meet her expectations even when we were married. I finally had to ask myself why in hell I was still trying so hard to please her. What was I holding on to? I think I'm a good father. I trust my instincts as a parent. Once I realized this, I became more detached, more businesslike with her. It was much easier.

DAN, *divorced 1 year*

3. *Focus on solutions.* Business is result-oriented; it is concerned with outcomes. Focus on solutions, rather than your personal feelings about each other. Evaluate the options in terms of benefits to the children and what is workable. Don't compete about who is right or who is the better parent. Limit yourself to the crucial issues in making decisions: Does this work? Will it benefit the children? Which option is most practical? Is there a better way to handle this issue in the future? Keep your personal relationship out of it as much as possible.

We used to have constant hassles about who had more time with the kids, who would take them for haircuts, soccer practice, medical treatment, or anything else. We were very competitive. It was a terrible power struggle. Through mediation we finally learned to do what is practical. George takes them to appointments because he can get off work early. It is strange not doing this dance anymore. We did it for so long. I feel kind of empty, but I also feel kind of free.

MARY, *divorced 1 year*

4. *Use teamwork.* Even when people in the business world are in unequal positions of authority, they are expected to work together as a team. Even if one parent has sole custody, the other parent's input and needs must be considered. Act the way you would want to be treated if the situation were reversed. If you make unilateral decisions that affect your spouse without first revealing your intention, you invite anger, mistrust, and retaliation.

Mary is still their mother even if I have custody. If she has strong objections to what is going on, I have to listen because the boys will pick it up anyway.

JIM, *divorced 2 years*

5. Use businesslike communication. Most significantly, you and your former spouse will have to change the way you talk with each other. Business mannerisms are different from the way you interact with friends. Businesslike communication is direct, explicit, to the point. Feelings are kept in check, and personal information is minimal. You exchange information, discuss possible solutions, formulate a plan of action, and confirm decisions in writing. In fact, being too businesslike is often perceived as being unfriendly. Communication between intimates, on the other hand, often has an emotional agenda, including an indirect testing of how the other feels or hinting at how you feel. Every couple has its own dance. You are going to be inclined to continue the familiar styles of relating to your former mate. But conversations that are short and to the point will be more successful, even though the coolness and distance will seem awkward and unfriendly. As a rule, if it feels unfamiliar and restrained, you are on the right track. If it feels familiar, you're probably headed for trouble.

> He stopped asking how I was. He just asked what time I would be back so he could pick up the kids. I'd tell him, he'd say thanks and hang up. It was so empty. It wasn't mean, just strange. I felt rejected at first. He was very detached. After a year it feels kind of normal. We rarely discuss anything personal, but we get along okay. Every once in a while, he even cracks a joke.
>
> DIANE, *divorced 1 year*

Step 2: Separate How You Feel About Your Spouse from How You Relate as a Parent

Develop objectivity about your spouse as a parent. As you move further away from your marriage, your spouse will occupy a more peripheral part of your life and the relationship that's left, being parents, will stand out. In the meantime, as stated earlier, you need to separate how you feel about your spouse from how you see that person as a parent. This kind of objectivity will be the basis of your future relationship.

For instance, did your mate relate to the children the way he related to you? If she was critical or unsupportive of you, was she more sympathetic and supportive of the children? If he was short-tempered with you, was he more patient with the children? If she buried herself in work to avoid the problems of the marriage, did that mean she wasn't interested in the children either? It is easy to see a person who has hurt and disappointed you as being unilaterally uncaring, selfish, uncommunicative. You need to carefully scrutinize these assumptions and determine the validity of your judgments.

> He left me for a younger woman after I had put so much of myself into that marriage. I helped put him through school, worked, and took care of the house and our daughter while he was at the office. I don't think he is a responsible parent to behave this way. He can't be trusted and only cares about himself. Our daughter feels the same way.
>
> SALLY, *separated 3 months*

> We stopped being good for each other years ago. For a long time I blamed him for not being there for me. Everything was for him. I thought he was selfish and didn't care about us. I later learned he didn't really understand what I wanted. I expected him to know without my telling him. Now that I can't fault him for that, I can see that he is a pretty good father and he is really there for the kids in ways he wasn't there for me. It's a hard pill to swallow.
>
> JANE, *separated 1 year*

Sally does not distinguish her daughter's sadness at her father's leaving from her own experience of rage, betrayal, and abandonment. Jane, on the other hand, after a year's time, can see her husband's qualities as a father and separate her experience of him from the children's experience of him. Not everyone is able to separate an evaluation of a spouse's adequacy as parent from that person's failures as a mate, particularly when the stress of an ailing marriage diminishes performance in both roles. It is easy to exaggerate the other's faults as a parent or to brand the other as the bad guy to gain a legal advantage, but if you are able to put your anger aside, you can see how your respective strengths and weaknesses as parents may in fact balance and complement each other.

The following survey will help you develop more objectivity about your spouse's parenting abilities and will help you separate the roles of spouse and parent. Try to be honest and answer the questions without anger. Think about these qualities the next time you see your spouse and write down any additional insights. If you can't list anything positive, you are probably still too angry to be objective. This is fine as long as you recognize it and are willing to try again at a later time.

ASSESSING YOUR STRENGTHS AND WEAKNESSES AS PARENTS AND AS SPOUSES

1. List your partner's strengths as a parent.
2. List your partner's shortcomings as a parent.
3. List your strengths as a parent.
4. List your shortcomings as a parent.
5. List your partner's good qualities as a mate.
6. List your partner's weaknesses or your disappointments in him or her as a mate.
7. List your good qualities as a mate.
8. List your partner's disappointments in you as a mate.
9. What is important to your spouse about being a parent?
10. What is important to you about being a parent?

Study your responses. What are the major differences in your parenting styles. Are there ways you complement each other in those differences?

Step 3: Focus on What the Children Need

The stress of separation and divorce reduces your availability to your children. Your patience wears thin, the children's demands feel excessive, and you often feel guilty. You are naturally more self-absorbed as you struggle to deal with the trauma you are undergoing. If you are the noncustodial parent, the pain at not being with your children can be overwhelming. If you are the mother of very young children, you may not feel ready for the extended absences when they are with their father. It is common to lose some of your objectivity and sensitivity to the children's needs as you struggle with your own increased emotional needs. Here are some of the typical ways parents confuse their own needs with the needs of their children.

1. You feel lonely and need your children more. You want the children with you as much as possible and feel anxious when they are away and you are alone. While it is absolutely normal to feel this way, especially in the beginning, needing your children too much blurs your ability to see their need to be with the other parent also. You may couch your own fears in what you think is best for them: for instance, you may feel you're protecting the children by limiting overnights with the other parent when in fact you're uncomfortable with them being away. Try to get more support for yourself so that you are less likely to use the children to fill the void. Consider joining a support group or increase your contacts with friends. Having prearranged plans when the children are not going to be with you reduces the anxiety of having all this time alone. As time goes, your discomfort will lessen.

2. You feel badly betrayed or rejected by your spouse and assume the children feel the same way. You are confusing your experience of loss with theirs. Remember the children are losing regular contact with a parent, not the relationship.

3. You feel that the children are all you have left. Unwittingly, you place the burden of your loneliness on them because they sense your vulnerability. The children may have trouble separating from you to be with the other parent because they are worried about your being alone; they may feel they have to take care of you. Many people assume that the children's crying and clinging behaviors mean they don't want to go with the other parent; in fact, such behavior may indicate that they are worried about you.

4. The children have heard you denigrate and complain about the other parent. When they return from time spent with the other parent they may say Daddy did this or Mommy didn't do that, echoing your very complaints. Children who love two people who

are hostile to each other tend to exaggerate or give information out of context, telling what each parent wants to hear. They want you to feel that they are being loyal. Be careful you are not taking everything the children say about the other parent or claim the other parent said at face value in order to further justify your preconceived notions of your former spouse.

Anger, more than anything else, can spill over into your relationship as parents and obscure the children's real need for both parents. If you don't recognize your own anger, neediness, or dependency on your children and haven't found more appropriate ways of dealing with these feelings, you may not fully recognize your children's need for the other parent and, as a result, resist their spending more time with that parent.

YOUR CHILD'S EXPERIENCE OF THE DIVORCE: AN EXERCISE

Here are some questions that can help you reestablish your sensitivity to your children's experience and separate your needs from theirs. To get maximum value from this exercise, take your time and imagine that you are each of your children. Then put your responses in writing.

1. What would you feel if you were in your children's shoes right now?
2. What are the hopes, fears, and worries of each child?
3. How do the children feel about each of their parents?
4. How is their experience of the separation and divorce different from your own?
5. Is there anything they need to help them adjust to the divorce better?
6. What is your picture of the best situation for them, given the current circumstances?
7. Describe your ideal future relationship with your ex-spouse as it will benefit your needs and the needs of your children?

THE PLEDGE OF NEVER TAKING A CHILD AWAY

Underlying many of the struggles between separated and divorced parents is a terrifying fear of losing the children. In my experience it is the single greatest anxiety of divorce for most people. Often this fear is irrational, sometimes it is not. As you face divorce, not only can you lose your children through the dangers that all parents fear—such as disease or accident—but now you have to contend with a former spouse who could try to get custody or move out of state and take your children away. Unless there is a high level of trust as parents or a strong commitment to coparenting, this fear of losing the children generates intense anxiety. It is often a vague and unspecified fear that you may not even be fully conscious of because it lurks beneath the surface. You may try to talk yourself out of it or unconsciously try to prevent the other parent's relationship with the children from getting stronger. Even though you may say to yourself that your spouse could never get the kids away, the anxiety is still there because the possibility, however remote, is always there. Losing the children is a shared risk, and you can increase the mutual threat or diminish it. I have found that anything people can do to reduce this anxiety is ultimately a mutual gain.

I have used a technique that I call the pledge of honor. This pledge needs to be executed like a solemn oath. It requires a quiet moment when each parent is ready to listen and be open with the other. Find some symbolic object on which to make your pledge; you can use a Bible, a picture of the family, or a picture of the child. Sit facing each other. You and your former spouse are to speak one at a time, without interruption, describing the reasons you would never take the child away from the other parent. Swear to the other on your word of honor, with your hands on the symbolic object, that regardless of your disagreements you will never do anything to deny the other parent the relationship and that any plans to move away would be discussed in advance. Shake hands when you are through stating the pledge. Don't speak; let the handshake linger long enough for the feeling of trust to sink in.

The purpose of this exchange is to begin to build a level of trust in the area of one of life's most fundamental concerns—the relationship to one's children. Conflict will begin to melt away if trust in this area can be developed. You may not need to perform a formal ritual or swear on a symbolic object, but it is essential to hit this issue straight on in your own way. To successfully employ the pledge of honor, you and your former spouse need to have a heart-to-heart talk and to offer the reassurance needed to reduce each other's anxiety.

SUMMARY OF BASIC GROUND RULES FOR PARENTING SUCCESSFULLY

1. Respect each other's privacy, and don't interfere in the other's household unless there is a real problem.
2. Extend common courtesy and manners as you would to a colleague or acquaintance, and make appointments to discuss things.
3. Give your ex-spouse the benefit of the doubt; don't make assumptions based on what the kids say but check things out with your ex.
4. When there are conflicts, search for solutions, not fault.
5. Be businesslike and keep your feelings in check, evaluate your partner's behavior not by how you feel but by how businesslike it is.
6. Be trustworthy; follow through on your agreements.
7. Concentrate on your own relationship with the children and let your ex-spouse parent in his or her own way.
8. Put things in writing. Make sure agreements and plans are explicit and detailed as to time, place, cost, and so on.
9. Keep the baggage from the marriage in the baggage compartment; don't keep bringing up the past.
10. Make the pledge never to take a child away.

III

HANDLING CONFLICT

Part III focuses on improving communication, avoiding the escalation of conflict, and understanding the nature of your disputes. You will learn how to create a less defensive atmosphere so that every discussion doesn't turn into a fight, how to deflect angry and provocative exchanges, how to bring up difficult subjects, and how to decipher the underlying issues that make some disputes so hard to resolve.

9

Border Skirmishes Don't Have to Turn into Nuclear War

How to Handle Conflict

> Better bend than break.
> SCOTTISH PROVERB

We had one fight in seventeen years. We did not communicate. In the end I knew I would die if I didn't stop stuffing my feelings and get out of a dead marriage.

SUSAN

We fought over everything, from how to make an omelet to how to make money. Neither of us could be right without the other's being wrong. We were never a team. We didn't know how to resolve our differences.

MARK

Most of us are ill prepared to deal well with conflict. We grew up in families where we could proudly state our parents never fought only to later learn that what we were really observing was peace at any price. Or we grew up in households filled with arguments, yelling, and screaming, where seemingly very little was resolved. We consequently either live in secret terror of confrontation or feel prepared to fight at the slightest provocation. Despite our best intentions, we often repeat the patterns of our families in the new families we create.

As you face divorce, you could enact one of these patterns one more time. After all, divorce mirrors marriage. The fights you had in the marriage tend to be the same fights you will have during your divorce. Here we will show you how to avoid some of these traps. Since your relationship is no longer based on the emotional vulnerabilities of intimacy, it is possible to successfully apply new skills for resolving your conflicts.

THE NATURE OF CONFLICT

In our culture, conflict is imbued with all sorts of negative connotations. When I ask classes of graduate students studying divorce mediation what comes to mind when they think of the term *conflict*, their associations invariably include the following words: fear, danger, intimidation, competition, winning, losing, arguing, fighting, escalation, out of control, hurt, anger, power struggle. The words are always negative. Conflict is threatening for many people. It is only when I ask the students to search for ways in which conflict is not negative that they begin to mention concepts like opportunity, increased understanding, better communication, closeness, creativity, learning, discovery, new ideas, and innovation.

Conflict in and of itself is not bad. It is an inherent part of life. Without conflict there would be no social change, no discovery, and no new technologies. Everything would remain the same if there were no opposing forces or points of view. However, our fear of and aversion to conflict limit the possibilities for constructive outcomes. Fighting is almost synonymous with conflict in language and thought. We have been conditioned to flinch in the face of conflict. We get defensive, we don't listen, and we counterattack. We avoid our discomfort by over- or underreacting. We need to learn how to put our reflexive responses into slow motion so that we can see what is coming at us and think about how to best respond.

AIKIDO: RESPONDING TO CONFLICT WITHOUT ESCALATION

The Japanese martial art, aikido, provides a good metaphor for dealing with conflict.[1] Aikido means "the way of blending energy." The aikido master accepts the energy coming at him instead of opposing it and joins with it to move it out of harm's way. His task is to disarm the attacker without injuring him. There are no karate chops or kicks to the groin. Translating the principle of aikido into a way of dealing with an ex-spouse yields the following rules: Don't immediately get on the defensive every time you feel attacked. Accept that the other person has a concern, and acknowledge that concern without necessarily agreeing or disagreeing with what has been said. Try to think of the other person's feelings simply as energy, as something to be dealt with creatively and not taken personally. Remain as detached as you can. Ask questions. Try to find out more about the problem and understand what the other person wants. The idea is to work *with* the other person instead of challenging him or her.

I've watched Tom Crum, author of *The Magic of Conflict*, give demonstrations of how the aikido metaphor is applicable to everyday life. The aikido master has enormous strength because of his ability to move *with*, rather than against, his opponent. He is not rigid. He gets out of the way of the intensity and direction of the attack but remains in contact with the person. The attacker is thrown off balance because he does not expect the force of the assault to be accepted. It is as if you were to say to someone who is yelling at you, "I can see you are very angry at me about this. What has made you so mad?" The other person, who was primed for a confrontation, is suddenly stopped by your comment, thrown off balance, and required to reorganize what he or she was going to say or do. It is similar to the way the unexpected calm of a customer service representative takes you by surprise as you launch into a complaint about the failure of a product. It is hard to keep yelling at someone who is considerately listening to your grievance.

The potency of the aikido metaphor lies in the paradox that there is more strength in accepting and working with an attack or criticism than in challenging it. You are in more control when you are not on the defensive. Attacks tend to diminish when the other's concern has been acknowledged. When you become the questioner instead of the defender, you take an initiating position instead of a reactive one and you direct the flow of energy instead of being pushed around by it. It is a more powerful position.

Think about how you might in fact have more control if you do the opposite of what you are probably doing now. Take a moment to visualize yourself acknowledging and working with your spouse's criticisms, attacks, or anger, either like an aikido master or a customer service representative. Write a list of four ways you could have more control if you acknowledged rather than refuted your spouse's complaints.

The aikido master prepares by grounding and centering himself. He takes a deep breath and focuses on his being, his spiritual connection to the earth. He feels his feet firmly planted on the ground and imagines shifting his center of gravity to his solar plexus to feel this connection. This gives him a sense of strength. He is ready to meet and accept the energy coming his way as an opportunity to practice his art. It takes practice to remain calm and centered in the face of an attack. When someone is yelling at you, you normally have a strong physiological response. Your heart races, your neck throbs, you become hot and flushed, and you can't think. Adrenalin is pumping through your body. Through breathing and grounding yourself you can become calm and take the time to think.

While most of us would not welcome conflict with open arms as an opportunity to practice our negotiation skills, our unwilling-ness to accept conflict as natural or prepare ourselves for it is equally unrealistic. It may be too late to resolve the differences that led to your divorce, but you can deal with the conflicts over the terms of your divorce constructively, especially with the help of a mediator or counselor.

CONSTRUCTIVE AND DESTRUCTIVE CONFLICT

Conflict is inevitable in your divorce negotiations. What determines whether these conflicts become destructive or not is whether you approach your disagreements *competitively* or *cooperatively*. Looking at differences competitively, arguing over who is right, and focusing on winning, almost always results in destructive conflict. You will feel more alienated and less trusting and will cling to your respective positions even more strongly.

Most couples are not even aware of how competitive they are. Whether overtly or covertly, dissolving marriages are often characterized by competition and power struggles. As the relationship disintegrates, an adversarial attitude develops in which neither person gives the other the acknowledgment and validation so desperately sought. As mutual acceptance diminishes, so does trust. Neither one listens to or acknowledges the legitimacy of the other's feelings or concerns. *Both* feel unappreciated and invalidated. In this atmosphere the only way to get what you need is to fight for it, and if you don't win, you lose. Ironically, each feels threatened by the other, and the need to use power tactics and manipulation becomes easily justified.

This is a self-perpetuating and vicious cycle. The loser almost always has a method of retaliation. Couples who have characteristically dealt with their differences competitively can become dirty fighters after the separation, using threats and ultimatums, intimidation, retaliation, or outrageous allegations as the modus operandi. They are closed-minded and try to make everything fit their preconceived notions. Winning, rather than findings solution, is the goal.

When two parties approach differences cooperatively, their overriding goal is to *problem solve, not establish fault*. This is a crucial difference. They recognize that differences are not necessarily tied to a right or wrong way and that their self-worth is not based on having to be right all the time. They do not lose sight of their common interests while also recognizing that they have separate and often conflicting goals. They work to compromise and reduce misunderstanding. They try to build trust. They listen to each other's perceptions about what caused the problem. They try to be open and not jump to conclusions. They provide honest and direct information and disagree without degrading each other. *They concentrate on finding solutions that will work in the future and focus their energy on where they want to go, not just on what happened in the past.*

WAYS TO INCREASE COOPERATION

The way to move from a competitive to a more cooperative atmosphere is to begin to *act* more cooperatively even if your spouse doesn't and even if you don't feel that you should have to be the one to initiate. Someone has to go first if the cycle is to be broken. A cooperative gesture tends to generate a cooperative response; an outstretched hand tends to be greeted by an outstretched hand. The experience of cooperating breeds a spiral of increasing cooperation. Each small success becomes a building block. Similarly, competition will breed competition, an attack a counterattack. The common accusation "You did this" almost always produces "I did not, you did that." A competitive approach to conflict is self-perpetuating and can be reversed only by *changing your behavior*. If competition characterizes the way you have been relating to each other during the divorce, it is important that you recognize this pattern as a cycle to which each of you contributes by reacting and counterreacting. As justified as it may feel, it is not accurate to say: "I am the innocent one and you are to blame, and therefore I don't have to take any responsibility for changing my behavior."

First, even if you feel that you have been the one who has tried to be cooperative in the past, see if you can think of new ways to extend cooperation in which you won't lose anything. For example, send an attractive card stating your desire to be more cooperative, or a peace offering of some kind. Follow with a concrete gesture; make a concession such as giving your spouse something you know is desired from the house, accommodating a request for time with the children or for use of the "better car," or offering a financial benefit. Send flowers from the children on Mother's or Father's Day or balloons on your ex's birthday. Start small but begin to look for ways in which you might be able to reach out by offering something your spouse would want, even if it is only a symbolic gesture. Second, look for solutions to problems, no matter how much you want to find fault. Say something like, "Where do we go from here? Let's not spin our wheels going over the past." Third, acknowledge your spouse's feelings and concerns even if you don't personally agree with them: "I can see you don't think this is fair, but I don't see it that way." Agree to disagree.

Competitive responses to conflict are very hard to change because they are based on a lack of trust. Each person believes that there is no other way to get what he or she needs. The following questionnaire assesses your tendency toward competitive and cooperative approaches to conflict. It is based on the research of Morton Deutsch at Yale University and applies to all sorts of conflicts, from family fights to organizational disputes to international conflicts.[2] Think about your fighting style in the past and how you relate now. Rate yourself on a scale of 1 to 5 to see how you may be contributing to the competition and escalation of conflict. As hard as it is, try to be honest in evaluating your shortcomings. You may not want to admit how poorly you handle conflict, but it is never too late to change even the little things you say and do that can be destructive.

RATE YOUR CONFLICT STYLE

Circle your response, using the following scale:

1 = always
2 = sometimes
3 = frequently
4 = rarely
5 = never

Cooperative Conflict Styles

1. Are you straightforward and direct?   1 2 3 4 5
2. Do you accept the legitimacy of your spouse's concerns?   1 2 3 4 5
3. Do you use persuasion rather than threats?   1 2 3 4 5
4. Are you open to new information?   1 2 3 4 5
5. Do you try to build trust?   1 2 3 4 5
6. Do you seek mutually acceptable solutions?   1 2 3 4 5
7. Do you emphasize common objectives and areas of agreement?   1 2 3 4 5
8. Do you give the benefit of the doubt and see misunderstanding instead of bad intentions?   1 2 3 4 5
9. Do you focus on finding solutions?   1 2 3 4 5
10. Do you try to enhance the power and resources of both of you?   1 2 3 4 5

Competitive Conflict Styles

1. Are you guarded and secretive? Do you make your spouse feel suspicious?   1 2 3 4 5
2. Is proving you are right important?   1 2 3 4 5
3. Do you use coercion, threats, or ultimatums?   1 2 3 4 5
4. Do you make assumptions and then blame your partner for them?   1 2 3 4 5
5. Are you ready to exploit an opportunity or take advantage?   1 2 3 4 5
6. Are you concerned only about your individual interests?   1 2 3 4 5
7. Do you emphasize your differences and areas of disagreement?   1 2 3 4 5
8. Do you impute bad motives and intentions? Are you looking to confirm suspicions and negative impressions?   1 2 3 4 5

9. Do you concentrate on what happened in   1 2 3 4 5
   the past?
10. Are you trying to dominate, gain power   1 2 3 4 5
    and win?

While there is no data to formally score this questionnaire, the following scoring method can be used as a guideline. For the questions assessing a cooperative conflict style, a score of 10–20 suggests that you have a highly cooperative problem solving orientation; 20–30 that you are generally being constructive; 30–40 that you may be trying to approach your conflicts constructively but you need to put more work into it; and 40–50 that you have problems dealing with conflict through mutual problem solving. On the competitive conflict style, a score of 10–20 suggests that you are combative and aggressively approach conflict; 20–30 indicates a generally competitive orientation to conflict; 30–40 suggests you can be somewhat aggressive in certain situations; 40–50 suggests you rarely approach conflict combatively and aggressively.

A mediator helps couples conduct themselves according to the principles implied in the cooperative conflict style by helping them redirect and control hostile, competitive behaviors, state things more positively, listen to each other, and say what they want instead of attacking each other. When nasty, destructive behaviors are controlled, a more cooperative atmosphere emerges. With self-discipline you too can control your destructive communication. You can reduce competition and animosity by trying to follow the principles implied in the cooperative conflict style questionnaire and by using the basics of good communication outlined in the following chapter.

If you have had a highly competitive marriage or if you feel you can't trust your spouse, it will be difficult to take the risk to relate more cooperatively. You probably believe that the only way to get what you want is to fight for it. That is not true. *Remember, a relationship is a system; if one person changes, the other is going to have to respond differently*. However, if dirty fighting has been a habitual pattern in your relationship with your former spouse, you may be so mired in escalated conflict and mistrust that you will need a third party to help you climb out onto higher ground. Consider seeing a mediator to help diffuse the competition.

The next chapter will show you the basics of communication that can reduce needless arguing and generate a more cooperative atmosphere.

10

How to Talk So Your Spouse Will Listen

> No one cares to speak to an unwilling listener. An arrow never lodges in a stone; often it recoils upon the sender of it.
>
> ST. JEROME

> The anger that both of us felt made simple communication end in arguments. This continued until she remarried.
>
> GREG, *divorced 3 years*

> We tried to talk once a week without a third party, but it was almost impossible.
>
> PAT, *separated 3 months*

How many times have you tried to talk to your spouse and gotten nowhere? You end up feeling shaky, incredibly frustrated, and, most of all, hurt. You started out trying to have a reasonable conversation. You hoped that this time it would be different. But somehow you wound up arguing over who gave more, who spent more money, who was more irresponsible, or who did the most around the house. Nothing was resolved and no matter what you were talking about, the past was invariably dragged into the discussion.

There is no mystery about the reasons that attempts at rational discussions go awry. After watching hundreds of separated couples in my office trying to talk, it is easy for me to see how the inflammatory phrase, the put-down, the closed mind, and the language of combat creep into the conversation. But it doesn't have to be that way. Skillful communication can be learned by anyone. I'm reminded of Jane and Brad who were separated for 2 years before coming to mediation to finalize their divorce. Words like Brad's have echoed in my office all too frequently. Brad spoke with deep regret:

> I've learned a lot since we've been apart. I've gotten tools I didn't have before. I can see I don't have to be right, don't have to win every argument. I can just say we disagree. I learned to listen. I never understood that I wasn't listening. I blamed her for a whole year after we split up. Now I accept more of what I've done. . . . I feel responsible for not being there, not paying enough attention to the marriage. I have a level of appreciation for her I never had before. I'm very sad we are getting divorced. We communicate better now than we ever did when we were married, but she doesn't love me anymore.

As I state throughout the book, you now have an opportunity to relate to each other on a totally different basis than when you were married. As your anger subsides and your emotional investment in each other changes, the door opens for communication that is based on practical decision making.

This chapter will give you skills to use when you want to be reasonable and have a discussion go well. It will provide you with the fundamentals of how to effectively communicate in difficult situations. Even though you may not be ready to stop fighting and won't be able to use these communication principles all the time, they will help you maintain a reasonably civilized relationship as parents over time.

CREATING A LESS DEFENSIVE ATMOSPHERE: GROUND RULES FOR REDUCING NEEDLESS ARGUMENTS

The cycle of conflict escalation usually begins when one person feels defensive. Much needless conflict can be avoided by a careful choice of words. Put quite simply, if you want your message received, you have to pay attention to how you send it. Building a nondefensive atmosphere means that each person's ego is left intact enough to be able to hear what the other has to say. As much as you may want to hurt, put down, or criticize your partner, realize that what you are really hurting are your chances of getting what you want. Much pointless conflict can be prevented by careful language and avoiding the guaranteed "button pushers."

Communicating effectively with your ex takes practice, conscious effort, and concentration. It is not automatic. It will undoubtedly be awkward because it is not the way spouses usually talk to each other. It is similar to learning any new skill, like tennis or skiing. In the beginning, before it becomes instinctive, you have to coach yourself about how to do it correctly. You tell yourself to throw the ball higher every time you get up to serve and to keep your eye on the ball; you remind yourself to put your weight on the downhill ski, plant your pole, and so on. Similarly, in learning to be a good communicator you must tell yourself to use "I messages," to ask for what you want, and to avoid complaining. You must ask yourself, Am I really listening? Did I acknowledge what I heard? By practicing the component skills of good communication discussed in the following paragraphs, you can reduce the defensiveness that results in needless conflict. Central to these ideas is the principle of speaking for yourself, describing your own experience, rather than characterizing the other person.

Self-Report Versus Accusation

Use statements that begin with "I" to express what you want or how you feel. Statements that begin with "you" characterize the other person, are experienced as an attack, and put the person on the defensive. People who feel attacked or criticized concentrate on their own defense and don't really hear your concerns. Even when you have a criticism, state it in terms of how the other person's behavior is a problem for you.

Negative communication:

> STATEMENT: "You never return the children on time. You are irresponsible, undependable, and always taking advantage."
>
> RESPONSE: You can't control my life; you think just because they live with you that you can tell me what to do. You are not exactly a perfect mother either; they are my children, too."

In this dialogue the "you" statement quickly moves the parties to a conflict of control and the issue of who is the better parent, instead of leading to a discussion about lateness.

Positive communication:

> STATEMENT: "I start to get worried that something has happened when the children are returned late. I would appreciate a phone call if you are going to be more than a half hour late."
>
> RESPONSE: "We got caught up in the picnic and baseball game and didn't want to leave. There was no phone. I will try to call in the future."

When you speak in the first person, using "I" statements to describe *your* experience of the problem, how you feel, and what you want, you leave the door open for the other person to respond. Using "I" statements is also a far better way to express anger than attacking your spouse for what he or she has done wrong: "I get very angry when you try to tell me how to deal with the children's bedtime. I feel like I can't do things my way," is more effective than saying, "You are trying to run my life."

Descriptive Versus Judgmental Language

Be descriptive about a problem rather than judgmental and critical. Even though you feel angry, describe the problem created for you rather than judging or blaming your spouse.

Negative communication:

> "You are trying to squeeze me out of the children's lives. As usual, you never tell me about school events until the last minute."

Positive communication:

"When I don't have enough advance notice of a school event, I can't arrange my schedule to be there and the children are disappointed."

Negative communication:

"You are leaving all the work to me just like you always do. You just expect me to do everything, pick up all the pieces."

Positive communication:

"I feel like I have been making a lot of phone calls to arrange the logistics when the children are going to be with you. I doesn't feel like I really get time off when I have to do so much to get ready. I would like you to get the information from the children and make arrangements yourself."

In stating how the behavior or situation is a problem for you, *focus on the consequences of what happens rather than whose fault it is.* Describing something as "not working" is another good way to broach a situation in which you might ordinarily want to blame the other person. For example, "This arrangement is not working for me," or "The way we are handling Sunday night, the summer schedule, driving, etc., is not working for me."

Recommendation Versus Complaint

Don't complain without giving a specific recommendation or suggestion for change. Complaining is a helpless act, stating what you would like is empowering. People complain when they are unhappy about something but don't believe they can do anything about it. Take the time to think of some suggestions for improving a situation you don't like before you register a complaint. You will feel more control over your life, and it will be easier for the other person to respond to a concrete alternative rather than defend against a generalized assault.

Negative communication:

"I am tired of paying for everything. You are sucking me dry, taking me to the cleaners. I never have any money, I'm paying all the debts and your mortgage, and you are always handing me another bill."

Positive communication:

"I cannot meet my monthly expenses and pay your mortgage and our debts. Until all of our joint debts are paid off, I would like you to increase your hours at work or find some way to reduce your expenses."

Negative communication:

"You are never here with the children when you are supposed to be on Sunday morning."

Positive communication:

"Dropping off the children on Sunday morning is not working for me because I need them there at a time I can count on. I could pick them up at ten o'clock in the morning at your house; or can you return them on Saturday night?"

Discovery Versus Assumptions

Separated and divorced couples are constantly making all kinds of assumptions about each other. They fall into the trap of getting all worked up about something before they check it out. They hear bits and pieces from other people or their children, fill in the blanks, and assume it is all accurate. In the absence of trust or direct communication, assumptions tend to be regarded as fact and are given more credence than a spouse's explanation. People who are angry at each other frequently jump to conclusions because unconsciously they seek evidence to justify their negative feelings. Be very careful about this because it is the source of much unnecessary conflict.

Speak only for yourself. Do not speak for your spouse or assume you know your spouse's thoughts or motives. Find out what really happened before assuming the worst. Give the benefit of the doubt and be willing to consider your spouse's explanation. Your interpretation has no more corner on the truth than your partner's.

Negative communication:

"Well, you certainly seem to have the money to go looking for a new car but not to pay half the debts."

Positive communication:

"I heard you were looking for a new car. I agreed to pay for most of the debts because you had to furnish your apartment and didn't have the money. It doesn't feel fair if you get a new car while I'm carrying our joint debts."

Negative communication:

"You are undermining our agreement. You let the boys ride their bikes after we agreed they were grounded. You never follow through, you are impossible to work with."

Positive communication:

"I heard the boys rode their bikes to the store. Is this true? I though we had an understanding that they are not allowed to ride them for two weeks."

Active Listening Versus Rehearsing

Listening without hearing is a common affliction of troubled relationships. Too often we are planning a response, judging and discounting what the other is saying, and not really listening because we disagree or because we think we have heard it all before. Active listening requires the receiver to suspend judgment and attend exclusively to the other person. This means being open to what the other is saying and putting aside your prejudices and preconceived notions. It is not a passive process. You are listening for the purpose of understanding, not to make a point. Listen for the underlying feelings or concerns, which are not always expressed directly or clearly. The key to really hearing is listening from the other's perspective, not yours.

The most lamentable and all too common example of not hearing is when a spouse expresses dissatisfaction with the marriage to a partner who doesn't feel that way and has consistently discounted or ignored these complaints. The more satisfied spouse hardly ever understands the problem from the partner's perspective and is shocked the day the divorce papers arrive. The comment I hear in my office is, "I didn't get it. I just didn't understand she was so unhappy. I guess I didn't really listen."

To promote active listening, paraphrase or repeat what you heard the other say, not your interpretation, but a simple summary of their words. Or ask a question to clarify your understanding. Get more details as to when, how, and under what circumstances the problem exists. You can use active listening even when you are being attacked by feeding back what you hear the other is angry or upset about.

Positive communication:

> "You are upset when the children are returned late because you are worried about their safety."

> "You are very worried about money because of what happened in your parents' divorce, and you want me to give you a lump sum instead of monthly support. It is not that I have been untrustworthy, but you just don't want to take a chance."

Focusing on the Future Versus Analyzing the Past

Rehashing the past is generally unproductive, particularly if you disagree about how you each remember a disputed issue. It works better to concentrate on what you can do right now to correct the problem or what you can do differently in the future. Looking to the future is more fertile ground than the hardened soil of the past. As a rule,

Don't attack a person for past action; concentrate on future change.

Don't go over and over whose fault something was in the past.

Don't spin your wheels trying to recreate a conversation from the past.

Don't prejudge the future based on the past; allow room for improvement and the possibility of change.

COMMON DERAILERS

How many times have you started a reasonable discussion and suddenly found yourself fighting about something that had nothing to do with what you started talking about? What happens to most discussions to make them unproductive is a comment—or even one word—that derails discussion because of the emotion the language incites. Staying on track is difficult in the best of circumstances. In the following paragraphs are common derailers. Try to eliminate them from your repertoire.

Globalization

Don't expand the size of the problem by using words like *always* and *never*. It is tempting when you are angry or trying to prove a point to put more evidence behind your argument; using these words is the easiest way to bolster your position. They are inflammatory and will derail the discussion into one about how often the problem occurs, which —while it may have some relevance—is not going to produce a solution. Keep the discussion confined to the specific time and place.

Negative communication:

"You never make accommodations to my schedule, I am always accommodating to you."
"That's not true. I am always doing what you want."

Positive communication:

> "For the last three weeks I have changed the schedule for you; it is
> very important to me that we switch this weekend."

Cross-Complaints

When your spouse introduces an issue, address that issue.
Don't respond by launching a complaint against him or her:

> "You are overprotective and won't let the kids go out and have a
> good time."
> "Well, at least I don't scare them with my temper like you do."

This is one of the most common ways a discussion gets
sidetracked. Instead of cross-complaining, ask for more information: "How do you think I am overprotective? Because I don't think
I am." As in the aikido metaphor, stay with the first person's
concern until it is dealt with. Then you may raise your concern.

Put-Downs

It goes without saying that a personal attack, name-calling, or
character assassination will derail even the most benign discussion: "You are selfish and only thinking about yourself, just like
you always do." Instead, use a self-disclosure statement describing what the problem is for you: "I get very frustrated when my
point of view is repeatedly disregarded in our discussions."

The other kind of put-down is an attitude of superiority. Give
your partner credit and acknowledgment when it is deserved, and
express appreciation when you can.

Should Statements

No one likes being told what to do. When you tell your spouse
what he or she should or shouldn't do, you place yourself in a
position of authority and superiority, which your spouse will
resent. Describe what you would like to see happen rather than

telling your ex what he or she should do. Rather than assert, "You shouldn't let the children eat so much junk food," you can say, "I am concerned about the amount of junk food the children eat. Can we discuss it so that we can have some consistency between households?" Notice how this statement meets the criteria for a nondefensive statement; it is an "I" statement, neutral, doesn't blame anyone, describes the concern without complaining, and offers a suggestion.

Lecturing

Lecturing is taking "should statements" to their extreme. Ever notice what happens when you move into the lecture mode with your kids? You are lucky if they are still listening by the third sentence. As much as you feel that you are right and have something to say and a right to say it, the truth is, the more drawn out you are the more lose your effectiveness. The more briefly you can make your point, the better. We tend to lecture when we are not sure we can make a point without providing a lot of justification for our position. We go on and on about all the reasons we feel we are right. Although we feel that we need to do this in order to state our case, the other has probably already tuned us out.

Either/Or Statements and Ultimatums

If you have a serious concern and want to express your final decision about it, do so by describing how you see the situation, why your bottom line is important to you, and what you see as your alternative if it is violated. Tell your spouse where you stand clearly and directly. Do not issue a threat or an ultimatum; for example: "Either you let me have the children on my birthday or I won't pay your car insurance." State it this way:

> "I feel I have been generous in accommodating your needs. It is very important to me to have the children on my birthday. This is a special day, and I have no one else to share it with. I do not feel I

can continue to be generous with you if you cannot honor some of my requests. I will not continue to make concessions to you, like paying for your car insurance, if there isn't more give-and-take."

HOW TO RESPOND TO ATTACKS AND CRITICISM: DEFLECT BY REFLECTING

The first step is to practice relaxing when angry criticism comes your way so you don't immediately get on the defensive. Step back, take a deep breath, listen and—like the aikido master—accept the energy and stay with the other's concern rather than defending yourself. Concentrate on listening, look for the concern underlying the attack, try to restate it neutrally without judgment, and ask for clarification about what the other wants. After you fully understand the other's complaint, you can then express your point of view. In a sense, you deflect by reflecting back. For example: "Let me see if I understand. What bothers you is that I keep changing my mind about agreements that you thought were final and that makes you think I am out to get you."

Acknowledging a concern in this way curbs the energy of an attack or criticism. This is the crucial first step. Acknowledging it does not take away the issue or your differences about it, but it slows the process down so that you can discuss the issue. In the following examples, notice that the reflective response feeds back the underlying concern without judging its merit or counterattacking.

> CRITICIZING SPOUSE: "You are sucking me dry. I never have any money. I am paying for everything. You are taking advantage of me and I won't put up with it."
>
> REFLECTIVE RESPONSE: "You are worried about money, and you think our arrangement is unfair. What specific part seems unfair to you?"

> CRITICIZING SPOUSE: "You don't care about your children. All you care about is yourself and your girlfriend."

REFLECTIVE RESPONSE: "You seem upset about my relationship with the children. What are you worried about?"

PARAPHRASING AND REFLECTING BACK: AN EXERCISE

The skill of paraphrasing and reflecting back is difficult, especially in the heat of emotion. Practice by writing down how you would deflect each of these attacks.

1. You are always coming after me for money.
   Reflective statement:

2. I am sick and tired of your bringing up this issue.
   Reflective statement:

3. You are not going to write me out of your life like a piece of used furniture.
   Reflective response:

4. You only care about yourself; you don't give a hoot about what happens to me or the kids.
   Reflective response:

HANDING ANGRY AND ABUSIVE BEHAVIOR: TIPS FOR REACTING UNDER PRESSURE

1. Center yourself: take several slow, deep breaths when you first feel yourself becoming tense, confused, or angry.
2. Listen fully and actively to the complaint.
3. Acknowledge or paraphrase the other's feelings or concerns without agreeing or disagreeing.
4. Ask questions to clarify the criticism. What exactly is the other person most upset about? When does this occur? What does the other want to improve the situation?
5. Do not defend yourself or counterattack.
6. After listening to the other and acknowledging the concern, state your point of view. Try not to get defensive but describe how you see the situation differently: "In my perception, . . ."
7. Don't countercomplain or bring up other issues. Stay on track. Say, "This is not what this discussion is about. We are discussing X, not Y.
8. Try to remain as detached and businesslike as you possibly can.
9. Look for opportunities to agree with something the other person has said, or acknowledge the other's point of view without necessarily agreeing with all of it.
10. Set limits. Be willing to take care of yourself and state what you will not tolerate in terms of abusive comments:

"I am willing to discuss this but not in this way." "I will not be ridiculed or attacked like this anymore." "I won't participate in these arguments for the sake of argument."
11. Remove yourself from a destructive or abusive situation. Follow through if the other person doesn't change his behavior: "I have to remove myself from this situation until it calms down."

HOW TO EXPRESS CRITICISM

Introduce the fact that you have a criticism or problem you'd like to discuss before you state what the complaint is. It is hard to receive criticism without being defensive in the best of circumstances. Blurting out a complaint doesn't give the other person time to prepare mentally and will usually result in a defensive response. State that you have a problem or criticism that you would like to discuss. Ask your spouse if he or she could just hear you out, consider your feedback, and try not to be defensive: "John, it's hard for me to bring this up, but I have a problem with the way you are dealing with Susie and her homework. I know it might make you defensive [or 'Please don't get defensive'], but just listen to what I have to say." The mini-preamble anticipates the other's reaction, which tends to modify the intensity of that response.

When you bring up your concern, describe what the problem is rather than characterize your spouse's behavior. Don't attribute motives, intention, or fault. Describe the situation as neutrally as you can and state how it is a problem for you or for other members of the family. If there is a positive aspect to the situation, you can mention it before you raise the criticism; that is, say the good news first: "I really appreciate the time you are putting in with Susie on her math and history, but she has been in tears because she feels she doesn't do well enough for you. I think she feels a lot of pressure to please you."

As was suggested before, when you have a criticism or complaint, have a suggestion in mind about what might help solve the problem. After raising your concern and allowing the opportunity for a response, ask if your spouse would be willing to entertain your suggestion.

HOW TO BRING UP A TOUCHY SUBJECT

To introduce a touchy subject, follow the same principles just discussed in expressing criticism. The key is raising the issue in a way that enables you to get beyond the initial defensiveness so that you might be able to have an open discussion. Again, first introduce the fact that you have a touchy subject to bring up. In your mini-preamble, express your own discomfort at talking about the particular issue. Admit that these kinds of discussions haven't gone well in the past, or say that you don't want the other person to get defensive even though you know that this is a touchy subject. Anticipate the other's reaction and state it in a neutral, nonblaming, way. By anticipating the other's response in an accepting way, he or she is less likely to respond that way: "I know that you will be upset about my bringing this up again." Express your hope that the discussion can go well this time: "Mary, I feel uncomfortable bringing up the subject of my time with the kids because I know it is a touchy subject and it upsets you. I can understand that. I really do understand that it is hard for you, but I feel like I just don't see the kids enough. It feels terrible to me, and I think it is rough on the kids. I hope we can find a solution that is good for everyone." Or: "Bill, I know the subject of child support is touchy between us, and I'm uncomfortable bringing up a difficult issue when we have been getting along so well. I do appreciate that from your point of view the arrangement is inequitable, but we do need to talk about the costs of summer plans for the children. I hope we can work this out so we both feel okay about it."

ARGUMENT BUSTERS: NEUTRAL PHRASES TO DEFUSE FIGHTS THAT GO NOWHERE

You know the feeling when you get caught in an argument that's going nowhere. You are not exactly sure how you got there or how to get out. As soon as you realize that you can't agree, use neutralizing phrases to help you move on, instead of going round and round about who is right and whose memory is correct. Neutralizing phrases make no one wrong and get you out of a no-win argument by acknowledging irreconcilable differences. Here are some examples:

"We see it differently; our perceptions are different, so let's just move on."
"We have different needs in this situation."
"Can we agree to disagree?"
"This is not working for me."
"There is no point arguing over who is right. Can we look at a way to handle this from this point forward?"
"This discussion is not productive. It is hurtful."
"What we are doing now is not helpful; let's stop."

REACHING OUT TO MAKE THINGS BETTER: WRITING LETTERS

I have found that writing letters is an effective method of diffusing a tense situation and promoting cooperation. In a letter you can organize your thoughts and say how you really feel without losing your cool, being interrupted, or being attacked. Decent intentions that are lost in the intensity of face-to-face interactions can be expressed in writing. On the receiving end, your spouse has the opportunity to think about what you've said without having to respond immediately. If you are able to speak from the heart of your desire to move beyond the anger and destructiveness, you can often cut through your spouse's animosity and touch his or her deeper concerns also.

The Goodwill Letter

To try to create a more cooperative atmosphere and extend goodwill, write a carefully worded letter expressing your hope and desire to improve the situation. If you blame or attack your spouse in any way, you will defeat the purpose. The letter should incorporate the language and principles discussed in this chapter.

Goodwill Letter Format

- State your desire to do what's best for the children.
- State your desire to have a cooperative relationship as parents and put the past behind you.
- State your hope that time has begun to heal and will continue to heal the hurts of the past so that the children won't be affected by the animosity between you.
- State your desire to resolve any issues on the table and not have them escalate into battles.
- State your desire for a meeting to try to talk about or formulate a plan to deal with a specific difficulty or impasse.

Deborah wrote the following letter to her ex-husband shortly after their divorce was final:

Dear Steve,

I know you still feel angry about the divorce and sometimes hate me. I didn't want our marriage to end up this way any more than you did. We tried in our own ways to fix it. I am truly sorry that I was not strong enough to make you understand how unhappy I was earlier. There is nothing more we can do now but help our kids grow up to be happy. I know you love them and are worried about them as much as I am. They miss you and need to be with you. I don't want our fighting to hurt them. You are a great father and I want to work with you as a parent. I would never try to take the children away from you. Please, please believe me. Even though you think Bob and I are going to move away and cut you out, that is the farthest thing from my mind. You will always be their father. I will never let anything change that.

My hope is for peace and healing between whatever new families these children become part of.

With respect and hope,

Deb

The Strategic Letter

Strategic letters can be used for a variety of situations. I do not mean strategic in a pejorative way. I call these letters strategic because the format includes specific principles mediators use to diffuse antagonism and invite cooperation. Such letters can be used for the following purposes:

- To improve cooperation and goodwill
- To deal with a touchy subject
- To keep an impasse from escalating
- To deal with the other's anger and hostility
- To ask your spouse to go to a mediator
- To deal with threats of court

Strategic Letter Format

Regardless of the problem you wish to address, the format of the strategic letter should include the following elements:

1. A statement of your desired goal and reasons for writing:

> "I am writing because I really want to be able to deal with xyz better than we have in the past."

> "I am writing because I am worried about the effects of our continuing conflicts on the kids. I would like you to consider going to a mediator."

2. A statement of your desire to cooperate and resolve the matter reasonably and fairly:

> "I know this is a touchy subject and hard to discuss in person, but I really would like to resolve our disagreement about child support equitably so that you don't feel ripped off and I have an amount that covers our needs."

> "I want to work with you on the visitation and come up with something we can both live with. I didn't mean for the attorneys to become so involved. Please can't we try to protect the children from our personal feelings about each other?"

3. An invitation to understand each other's viewpoints and concerns:

> "I want to understand your point of view and come up with something fair. I would like to lay down the hatchet."

> "Please can't we try to put the past behind us? I am not trying to take advantage of you. I want to understand what you want out of this."

4. Anticipation of the obstacles and a matter-of-fact statement of what you think your spouse's objections are going to be:

> "I know we haven't had much success talking in the past, but I feel that enough time has passed that we can do better now."

> "I know we haven't trusted each other, but I am willing to extend good faith if you are."

> "I know you think my lawyer is going for broke, but that is just not the case."

5. Language that describes your feelings and desires rather than attacks or blames your spouse:

> "I feel very bad that this has been so difficult and we have hurt each other so much with our constant bickering."

"I'm lost without the children. I'm worried they will think I've abandoned them and the same thing will happen to them as happened to me in my parent's divorce."

6. An emphasis on mutual concerns:

"We both want to keep the costs down."

"We both want our daughter to feel comfortable about being able to go to college."

"We both want what is best for the children."

7. A concluding statement about how you would like things to be in the future (i.e., a picture of what future success would be like):

"It would be nice for us to be able to change the schedule with one phone call and for little Johnny to be with either parent without always worrying whether it's exactly fifty-fifty."

"I would like for the kids to be able to have both of us at their sport events. I hope someday we can both give Susan a hug when she scores a goal."

8. A bottom line, if the problems are serious: Communicate this as a last alternative, without threat or blame but simply presented as the last choice you see if the issue can't be resolved. Always restate your desire to try to work the problem out:

"If we cannot be more accommodating of schedule changes and these fights continue to escalate into threats, I seriously think we won't be able to continue joint custody. As I said, I don't want us to have to go to court; I would like to go to a mediator to deal with the continued tension and fighting, but this can't go on much longer."

"I really want to work with you to establish a more reasonable visitation schedule now that the children are older. As I said, I will pay for mediation so we can try to talk about it. However, I cannot tolerate the restrictions you have imposed, and if we can't try to work this out on our own or with mediation, I will take legal action to modify the schedule. I hope you will consider mediation."

It is probably hard to conceive of communicating with your spouse as I have suggested in this chapter. You have so much history, so many automatic reactions. There will be many times when you will simply want to yell and be nasty.

In the years after my own divorce, there were times when I would become furious at my ex-husband. I wanted to draw the line, give an ultimatum, and call a lawyer. I usually didn't do this. At times it took all the skill I possessed to have a civilized discussion about our differences so that the problem did not escalate. Even as I write this, I cannot emphasize enough that *there is little about the language of effective communication that comes naturally*. You have to think about what you want to say and how to say it. You have to choose words carefully. As hard as it is in the beginning, it does become easier over time, and most importantly, it sets the tone for a more cooperative atmosphere in the future.

11

Diagnose the Dispute

What Is This Fight Really About?

> The truth remains hidden from him who is in
> the bondage of hate and desire.
>
> BUDDHA

Conflict is misleading. It is hard to know what a fight is really about. Are you angry because you actually want more help in the kitchen or because you feel ignored, unloved, or unappreciated? Are you arguing over the money your wife spent on a new dress or the fact that your sexual advances have been rejected? Fights are often not about the ostensible issue but, rather, about something else that is not clear or safe to express. If you can't decipher the underlying concern, you won't be able to resolve the dispute. This is especially true for divorcing couples. The real concerns are often hidden. A dispute about overnight visitation may cloak fears about separation from young children. The dispute about who gets the favorite antique is more often about the value of the relationship rather than the value of the antique. If you can't get to the underlying issue or real concern, these disputes will continue.

Perhaps the most important distinction in terms of your ability to resolve conflict is to recognize the difference between disputes based on actual conflicts in needs and desires—for example, when both have a legitimate need for the washer and dryer or cash for a down payment on a house—and disputes that are fueled from the hurts and resentments of the past, as expressed in the common statement: "You left me; my life shouldn't be disrupted, so you find the money for the washer and dryer and the down payment." Conflicts based on genuine opposing needs and desires can be resolved through negotiation, trade-offs, and compromise. Conflict with an emotional agenda or conflict which expresses aggression to hurt or defeat the other cannot be dealt with effectively by negotiation or problem solving. The emotional part must be dealt with separately.

This chapter helps you identify the underlying issues that make some disputes so hard to resolve, recognize your real points of disagreement, and separate past issues from present concerns. It also shows you how to deal with the different types of conflicts divorcing couples typically face: conflicts generated by old history, conflicts based on differences in values, conflicts caused by limited resources, and conflicts that arise because of the lack of trust.

CONFLICTS BASED ON OLD HISTORY

Most of the intractable disputes during divorce are a continuation of conflicts from the marriage or a response to the pain and anger of ending the marriage. These disputes are driven by injured pride, feelings of abandonment, desires for retaliation and control, and, oftentimes, looming fears and anxieties. When these feelings are strong, reasonable problem solving is almost impossible to achieve unless you can identify the underlying issue and either deal with it separately or agree to set it aside.

Sometimes the underlying emotion is not recognized and not consciously intended to undermine negotiations. A man in mediation whose wife couched all of their discussions about financial support in terms of his "owing" her, because he had left her, finally said outright, "I'm tired to sitting here being blamed. We both know the marriage had terrible problems. I'm not going to be painted as the bad guy and be made to pay just because I don't think our marriage can work anymore. I'll be fair, but that's it." Surprisingly, the wife said she was sorry she was acting that way. She knew what he said was true, but it was hard for her not to blame him because the family life she had so cherished was gone.

How to Handle Disputes with Underlying Issues

Acknowledge the Emotional Issue

In a nonblaming, nonaccusatory way try to bring the underlying emotion out in the open. You can do this in several ways. You can ask your spouse if there is something upsetting about the subject under discussion that makes this issue so hard to resolve. Or, as in the example cited, you can describe what you think is going on: "Anger is getting in the way of being reasonable. I feel I am being punished for wanting the divorce." Notice the husband used "I" statements describing his own feelings and where he stood. He did not launch into a character assassination or accuse his wife of being malicious. He described his own experience, was not judgmental, and set limits on what he would tolerate. Sometimes just labeling the undercurrent diffuses it.

When a dispute has a strong underlying issue, the person experiencing it is in distress. Acknowledging the other's distress can be very helpful if you do it sincerely, respectfully, and without being patronizing:

"I know you feel abandoned, but I am trying to be fair. Can't we just look at our finances realistically."

"I know you are worried about being away from the children, but I'm not asking for an unreasonable amount of time and I support your relationship with the girls."

"I know you are angry about my involvement with Patrick, but that is not the reason our marriage fell apart and we have to come up with some fair way to deal with the equity in the house. I am truly sorry this is so painful for you."

Remember to speak briefly, to the point, and from the heart.

You can't always ease another person's pain, but you can acknowledge it. *Some disputes are really about not being acknowledged.* The fight is to have one's experience understood and acknowledged even though there may be nothing that can be done to change the situation. Any mediator will tell you that the tension diminishes significantly once a person's feelings, concerns, or points of view have been honestly acknowledged rather than judged or debated. A wife arguing with her husband over child support finally said, "I really don't want more money. I know you don't have it, but I just want to be acknowledged for carrying the lion's share of the support of the children right now."

Honestly Express Your Real Feelings

Strong feelings honestly expressed can break through long-standing barriers. Expressing your sorrow, your anger, or your disappointment from your gut, without attacking the other person, can cut through to the heart of the matter. How can you continue to argue with someone who is bleeding in front of your or has just seen the depth of your own wound? I have found in mediation that the fighting stops and the whole tone shifts when a couple gets in touch with the depth of the pain and the sorrow at the loss, instead of blaming each other for it. One client, who had been dealing with a very angry spouse for months, burst out with anguish in her voice, "I am in such pain, this is killing me. I am so sorry our loving stopped; please let me be, please, please, please." Her husband had no more words, but his eyes welled up with tears. Encounters like these can be turning points, where the rage diminishes and reasonableness begins.

So don't be afraid to speak from your heart. Real feelings are potent. You are often more empowered if you stop arguing and express the emotions that lie beneath your anger. Let your battle fatigue show. Say you're sorry and you wish things hadn't turned out this way. Say how tired you are of struggling and how much you would like peace for everyone. Remind your spouse of your mutual love and commitment to your children.

If an honest expression of feelings doesn't break through the cycle of fruitless discussions, then discontinue the conversation. Simply say, "There is an emotional agenda here that I can't deal with. It is preventing us from looking at options to resolve this problem. I want to end this discussion for now."

Separate the Past Issues from Present Concerns

As noted before, one of the frustrating disputes divorcing couples encounter is the rehashing of major problems that plagued them throughout the marriage. These same themes recycle themselves into the settlement discussions, and the couple ends up fighting the same fight but in a different forum. For example, one couple I saw was discussing dividing the husband's retirement plan when the husband suddenly blew up and began ranting about how his wife was playing helpless again, how she was just trying to make him feel guilty, how nothing was ever enough, and how she better understand that he wasn't going to take care of her forever. Though the wife was expressing a legitimate anxiety about her future, the husband could see her concern only in terms of the past. When an issue is emotionally loaded because of its history, many people feel justified in their reaction. There is a tendency for them to react as they always have or to compensate for underreacting in the past. Often there is a feeling of "I'm not going to let him do that to me one more time!" While this kind of response often represents personal growth, be careful about overcompensating or taking an unyielding stand.

If you find yourself in a frustrating, recurrent pattern of conflict with your spouse that echoes scenes from your marriage, you need to change the way *you* respond. Respect your anger and acknowledge the part of the argument that is old history but focus on the present circumstances in practical terms. You have to ask yourself, How much does this matter now that I am not going to be living with this person anymore? What matters more, making an issue of this or a swift resolution?

George and Margaret, who had been separated for 8 months, couldn't seem to get beyond their old games. They came to mediation because their fights about money were escalating into a custody battle. Money had been a major issue in the marriage, with George trying to control the expenses and Margaret rebelling, doing what she wanted, and resisting George's control every step of the way. Whenever Margaret asked George to contribute to the extra expenses for the children, George reacted to her requests as he always had—by launching into a tirade about her irresponsibility with money. Margaret typically defended herself by attacking George for his drinking habits. They were not even aware that they were engaged in the same game. All they recognized was the familiar fury that left nothing resolved. George used a technique a colleague of mine calls "getting present."[1] He had to ask himself, What does this issue have to do with the past and what does it have to do with the present? George looked at the money conflict in terms of the practical realities now, as if it weren't a loaded issue weighted down by a factor of 75 percent past history. He saw that some of Margaret's concerns were reasonable and needed to be addressed. There were circumstances that could not have been predicted, such as contact lenses being lost and summer tutoring, that increased Margaret's expenses for the children. George also realized that to some extent Margaret was manipulating him as she had in the past and that he needed to be cautious. But rather than yelling at her and starting up the usual cycle, he respectfully set a limit on what she saw as his role in contributing to "extra" expenses.

Using the "getting present" technique, you can separate the past history from present concerns by using the following suggestions:

1. Write down the recurrent issue or theme that causes the most conflict in your negotiations and discussions.
2. What percentage of your reaction would you attribute to past history? Briefly describe what the problem was and what made you so angry in the past.
3. Then describe how this issue is a problem for you now, in your current circumstances.

4. Write down in practical terms what *you* want now or need now to handle this in the present circumstances. Focus on practical solutions rather than passing judgment on historical events.
5. Formulate a plan of action.

Another client, Jill, who had a 4-year-old daughter and was separated from her husband, fought with him over visits continually. Her ex, Tom, would press for more time, and Jill would refuse and become irate at his demands. Jill realized that her anger was excessive and had to do with the past. Her "getting present" list looked like this:

Issue: He is always asking to spend more time with our daughter after we have already agreed what the schedule will be. He calls me Sunday night and asks if he could keep her until Monday. I just can't believe he is doing it again. He is incapable of sticking to agreements. No matter what limit I set, he pushes it.

Past feelings: Seventy-five percent past. I can't trust him and I am angry. He always says one thing and does another. Why should I give him latitude about anything after he practically deserted us when she was a baby? I am just sick and tired of being jerked around by him.

Present concerns: Our daughter needs a predictable schedule. It is confusing to her to have all these last-minute changes. It is also disruptive to me. With so much going on with school and work, I simply need order in my life and as little contact with Tom as possible.

Plan of action: I could try to set up a schedule that gives him more time with our daughter —maybe on the nights I have evening classes. I will let him know that if I agree to more time on a regular basis in writing, it won't be changed unless there is an emergency.

Another approach for "getting present" is to ask yourself the questions, If this weren't a "loaded" issue, how might I respond or see a solution? Take a few minutes to think about your response in some detail. Imagine addressing the dispute as if it were an issue between you and someone you respect, instead of between you and your spouse. Experiment with acting as if the issues you have these strong emotional responses to didn't have a history. Acting "as if" something were not a heated issue can change a habituated response, interrupt the escalation cycle, and enable you to concentrate better on practical solutions. The important thing to remember is to focus on taking care of your own needs without overcompensating for the past.

Stay Solution-Oriented

The last technique for dealing with the undercurrent is to recognize its existence and simply try to bypass it. State when you think an old issue is resurfacing and ask your spouse to just look at the current problem from this point forward. You can say something like the following: "Can we leave our relationship out of this and just deal with it on a practical level?" or "We already know that we don't trust each other and feel the other was at fault. Nothing is going to change our views of the past. Can we just drop the argument and try to figure out what to do now?"

CONFLICTS BASED ON DIFFERENCES IN VALUES

Disputes based on deeply held values and principles are usually not negotiable and are not going to be resolved by trying to change the other person's mind. You are no longer going to be married so there is no point in continuing to fight over whose values are better. You need to develop a mutual respect for your differences —and agree to a minimal level of consistency where the children are concerned —or work around your differences. For instance, some parents who do not support organized religion are willing to take the children to Sunday school when the children are with them because that activity is meaningful to the children. Others are not willing to do this. They may want to expose the children to an experience that they value more, like doing things together with a new stepfamily. When you divorce, each person has a right to function autonomously within reasonable community standards and without the other's interference. There is no point in trying to change your ex-spouse's values anymore.

How to Handle Value Disputes

If you suspect that value differences are creating disputes in your parenting arrangement, make a list of what you see as your major value differences. Stan and Connie compiled this list:

1. Health and diet: natural food, naturopathic medicine versus traditional medical care and unsupervised nutritional habits
2. Importance of religious education and belief in a deity versus religious skepticism
3. Private school versus public school: belief that it is a parent's responsibility to provide children with the best educational opportunity that can be afforded versus the belief that it is the children's responsibility to get the maximum out of whatever situation they are in
4. Belief in the importance of providing children with extracurricular activities, camps, lessons, and equipment versus the belief that children should earn money and work for what they want

Sometimes value differences can be negotiated if they are first acknowledged and there is a willingness to tolerate the children's exposure to the other parent's values or lifestyle. The significance of negotiating where children are concerned is to provide some continuity so that the rules in each house are not in total contradiction. As you can see from their list, Stan and Connie had conflict over the children's diet and medical care as well as over how much they should be given and how much they should earn. In mediation they negotiated a minimal level of what each would do in recognition of the other's values: Stan agreed to cut down on sugar and additives in the children's diet, and Connie agreed to call Stan and take the children to an M.D. when they were sick for more than a few days or had a high fever. They decided they would each expose the children to their own religious beliefs without interference from the other parent. Stan agreed to contribute half the tuition for private school for one year until Connie could enroll the children in a better school district. They also agreed that Stan would pay 25 percent toward extracurricular activities and Connie and the children would share the remaining costs.

When there are impasses that relate to differences in values, see if there is a minimal level to which you can both agree, like the minimum each parent will contribute toward college costs or summer camp. Then, if one parent wants to or is able to subsidize further, that is an option.

Another way to approach values disputes is to ask, Is the disagreement really over substance or about how the values are expressed? For instance, in her emphasis on natural foods Connie was trying to teach the children to take good care of themselves and to take responsibility for what they eat. Stan also wanted the children to learn to take care of themselves but did not choose eating only "health" food as the way to do this. He had other family rules to teach this same lesson. Both parents wanted the children to develop a sense of responsibility and to work hard to achieve success, but they disagreed about how much support parents should provide as part of this learning.

In sum, concentrate on teaching and exposing the children to your values through your example rather than opposing your spouse's values. Learn to recognize when conflicts represent differences in values and try to see where the common ground might be.

CONFLICTS CAUSED BY LIMITED RESOURCES

Many disputes arise because there isn't enough to go around. These disputes become intense because both parties feel that their survival is at stake. Disputes over scarce resources are often not recognized as such, and couples desperately argue over who deserves what there is, not recognizing that what is involved is a loss for both. These disputes are fueled by a lack of understanding of the realities of the financial situation and the myth that there is more money than there is.

Families with more financial resources, flexible work schedules, and adequate housing tend to have less difficulty resolving these conflicts than couples who have limited options available. Couples with limited resources can't always meet the basic needs of two households. When there isn't enough money to afford an apartment large enough to accommodate children, it puts a terrible strain on that parent's ability to have quality time with the children or to have them overnight. When what little there is has to be divided, it is hard not to want to blame someone. There is a rage at having worked so hard and ended up with so little. The reality is that there isn't enough for both parties to have what they need, and this is no one's fault.

One couple I know sold their house because it was too big and costly for a single income and it needed repairs. They fought for a long time about what was fair. If the husband didn't get half of the cash from the sale of the house he would never be able to save up enough to buy another house; his child support payments and credit card debt would preclude the possibility of his buying another house until the children were grown. But if his wife didn't get all of the cash from the house, she wouldn't be able to make a big enough down payment to buy a house with monthly payments she could afford. The only other asset was the husband's small pension, whose value was similar to the equity in their home. It was a very emotional situation, with both sides arguing over why they deserved to get the cash from the house instead of the deferred retirement monies. The husband had the teenage son, who had problems with drugs, living with him, and the wife had the two teenage girls living with her. It wasn't a question of deserving or fault; there were simply not enough resources for them both to get what they needed. It was finally resolved by their lawyers: the wife got most of the equity from the house and the husband kept his pension.

When partners stop blaming each other and recognize the limited resources as no one's fault, it becomes possible to mutually approach the problems created by a financial pinch. Some of the antagonism can be avoided by having a complete picture of the financial situation early on. Many people never kept a budget before their separation, and the emerging financial picture can be a real shock. Inventory your assets and debts so you can adjust your expectations. Realize that when the pie is small each person gets a smaller piece. Try to be creative but be willing to accept that it often takes years to get back on your feet financially after a divorce. This is just another painful reality you have to deal with.

CONFLICTS GENERATED BY MISTRUST

The nature of divorce creates a breeding ground for disputes that might not otherwise arise. Many conflicts are born of mistrust. When you have been hurt and betrayed, when you thought a promise of love was forever but it wasn't, the person you once trusted no longer seems worthy of any faith. This person who was once everything to you suddenly becomes nothing. There is a feeling that you just can't trust your spouse anymore about anything. It is hard to be objective about a former lover's trustworthiness as a human being or as a parent, yet that is precisely what you must learn to do. You need to ask yourself what specifically your spouse has done to become untrustworthy as a parent. Was he or she a bad parent before? What specifically don't you trust about him or her now? What evidence do you have for this feeling, or is it just a feeling? Has your spouse broken agreements, done things behind your back, threatened or harassed you? While there is good reason not to trust someone who is clearly acting like the enemy, feelings of mistrust can't always be accepted at face value.

The breakdown of trust is difficult to reverse because you are caught in a vicious cycle of not believing what your spouse says, thus eliminating any possibility of the other setting the record straight. Lack of trust feeds on itself. Your interpretation of events reinforces your feelings of mistrust and not trusting generates a negative interpretation of events. No matter what happens, there is a tendency to impute negative motives, to see the other guy at fault, trying to get you, defeat you, or do "it" to you again. You don't give the other the benefit of the doubt, and you easily jump to conclusions. Sometimes you are correct and sometimes you are not.

Perhaps the most common problems I see are those where mistrust turns ordinary misunderstandings into major disputes. This is what happened to Phil and Susan, whom I met a year after their divorce. Phil believed that Susan was trying to systematically diminish his role as father. It began with her refusal to agree to joint custody. Even though Phil saw his son, Jason, frequently, he had no control in an area in which he felt most vulnerable—his relationship to his son. Phil was a high-powered attorney, used to having his way and having control. He was very attached to his young son and didn't trust Susan. Whenever something in their parenting agreement didn't work out, he became more convinced that Susan was just giving lip service to her commitment to share parenting. He regularly launched into a tirade and demanded that she respect his "fundamental rights." Susan would try to defend herself but usually ended up in tears, after slamming the phone down. The situation came to a head when Susan enrolled Jason in a special educational program without consulting Phil, as they had agreed. It was the last straw. It was the last straw for Susan also. She had it with Phil's continual demands and accusations.

Three thousand dollars in legal fees later, they came to mediation. It was apparent that Phil's distrust of Susan translated into his seeing everything through the prism of her insidiously trying to diminish his role and influence. He felt her behavior was calculated and purposeful and that she never had any intention of adhering to their agreements about Jason. Phil reacted this way on many occasions, such as when Jason had pizza before Phil was to take him out to dinner or when a friend, instead of Phil, was called when Susan had to go out of town. In all of these situations a logical explanation existed. But Phil always assumed the worst, became angry, and demanded that Susan be held accountable for denying him his "parental rights." The more Susan felt pressured, the less she consulted with Phil, which only increased his mistrust. While Susan truly valued Phil's relationship with Jason, she wanted minimal contact with her ex-spouse. It was only when they could understand each other's perceptions of the problem and when Susan could reassure Phil that he was valued as a parent that Phil was able to feel more relaxed and see how quickly he'd jumped to conclusions before.

There are many times when the lingering feeling of mistrust is no longer founded and the other person's actions are indeed misread, as happened with Phil. Some spouses, however, are deliberately dishonest. They do things behind their partner's back, break legal agreements, clean out bank accounts, try to hide assets, and deny the other the right to see the children. There is good reason not to trust such a person, and legal protection is needed. I recently saw an old friend whom I hadn't seen in a number of years. She had been through what she described as the "divorce from hell"—3 years in and out of court and $60,000 in legal fees. She said her husband had totally changed from 30 years of Mr. Nice Guy to a person who hid community assets, forged her signature, brought her into court on frivolous motions, and lied under oath. Her life was in total chaos during this time. While my friend's situation represents the minority of divorces (less than 10 percent of all divorces go to trial), the problem of mistrust is an issue, to different degrees, in almost all divorces. I can't tell you whether or not to trust your former spouse, but I can suggest that you examine your feelings and consider giving your ex more of the benefit of the doubt. If you have children, it is essential to try to rebuild trust because its absence causes so many continuing problems after the divorce.

In a sense you have to build a track record all over again. You have to extend some trust, knowing that it could fail. You have to think, What is the worse thing that can happen if this trust is misplaced? Try to understand where your feelings of mistrust are coming from and whether they are valid. To some extent, rebuilding trust requires an act of faith.

Evaluating the Trust Factor

Here are some questions that might help you clarify your feelings about your spouse's trustworthiness:

1. Were there patterns of dishonesty in the marriage? List the recurring things your spouse does or has done that make him or her untrustworthy in a *particular area*, for example, overspends, abuses credit cards, has had affairs, doesn't bring the children back on time, breaks scheduling commitments. How often does this really occur? Are there mitigating circumstances? Be specific in your answers. The purpose is to get some data to make sense of your feeling.

2. List the ways in which you feel your spouse is trustworthy, for example, honest and responsible about money, will not take advantage or break agreements about joint assets, has the children's best interest at heart, is careful about safety.

3. As an experiment, give two other (i.e., besides untrustworthiness) possible interpretations to everything your spouse does that you are inclined to interpret negatively. Do this for 2 weeks. For example, if your spouse didn't return the children's clothes clean as agreed, consider other interpretations, such as getting home late, not having time to do laundry, running out of detergent.

4. Think about the ways you and your spouse feel threatened by *each other*. How does feeling threatened contribute to the mutual mistrust?

5. If your spouse doesn't trust you, try to find out why. What does your spouse fear about what you can or will do? Give whatever reassurances you can honestly offer. Express your sincere desire to try to rebuild trust as parents. Point out the areas where your spouse may have misread your actions or intentions.

6. Get a reality check from mutual friends. Sometimes friends can be objective and give you feedback about whether you have a basis for mistrust or are just overreacting.

7. After identifying any area of mistrust that can be supported by facts, make a list of what you can do to protect yourself. Consult with your lawyer about this list and your concerns that relate to legal matters.

The Self-Fulfilling Prophecy

Another cause of continuing conflict that relates to the problem of trust is the belief that things will not change and that there is little you can do to improve your situation. We all know how self-fulfilling prophesies work. When you don't believe something will change, you unconsciously act in defeatist ways, ensuring or inviting the outcome you have negatively prophesied. When you don't trust your former partner, it is indeed difficult to believe that goodwill or cooperation will be extended when you ask; so you either don't ask or you ask aggressively. You may not even be aware that you have an emotional investment in gathering data to justify your negative feelings.

This is what happened to a client whose former wife wouldn't let him see the children more than the minimum specified in the decree. When he asked for additional time, as allowed in the decree, she would snap some excuse. He felt defeated and hopeless that the situation would change. He despaired of ever becoming close to his toddler son, whom he loved very much. I suggested that he explain to his ex-wife, using his best communication skills, how painful it was for him to see the boy so infrequently and that he try to reason with her rather than be confrontational. He returned to the next session and reported that he'd tried but she was just as nasty and controlling as ever. I asked him exactly what he had said to her. He said he had asked if he could keep Joey Sunday night and she had said no, Joey needed to be in his own bed to get ready for school. He then told her that that was a poor excuse since Joey was his kid too and that he had just as much damn right to him as she did. My client's idea of trying to "reason" with his former wife was basically yelling at her. Unconsciously, he sought to justify his frustration at the denied requests, and in fact he provoked her aggressive responses by his own behavior. It took many more practice sessions for my client to learn how to change his self-defeating response to his ex-wife. Even though she was difficult and unwilling to be generous or flexible, my client's beliefs that she would never change and was out to get him interfered with his ability to act in ways that might have promoted a different response from her.

THE EIGHT DANGERS OF DIVORCE MYOPIA

Many conflicts occur because the stress of divorce creates perceptual distortions. You think you have the whole picture, but you don't. I refer to this as the "divorce myopia syndrome" because your vision is impaired. Most divorcing couples are afflicted to some degree or another, although they rarely recognize their own symptoms. The syndrome doesn't cause death, just combat. It is characterized by the following traits:

1. You only see issues from your side but think that you have an objective view. This stems from your unwillingness to understand or empathize with someone who has hurt you.
2. You believe that your interpretation is the correct interpretation. This derives from anger and the need to justify that anger by the conclusions you draw.
3. You make assumptions that are confused with facts. This occurs because there is little direct contact with your former spouse and you frequently jump to conclusions to fit your preconceptions.
4. You tend toward a negative, rather than benign, interpretation of events in a climate of mistrust.
5. You become shortsighted in any crisis. You see only the

present. You don't look at the long-term consequences and implications of present decisions.

6. You can't or don't want to remember anything good from the past. This concentrating on the negative creates a distorted outlook and increases suspicion and mistrust.

7. You tend to see the losses and suffering only in your own situation and not in your spouse's. You see your spouse as having the better deal rather than as someone with a different set of losses and problems.

8. You predict the future based on the past, not recognizing that you are in the middle of a transition that means that *everything* is undergoing change. The truth is you don't know how things will be in the future. The only thing you can be sure of is that they will change.

The chapters in this section have focused on helping you understand the nature of conflict, see how careful language can prevent disputes from arising, and learn how to recognize underlying issues that make some disputes so hard to resolve. It is important to understand the conditions that promote conflict so that you can take steps to reduce these risks. The divorce myopia syndrome summarizes many of the themes I discuss throughout the book. Learn to be aware of these distortions, and make a conscious effort to be more objective. The next section moves on to the fundamentals of win–win negotiation and will show you step-by-step how to resolve disputes and negotiate the final settlement issues.

IV

THE FUNDAMENTALS OF NEGOTIATING

Part IV shifts gears and focuses on the nitty gritty of how to negotiate agreements with your spouse, both in terms of everyday matters as well as in terms of your final divorce settlement. It describes the steps of win–win negotiating, how to have productive 'business' discussions, and how to generate creative solutions. If you are trying to work out your own divorce agreements, this section should prove essential. If you are mediating your divorce, this section will help you get the most out of your mediation effort. Even if you are using attorneys to handle your divorce, there are still things you will have to discuss with each other. If you have children, you will have continuing negotiations about holiday schedules, summer plans, unanticipated expenses, and a host of other topics. By increasing your conflict resolution and negotiation skills, you will be able to work more effectively with your ex-spouse and can avoid having to call a third party every time there is a disagreement in the future. The section concludes with chapters on mediation and on understanding and working with the legal system to reduce escalation.

12

Getting Ready to Negotiate

Let us never negotiate out of fear,
but let us never fear to negotiate.

JOHN F. KENNEDY

This chapter is aimed at helping you strengthen your skills as a negotiator. This way you can plan for negotiation sessions and be at your best at these meetings.

In most negotiations there is a point at which real bargaining takes place: "I'll give you this or do that, if you do this or give me that." This kind of bargaining is uncomfortable, if not repugnant, to many people. The idea of trying to strike a deal over how many days of Christmas vacation the children will be with you or how much money will be traded off for the treasured antique tea service diminishes the value of these things.

You will find it painful to put dollar values on a life created together and to treat the ending of a marriage as a business deal. Your possessions are symbolic of the life you created together. Each item partitioned is a reminder of what was once whole. Each item traded and divided brings you closer to facing the imposing reality that it is over. On one level the settlement negotiations are really about how much you were valued, cared about, and respected. They are about wanting to be acknowledged. Negotiating in the framework of our adversarial legal system can create such animosity, competition, and conflict that people who once shared life dreams with each other feel like they never mattered to each other at all. It is a terrible way to bring 5, 10 or 20 years of your life to a close. Underneath it all, everyone wants to know that he was valued.

When an attorney handles the divorce negotiations at arm's length, the discomfort and pain of bargaining over the value of a life built together is somewhat removed. In many ways it is easier emotionally to have someone else handle it for you. But an attorney can't do it all. You still have to deal with each other. As you prepare to talk to each other, remember that *your spouse has also anguished over the failures in your marriage and has experienced all the hurt and angry feelings that you have*. In your heart of hearts, neither of you wanted things to turn out this way. As much as you disagree about what is fair and as heated as the settlement negotiations may get, try to be respectful of the fact that you are undoing what were once sacred vows.

ARE YOU READY TO NEGOTIATE?

The failure to deal sensitively with the other party as a human being can jeopardize even the most high-level negotiations. The first question is, Are you ready to be reasonable? Has enough time passed that you are able to put aside the hurt and angry feelings and deal rationally with the decisions that need to be made, or are you still reeling from the aftershock, hating or missing your mate? You have to ask yourself if you are fundamentally ready to do "business" with your spouse, and if your spouse is ready to be reasonable with you. Here are questions that will help you examine your readiness. Answer yes, no, or sometimes.[1]

1. Do I want to resolve these issues equitably?
2. Am I willing to put aside my anger and deal with the issues in a rational manner?
3. Are the issues negotiable? Am I willing to make compromises and give some things up?

4. Do I value the importance of the children's relationship with their other parent despite my feelings about him or her as a spouse?
5. Am I willing to work to keep the channels of communication open?
6. Can I accept that we will have differences of perception and in what we think is fair?
7. Have I stopped blaming my spouse for the divorce?
8. Do I feel that my spouse is basically fair-minded?
9. Am I ready emotionally to deal with the final settlement?

If you have answered no more than twice, you may not be ready to embark on the final settlement negotiations. Your feelings may be too raw, you may still feel too angry, or you may not have come to terms with your role in the divorce. Consider waiting until you have had more time to heal and gain perspective. The same is obviously true of your spouse. One of you may be more ready to be reasonable than the other. It is best to wait until you are both ready. Pushing it only leads to a more conflictual settlement process. If you need help with interim decisions, seeing a mediator can be very helpful.

WHAT WORKED WELL IN THE PAST?

There have undoubtedly been times in the past (think hard now!) when you did resolve your differences well and were able successfully to solve a problem together. These will not necessarily stand out in your mind as you struggle with the conflicts of the divorce negotiations. You bring out the worst in each other now. It is hard to remember that it wasn't always this way. If you can recall what worked well in the past, you can use it now. One of the new approaches to short-term psychotherapy is called "solution-oriented" therapy.[2] The idea is that instead of just analyzing a problem, the therapist helps you examine what is going on when the problem is *not* occurring. This way you can get a clear picture of your interactions and relationships when they go well and can learn from your successes. We are conditioned to see what isn't working, what we don't want to happen anymore, and what the problems are; we rarely have as well defined a picture of the successful parts. It is useful to look back at your problem-solving and negotiating successes in this respect, even if they were few and far between. Past successes are resources. The more you are aware of the skills you possess, the more you can consciously and intentionally tap into them.

TAKING INVENTORY: AN EXERCISE

1. Take a moment to think back in your marriage and recall three instances in which you successfully resolved an issue with your spouse or former spouse. Remember how you each handled yourselves and what you each did or said. Write down what characterized those situations and their successes. How did you contribute, and how did your spouse contribute? When the list is complete, think about how you can apply any of those successful behaviors to your current situation.

2. List two things your spouse or former spouse does now that contributes to discussions or interactions going well. My former husband, for instance, once said in the midst of a heated argument full of accusations and counteraccusations, "This is not helpful; we have to look at what we can do about this now." His comment cut through a situation that was out of control and enabled us to get back on track.

3. List two things that you do now that contribute to having successful discussions. I have learned to take deep breaths when I get angry and flustered during discussions with my ex. I am careful to use "I" messages and simply describe my own feelings, and what I don't like about the discussion. This takes great self-control and conscious effort but ultimately makes me feel that I have more power to affect a hostile interaction.

4. What have you found to be the most effective means of getting along with your spouse since the separation?

5. What does your spouse do that infuriates you or pushes your buttons? List three things you can do that are "solution-oriented" when this happens.

6. Are you aware of what you do or say or how you come across that frustrates or infuriates your spouse?

7. When do your discussions go best? What approach to each other seems the most helpful? (Describe the approach in terms of the presence of positive behaviors rather than the absence of negative ones.)

8. What are the two things you have to remember that will help you get along better? Write them down in big letters on the cover of your divorce file, next to the phone, or wherever you can be reminded of them before dealing with your spouse.

RED FLAGS: ANTICIPATE THE MOST SENSITIVE ISSUES

When you can anticipate sensitive or inflammatory issues, you can deal with them more delicately. These issues exist in every divorce. Sometimes they are related to a person's past, sometimes to the circumstances of the breakup. They violate a profound sense of what is fair or touch a deep emotional wound. A client who had alcoholic parents and had to make it the hard way, supporting himself all through high school, college, and graduate school, was adamant about not supporting his ex-wife to finish college. Another client was unwilling to tolerate the children's being around her husband's new lover, who had been a mutual friend.

Exercise: List any red flag or highly sensitive issues in your divorce.

My sensitive issues:

Spouse's sensitive issues:

These issues run to the core. They tend to cool down with time if their intensity and meaning are respected. Deal gently with these matters. Choose your words carefully. Acknowledge your spouse's right to his or her feelings, although you don't have to totally accept the demands that come with them. Try putting yourself in your partner's shoes. If this had been your life circumstance, how would you feel? How would you react? If you are the one having an intense reaction to a settlement issue, try to identify what is behind your reaction. How does your reaction relate to your personal history?

ACCESSING YOUR RESOURCES AS A NEGOTIATOR

You may be wondering, How can I negotiate with my spouse? We have had little success resolving conflicts in the past. My spouse is stronger than I am, I won't be able to get what I need, and I have rarely won an argument in the past.

Ultimately, you will have to be the judge of how much you can negotiate directly with your spouse. But you may, in fact, have more negotiating skills than you realize. If you think about it, you negotiate all the time, in all kinds of situations. Often you are not even conscious of these behaviors. For example, you negotiate with children (if you keep your room clean, I will take you to the movies), and with friends (if you can take care of Susie for me tomorrow, I'll take care of your kids over the weekend). Even if you are the kind of person who wants to please others and has difficulty asserting what you want, there is probably a situation or time in your life where you have successfully negotiated for what you needed.

As an exercise, take a few minutes to recall one situation in which you successfully negotiated for something you wanted. Maybe it was when you were a child lobbying for ice cream or candy or a teenager angling for use of the car, money, or a shirt you really wanted or an employee asking the boss for time off or even a motorist talking a policeman out of giving you a ticket. Notice what you said and did, how you felt, what allowed you to be successful. Take 5 minutes with your eyes closed to recall this occasion. Then write down what you said or did in that situation that could be useful in dealing with your divorce negotiations. Next, write down your fears or concerns about negotiating with your spouse. Can you use any of the abilities you just listed to help with these anxieties? Can you think of three ways to be more businesslike and assertive that work in other situations—for example, at the office or even with your children—that you can try the next time you have to negotiate with your spouse?

Are You a Soft or Hard Negotiator?

All negotiators have two primary interests: how strongly they feel about what they want and their concerns about the relationship with the person or parties with whom they are negotiating. These two factors are a part of every negotiation. You may not be aware of the role they play. Sometimes you are more concerned about getting along or not rocking the boat, other times all you care about is getting what you want. Folger and Poole[3] describe conflict management styles in terms of a model of two intercepting continua—concern for self-interest and concern for the interests of others. You may be a person who tends to yield in the face of opposition, not wanting to hurt the other's feelings and not wanting to be disliked. This kind of negotiator typically cares more about the relationship and being accepted than about personal needs and goals; such people would rather give up what they want in order to avoid the discomfort of potential conflict or the risk of not being well regarded. They are "soft" negotiators. At the other end of the continuum are the "hard" negotiators, who seek to meet their own goals without concern for the needs or acceptance of others. To varying degrees these people can be aggressive and bullying, believing that this is what it takes to survive in the world. They go after what they want and don't care what other people think about them.

Either extreme obviously creates problems. See where you would place yourself *in general* on the grid below measuring how much emphasis you place on concern for your personal goals and how much emphasis you place on your concern for relationships. Then rate yourself on each continuum a second time specifically in regard to your divorce negotiation behavior. Did you place yourself on the same place on the grid? The X is Susan's rating. She feels she is much more concerned about the other person than herself. The Y is where she rated herself as a negotiator in the divorce. You can see this time she is more concerned about her own interests than her spouse's.

Concern for others (high)			
5			
4	I X	II	
3			
2	III	IV Y	
1 (low)			
	(low) 1 2 3 4 5 (high)		
	Concern for own interests[1]		

If you are in quadrant I, you are overly concerned about others and are not looking out for your own interests carefully enough. You care too much about the relationship and could sacrifice what you need. If you are in quadrant II, you have a good balance between focusing on your needs as well as other's concerns. In quadrant III, you tend to avoid conflict situations and do not assert yourself to satisfy your own needs or focus on the other person's. In quadrant IV, you tend to ignore a relationship or other people's concerns in pursuit of your own goals.

If you are the overly accommodating kind of negotiator, (quadrant I or III) you will have to practice paying more attention to your own needs, perhaps even more than you are comfortable with. You will have to learn to take deep breaths so that you can think more lucidly under pressure. Prepare well for meetings so you aren't so easily flustered. And, perhaps most important, know where you stand. If you know exactly what you want, it will be easier to negotiate for it. Often you know what you *don't* want but don't have a clear picture of what you do want. Before a meeting to discuss divorce matters, take the time to write out your needs and concerns about the issue on the table, whether it relates to the furniture, spousal support, or Christmas vacation. Use this as your standard. Ask yourself if what is proposed is bringing you closer to your goals. *Remember, it will probably be easier to stand up for yourself now than in the past because the approval of and relationship with your spouse is not so important to you anymore.*

If you tend to have a dominating style of negotiating, you might not want to admit it. I am sure you have had experiences where winning and self-righteousness may have felt good but cost you in your relationships. Domination is power. While it intimidates, it frequently generates passive resistance and opposition because the other side is afraid to confront you directly. If you are in quadrant IV, you will need to pay more attention to your spouse's concerns and needs if you want your talks and negotiations to succeed. You will have to listen more carefully without interrupting, ask more questions about the other's concerns, and offer proposals that meet your spouse's needs as well as your own. *If you overpower your spouse or take advantage of your strength, you will simply push your spouse into the hands of a strong attorney who can handle you.*

IS THE POWER BALANCED? WHAT IF YOUR SPOUSE IS STRONGER?

Power in any relationship derives from many sources. Most couples have found ways to keep the power in a relationship balanced, even though on the surface it may appear as if one person wields greater control than the other. When one party dominates the other, the "weaker" party will usually find some way to rebel or resist. Resistance is potent, though not necessarily recognized as a source of power by the "weaker" party. The paradox of power struggles is that each person truly feels he is the weaker one struggling to maintain equanimity in the face of a formidable opponent. You may see yourself as the weaker party without realizing your internal sources of power.

Let's say you are worried about being able to hold your own in discussions with your spouse because he knows more about finances, can think faster on his feet, or is more persuasive. There are things you can do to help offset this disparity of power. For one thing, knowledge is power. You will need to become educated about what you are going through. Read a do-it-yourself guide to divorce for your state so you will know what to expect from the legal process. Consult with an attorney to understand your legal entitlements, and develop proposals to discuss with your spouse. Review things you don't understand with your attorney as they arise. If you don't understand the family finances, meet with an accountant, a financial planner, or an appraiser. As overwhelming as it may seem at first, take one step at a time to become more prepared in the areas in which you are lacking knowledge. You will soon be totally responsible for your own assets and financial security. Future choices will be affected by the decisions you make now, so becoming informed is very important. Make sure you are well prepared for any "business" meetings with your spouse and that you have thought through what you want, have supporting data for your position, and have the important points written down, even for small issues.

Sources of Power or Vulnerability[5]

As you go through the negotiation process, you will see that you and your spouse each have strengths and weaknesses that will contribute to the balance of power. Study the following list of factors that contribute to power and vulnerability in a divorce situation and rate yourself in each area on a scale of 1 to 5 according to whether you see yourself as being strong or vulnerable. Then rate your spouse and see if your scores are similar. Notice that there are emotional vulnerabilities as well as negotiating deficits. The person who no longer wants the marriage, for instance, is in a stronger emotional position.

Power and Vulnerability Rating Scale

	Power	$\rightarrow$	Vulnerability		
Readiness to accept the divorce	1	2	3	4	5
Desirous of reconciliation	1	2	3	4	5
Ability to assert your needs	1	2	3	4	5
Knowledge about family finances	1	2	3	4	5
General financial sophistication	1	2	3	4	5
Experience in negotiating as part of your job	1	2	3	4	5
Experience as primary caretaking parent	1	2	3	4	5
Ability to persuade	1	2	3	4	5
Skills in handling conflict	1	2	3	4	5

Legal rights or "bargaining chips" are also sources of power. However, your legal entitlement is not always clear. There are many gray areas in the law. Given the same set of facts, two judges are unlikely to come up with the same rulings. In addition, your attorneys may be advising each of you that you have a strong case; thus, when you sit down to talk, each of you may think that the law is on your side. Power related to legal entitlement is ambiguous. It is subject to games, leverage, and strategies.

TIPS FOR NAIVE NEGOTIATORS: HOW TO IMPROVE YOUR CHANCES OF GETTING WHAT YOU WANT[6]

Whether you are working on your divorce settlement or are divorced and dealing with the myriad of negotiations around arrangements for the children, often what you are actually doing is bargaining. The more you understand the basics of bargaining, the more strategically you can plan your negotiating moves, whether it be for the equity in the house or for a different weekend with the children. Here are some basic strategies that should help improve your chances of getting what you want:

- *Don't make new demands every time you get a concession.* This creates the impression that you are never satisfied and are negotiating in bad faith. Think about what you want and state your full request up front.
- *Acknowledge a concession.* Thanking the other for a concession creates a feeling of goodwill. Be willing to reciprocate as an act of good faith.
- *Don't start out from an extreme position from which you intend to back down.* This leads to escalation as each person becomes angry at the other's outrageous demands and increases his own.
- *See if there is room for "movement" on an issue that seems to be deadlocked.* Ask if your spouse would consider any single part of your request or consider it at another time, if there is anything you could do to make your proposal more acceptable, or if there is anything your spouse would want in return. For example: "I really want the kids this spring break. Would you consider trading with me if I gave you Christmas Eve, Christmas Day, and Thanksgiving?"
- *See if you can find some benefit in your proposal for your spouse.*

"If the children lived with me in the summer, you would have the time to take the extra credits to get your master's degree." Or, "If you take less money in a lump sum spousal support, you will still have the money even if you remarry next month!"

- *Test a proposal against reality rather than criticizing it.* If a proposal seems outrageous and unworkable to you, rather than jumping all over your spouse, ask questions *calmly, without being accusatory*, about how he or she envisions the proposal working, that is, where is the money going to come from, how will back debt be handled, how will you get money to put down on a house, what will happen to the children after school, and so on. Using a "Colombo" type approach, follow your spouse's logic by simply asking for further clarification at each point until the impossibility of the idea becomes apparent or until you get enough information to satisfy your concerns.

- *Anticipate an objection.* Ask if your spouse would be willing to simply think about an idea that you expect will be automatically rejected. For example: "I know you don't want to sell the house right now and I appreciate your reasons, but would you just be willing to listen to this idea?"

- *Be conscious of your spouse's need to look good and maintain self-esteem.* In negotiating language this is called "saving face." It is to your advantage to state things in ways that preserve your partner's self-esteem. A person will not make concessions if his or her ego or self-esteem is assaulted.

- *Do not use take-it-or-leave-it tactics.* This backs the other person into a corner, arouses hostility, and puts his or her ego on the line.

- *Look for the anxiety underlying strong resistance to a request that seems reasonable.* Behind every resistance is a fear or an emotional threat of some sort. When practical proposals are repeatedly rejected, try to find out what your spouse is really worried about. Can your proposal be modified to address or reduce these anxieties?

- *Use written memos to bring up sensitive issues, clarify points of disagreement, or review previous decisions.*
- *In any telephone negotiation the caller has the advantage because he or she has thought about the issue about to be raised.* If you are calling, always ask if your spouse has the time to discuss a particular topic. If you are the person called, don't feel pressured to make a quick decision.
- *Consider shaking hands on agreements, however small.* Even though this may be uncomfortable, a handshake goes a long way toward creating a feeling of commitment to whatever agreement has been reached.
- *Balance short-term gains against long-term goals.* Consider what you might gain now against the cost of future antagonism. Don't undervalue the benefit of getting along just because you are getting divorced.

FIFTEEN STEPS TO MORE SUCCESSFUL "BUSINESS" MEETINGS

Here are some very practical guidelines to help structure business meetings with your spouse or former spouse. These guidelines should be helpful whether you are having a major business meeting or just discussing everyday arrangements.

1. Schedule a specific time. Agree before you start how long the meeting will be. Structure makes difficult discussions feel more manageable. For example, you can say, "I need fifteen minutes to discuss the medical bills. When is a good time for you?"
2. Create an agenda and stick with it point by point. This keeps the meeting more businesslike and less personal.
3. Do not try to discuss your relationship or use the meeting to influence your partner's feelings about the marriage.
4. Do your homework. Get the information you need—exact values, costs, or work schedules—before the meeting.

Have the information to support any new requests you make.

5. Develop a realistic picture of your financial situation. Prepare budgets of the fixed expenses for each household and the joint debts, look at the gross and net incomes, and see what kind of money for variable expenses and discretionary spending is actually available. Many conflicts over money can be prevented by honestly reviewing budgets together at an early point.

6. Designate any red flags or loaded issues—those feelings or issues that require great sensitivity in handling.

7. You can assign one of you as meeting facilitator to help make sure the discussion stays on track and the agenda is followed. Rotate this task. If you choose this technique, the facilitator's job is to (1) write down the agenda; (2) keep the discussion focused on one issue at a time; (3) periodically summarize the progress (where there is agreement, where things are bogged down, or where further information is needed); and (4) keep mutual goals and concerns in focus.

8. Use businesslike communication, as discussed in chapter 10. Use note taking to help maintain a businesslike focus.

9. Before beginning a discussion, summarize the points of agreement and disagreement about the issues under discussion. For example: "We agree there will be family support for you to finish your degree, but there is no agreement about support beyond those three years."

10. Start with the easier issues. Success builds on success.

11. Introduce difficult issues by giving an acknowledgment or expressing appreciation. For example: "I am very pleased with how we have been handling the credit card problems, but there are some new expenses related to the house."

12. Be sensitive to timing. Take breaks in the discussion to think things over or to regain composure. Don't continue a meeting that is no longer productive: say that you think

you have gone as far as you can go today or that perhaps
you are just not ready to deal with a particular issue.
Schedule another meeting.

13. Don't pressure your spouse into immediate decisions.
Allow time to think about new ideas or proposals. New
information tends to become more comfortable over time.

14. If you cannot agree on all points, settle on those on which
you do agree. Do not allow the fact that you don't have
full agreement to negate the decisions you have already
reached.

15. Write down all agreements and plans. Don't try to trust
your memory.

TENSION BUSTERS

Unfortunately, even the most well intended business discussions get sidetracked because tensions are high and tempers flare.
Most people don't know what to say to cool things down again.
There are specific statements mediators make to ease tension and
keep a discussion from escalating into an argument. These are
skills that any good negotiator must have. You can easily apply
these techniques to your own discussion. Study this list and
practice making comments based on these principles, particularly
when things heat up. If one person is acting as meeting facilitator,
part of that role would be to diffuse the tension and hostility by
making these interventions.

- *Restate goals and desire for agreement.* "I really want to work
  this out"; "I want to be on civilized terms with you and be
  able to talk afterwards"; "I want the children to still have
  both of us as parents."

- *Restate areas of agreement, however small.* "Even though we
  are stuck now, we have made progress on how to deal with
  back taxes."

- *Emphasize mutual concerns.* "We both want to avoid court"; "We both want to reduce stress for the children"; "We both want to come out of this with enough money to live on."

- *Restate superordinate goals.* "We know, above all else, that our primary concern is the welfare of the children. We both want them to have a good life despite our problems."

- *Redirect accusations from the past into requests for the future.* "Blaming is not helping. How shall we handle notification of school events in the future?"

- *Be aware of opportunities to compliment your spouse or express appreciation.* "I appreciate the work you put into organizing our financial statement'"; "I appreciate how reasonable you are being even though you are very upset by this"; "I think you handled that situation with Johnny very well."

- *Ease tension with humor.* Lighten things up from time to time by laughing at yourselves.

Now that you have a sense of your negotiating style, and how to set up productive business meetings and ease the tension in those meetings, we are ready to move on to the fundamentals of negotiating agreements.

Win–Win Negotiating Strategies

Quarrels never could last long,
if on one side only lay the wrong.
BENJAMIN FRANKLIN

All Bob Brown wanted when his wife said she didn't think she loved him anymore was to lick his wounds. It was true that the life had gone out of their marriage, but he'd never had the courage or the strength to face it. Now in the solitude of an empty apartment, he reflected on the chasm that had grown between them. A giant glacier had slowly, imperceptibly, moved in on their lives. He must have been somewhere else. He saw it, but he didn't really want to. She said he was married to his career. He couldn't even remember when that had happened. She was right, though. He sighed deeply. She had slipped away, too—the kids, the perfect house, the community boards. He didn't understand how they had allowed all these other things to become more important than each other.

Somehow, they were civil about it all. It was eerie. Maybe they were just numb. Then it started to get real. She said she wanted to be home with the children and wanted the financial support due her for all the emotional support she had given him through dental school. She didn't want her life to change. He owed it to her.

She had to be kidding. His life was being blown apart.

213

Everything he had worked so hard for was gone, and she wanted him to continue to break his back so that her life wouldn't change! He was tired, very tired. Then the anger started to seep in. He had become a money machine. He was sick to his stomach. He had lost touch. How many soccer games had he given up to teach clinics on the weekends? How many bedtime stories were never read? He missed the kids terribly. It was now or never, something had to give. His life had to change.

For 16 years, Carol Brown put everything she had into her marriage. She had wanted things to be perfect. Her husband and children always came first. They were her life. She was what she thought Bob had wanted and what her parents wanted her to be. The house was immaculate. Dinner was always ready. She kept up her appearance. Still, she knew that something was wrong. Bob was never home and when he was, he was distracted. They didn't talk much except about the kids. They were drifting apart. She ached inside but threw herself into the children, her friends, and daily activities. Outwardly, they got along well but the pain got worse. She thought it would go away. They avoided sex for 2 years. They saw a marriage counselor, which helped for a while but the feeling never really came back. The emptiness was killing her. She had to break away from him.

As she sat in the big house on the hill, Carol could barely believe she had told Bob she wanted a separation. She was so used to depending on his judgment, his decisions. For the first time she was going to take the risk to make her own judgment calls and stand up for what she wanted. She wasn't sure what she wanted or what she was going to do now. She needed time to regroup. She had exhausted herself meeting other people's expectations. Now she was owed. She didn't want to be pushed around anymore. He had better back off from his demands to have the kids with him half of the time and for her to get a job. She was not going to be steamrollered on this one.

* * * * *

However well you have managed to communicate rationally and calmly with your former spouse, real conflicts of interest are inevitable. When marriage ends, most of the givens in your life are open to renegotiation, from keeping the family residence, to being a parent, to how much can be spent on groceries. Like Bob and Carol, you are bound to disagree about what is fair, what each person contributed, what each is owed, what the children need, or about any of the other details that arise when you try to separate joined lives. Some decisions come easily because your needs do not conflict. More often, you both want the same thing, like the better car or the family residence. Or you are vying for limited resources, like time with the children or enough money to maintain your lifestyle. These are the conflicts of legitimate needs and goals that exist independently of all the hurt and angry feelings about the marriage's ending. *Use negotiation to resolve these differences.*

NEGOTIATE AROUND NEEDS AND INTERESTS, NOT POSITIONS

Most divorcing spouses, in my experience, are poor negotiators. Marriages fall apart because they can't handle differences well. It is fight or flight, instead of negotiate. And when they do negotiate, there is a tendency to turn differences into "positions" and take immovable stands. When couples argue over who has the better idea or who is right, creative problem solving cannot take place because each person defends his position. For example, a wife says to her husband, "We need to remodel the house." The husband responds with, "We don't really have the money and, besides, if we did my new car comes first." The wife takes a stronger stand: "I earn money too. Why should I live in a world of linoleum when my friends all have tile? You are selfish and only think about what you want and, besides, there is nothing wrong with your car." To which the husband replies, "My new car is more important because I have to drive customers around. We don't need a new kitchen floor just so it will get splattered with strained asparagus and Cheerios." As the wife continues to advance her position, bringing in more data about the sorry condition of the house and the good condition of her husband's car, he will refute her, going on about the transmission, clutch, and how because of the greenhouse effect he really needs a car with air-conditioning. The argument will go on and on, and nothing ever gets resolved.

When you take a position, it is very hard to look at other options because positions force you into my-way-versus-your-way arguments. As you defend a position against attack, you tend to take a stronger stance and dig in your heels. As you assert what you will or will not do and try to convince the other to change positions, a contest of will develops. As you go round and round, you become more identified with your position and it becomes harder to back down without admitting you were wrong and losing face. Look what happens when you tell teenagers what not to wear or to cut their hair. They dig in when challenged.

What works better is to find the *needs and concerns* that are represented in each position. By focusing on what is important to the wife about remodeling and what is important to the husband about a new car, it becomes possible to more creatively address both sets of concerns. Maybe the wife's major concern is the inconvenience of old appliances and she would be willing to postpone a remodeling project if new kitchen appliances were purchased now. If the husband's major concerns about the car are image rather than mechanical, creative ideas might include leasing a car, buying a used "status" car, or having his car painted. With this approach the focus is not longer a matter of either/or, your way or mine.

Many divorce negotiations get bogged down in power struggles because neither person will back down from the position held. Bob and Carol's situation, described at the beginning of this chapter, turned into this. Bob wanted the children half of the time, and Carol wouldn't agree. Bob argued that he had a right to joint custody, to be an involved father. Carol argued that the children needed a stable home base. The more Bob asserted his position, the stronger Carol asserted hers. They were headed for a collision. Let's analyze their dialogue:

Bob (stating his position): I want the children to be with me half of the time. I want joint custody. I'm their father and it's my right.

Carol (stating her position): They need a stable home base. I won't agree to joint custody.

Bob (defending his position): They are my children too. They need me just as much as they need you, and you don't have the right to strip me of my fatherhood.

Carol (responding and digging in): I'm not stripping you of your fatherhood. They are used to my taking care of them. Where were you in the middle of the night? Where were you when they had to go to the doctor? Who disciplines them? You weren't there.

Bob (defending himself and counterattacking): That's patently not true. Who set them up with the computer, helped them with their homework, taught them to ski? You think you have the right to control this just because you are the mother. This is the 1990s. I have my rights. You are not going to push me around.

Carol (countering with a secondary issue): Don't talk to me about being pushed around. We have done what you wanted to do for sixteen years. How many times have I put aside what I wanted for your career?

Bob (counterattacking): That's just another one of your little Miss Innocent myths. You did plenty of what you wanted to do without any interference from me. I'm getting sick of your victim mentality. I never stopped you from doing anything.

As you can see, this discussion escalated into an argument about who was the better parent, who controlled what happened in the past, and who has the right to control what happens now. The discussion quickly moved from conflicting needs (in this case, both wanting to be fully involved parents) to a personal attack and power struggle.

By focusing on what in negotiating language is called the

"needs and interests" of the parties (i.e., what is important to Bob about having the children half of the time and what it means to Carol for the children to have a stable home base), it is possible to find solutions that address both sets of concerns. What was really going on for Bob was a feeling that time was running out. The children were almost teenagers. He felt he'd missed out on a lot of things when he had been building security and making money. Now he wanted to be with the children before they were grown-up and gone. Carol, on the other hand, was scared. Motherhood defined her. Her life revolved around the children, and she felt in danger of losing her identity if her familiar role was taken away. She didn't want things to change. If the Browns had been able to look at their real needs and interests and work with them, their "needs lists" might have looked live this:

Carol

Maintain closeness and bonding with the children.

Be there when the children need me.

Feel like a full-time Mom and be able to do the little things along with the big.

Feel comfortable that the children's safety is being protected.

Not lose their affection and loyalty to a father who has more money.

Give children stability and security and a sense of where they belong.

Not have long periods of separation from the children.

Bob

Be a real father, not a Sunday, good-time, carnival dad.

Influence my children's development.

Be involved in their everyday activities.

Have extended periods of time together with them.

Share my knowledge and skills with them.

Have some control over the decisions that affect their lives.

Not have ex-wife tell me how to parent.

Have my children know that I love them and will always be there
for them.

Looking at these lists, you can see that the needs expressed
are not necessarily irreconcilable and that many of the concerns in
essence are shared, particularly each parent's desire to "be there"
for the children and for the children to be able to count on that.
By addressing the underlying needs, it becomes possible to invent
a variety of ways to respond to these concerns besides the limited
alternatives that snared Bob and Carol. As it turned out, they
negotiated that the children would be with Bob Tuesdays for
dinner and every Friday evening and Saturday, as well as the last
week of each month, thereby providing a balance between Bob's
desire to stay in touch with the children during the week as well
as have an extended block of time with them. The children also
had the benefit of continuity of their home base during the week,
which was so important to Carol. The parents agreed to joint legal
custody with Carol managing the day-to-day affairs and Bob
taking on special projects like the children's sports activities and
their computer interests.

Negotiation around "needs and interests" instead of positions
is the basis of the strategy developed by Roger Fisher and William
Ury in the bestseller *Getting to Yes* and the method used by
professional divorce mediators to help couples develop agreements that work for both.[1] It is a win–win method of resolving
conflict, which seeks to find solutions that address the real needs
and goals of both parties. The next two chapters show you, step-
by-step, how to apply these methods to the issues in divorce and
negotiate plans and agreements where you can both win.

Always Look at Both Sides

Many disputes escalate because the parties fail to recognize
or consider the other person's side. It is a knee jerk response that
we all do—thinking that only our position is right and absolutely
defensible. This is a major obstacle in every level of conflict reso-

lution, from corporate lawsuits to neighborhood disputes to arguments between parents and teenagers. We are not even aware of
how one-sided we are because we are focused on defending our
position. Often we have not really listened even though both sides
usually have some legitimate points. It goes against the grain to
want to understand the feelings or concerns of a former lover. Whatever understanding we may think we have of our spouse's situation,
our opinion is often based purely on our assumptions about it.

My clients Barry and Linda got caught in this trap. They were
about to go to court because they could not see beyond their own
situations. It started when Barry received an unexpected inheritance
a year after the divorce. Linda heard all about it from friends—the
sports car, the new girlfriend, the trip to Hawaii, and Barry's cutting
back on work. The more she heard, the angrier she became. She saw
Barry playing golf and buying new clothes while she struggled to
support three children. It wasn't fair. She confronted him with his
responsibility to contribute more child support. Barry was furious.
As far as he was concerned, she was a money-grabbing parasite just
trying to get more money out of him. He felt he had been generous
where the children were concerned and always bought them the
things they needed. He couldn't believe she was doing this, again.
Whatever he gave, it was never enough, just like in the marriage. It
enraged him.

Linda, in fact, was a nurse working the night shift and was on
call over the weekends because she needed the extra money. She felt
she was carrying the lion's share of their joint responsibilities and
Barry was off doing whatever he wanted to do, just as he had when
they were married. Now that they were divorced, she felt that she
had to draw the line. She insisted on getting more child support.
Barry wasn't going to be pushed around. He got the best lawyer in
town. The tension was terrible, communication stopped, and the
children were upset. Finally, friends persuaded them to see a
mediator first.

When they finally sat down to talk openly, Linda learned that
Barry was planning to use the money to start a software business.
While he had cut back on his regular job, he was working on the
new venture and was not about to become a millionaire. Barry

could see how difficult working nights was for Linda and how it affected her energies as a mother. He realized that she actually needed more money each month just so that she could get on a day shift and not be on call on weekends. They agreed to $300 a month increased support, a sum they would review in a year, after the business got going. Barry also agreed to pay directly for piano lessons and sports equipment for the children, since he now had additional cash. Because Linda was not working nights and weekends, she was able to let Barry have more flexibility in scheduling time with the children. This was an unexpected plus. She was willing to be more responsive to his needs because he was being more responsive to hers.

Barry and Linda's struggle is typical of positional disputes that lock couples into downward spirals. They happen quickly and are often the result of misinformation and assumptions that are taken as gospel. Using the principles of negotiating around common interests, you can avoid these pitfalls. Go to the level of needs and find out why something is important to the other person. Ask yourself, If I were in my spouse's shoes, why would I take this position or want these things? Go out of your way to understand your ex's concerns even though it goes against your instincts.

STATING THE PROBLEM WELL: THE CRITICAL FIRST STEP

Describe the Problem in Neutral Language without Blame

The way you introduce and describe an issue affects the discussion that follows. If you antagonize your spouse with fault-finding or blame, you are going to have a fight instead of a negotiation. If you haven't clearly described the real issue, you will be negotiating about the wrong thing. *The way you define the issue is a critical first step.*

Here are three guidelines for establishing a clear description of a problem: (1) Know exactly where you stand, what your concern is really about, and what you want before you bring an issue up. Break it down as to when, where, and how this is a problem for you. (2) State the problem as a broad *factual* description of the issue, not a judgment. Your problem definition should be in carefully chosen neutral language that is descriptive without blaming or attributing fault. (3) Don't include a solution in your description of the problem. Including a solution—your solution—limits the flow of other, perhaps more creative, options. It tends to antagonize the other party because your solution is unlikely to serve the other's needs and may result in the feeling that you are telling the other what to do.

Here are examples of typical poorly phrased problems and more effective ways to state them.

Wrong	Right
"We *have to* sell the house because I need my share of the equity to buy a new house."	"How shall we finance a second house?" or "How can we each have affordable adequate housing?"
"You will have to skip the visit this Wednesday because the children have a game after school."	"How shall we handle visits when they conflict with the children's activities?"
"I have to work this weekend; you'll have to keep the kids."	"There is a problem with child care this weekend because I have to work."

Each of the solutions contained in the problem statements on the left represents only one alternative. Stating "we have to sell the house" as the problem when, in fact, it is only one of several possible solutions, inhibits looking at other options. There are many ways of looking at family finances to get the down payment for a second home besides selling the family residence, just as there are many ways to handle a visit when the children have an activity besides canceling the visit. In the examples on the right, the problem is stated in the *broadest and most general terms*. No one is blamed or judged, and no solutions are presented. This leaves the door open for both parties to consider many solutions and be creative.

Using the last example—the husband who has to work on his weekend with the children—let's contrast how the dialogue typically escalates when the solution is included in the statement of a problem:

> Husband: "I'm sorry but you'll have to keep the kids since I have to work this weekend."
>
> Angered by the presumptuousness of his solution, the wife says: "You are going to have to handle it. I am going out of town."
>
> The husband responds by justifying his solution: "I am always accommodating your schedule; you owe it to me."
>
> The wife defends herself: "That's baloney—what about all the times I changed for you so you would get away for the weekend with your friends? You never make a change for me unless I'm absolutely desperate."
>
> The husband escalates: "You only did that once, and what about all the times I've helped you with money?"
>
> The wife counters: "What about all the times child support was late and the time you didn't. . ."

As this couple argued over the *one* unacceptable solution, they got further and further away from the problem at hand. Even though the husband was not antagonistic initially, pressing *his* solution as part of the problem statement hindered open discussion. If he had said something more neutral—like "I have to work this weekend; I don't know what to do about the kids"—he would have left the door open for jointly looking for solutions and might not have antagonized his wife.

Another way to keep the statement of the problem neutral is to use the third person and avoid personal pronouns. For example, "You don't give us enough money for xyz" becomes "*There is* not enough money in the budget for xyz"; "You never return the children's clothes clean" becomes "*There is* a problem with laundering the children's clothes."

Any statement that begins with or contains the expression "you'll have to" is earmarked for failure: "You'll have to pay for the orthodontia because I don't have the money"; "You'll have to change shifts because I can't get child care"; "You'll have to take Susie out of private school because I can't afford it." Again, always express the problem as an open-ended question, as a very general statement, or in a way that avoids the accusatory "you" and the inclusion of your own solution.

- How shall the orthodontia be financed?
- How should child care be handled when we have conflicting work schedules?
- There is a problem with continuing to pay for private school.

The way a problem is defined also affects the types of solutions you will seek.[2] For example, is the problem that a father is irresponsible and doesn't return the children with clean clothes or that there are simply not enough clothes? Will solutions be sought in terms of the father's behavior or buying more clothes? Is the issue selling the house or is selling the house just one possible solution to an as-yet-unclear and larger financial problem? Will solutions be sought in terms of the particular conditions of the sale of the house or will you evaluate all of your financial resources and obligations?

One of the most common examples of this failure to accurately define the problem that I see in my office occurs when children return from time with one parent and they are moody, aggressive, "hyper," or more difficult to handle. One parent typically says to the other: "We have to eliminate weekday visitations because the children can't handle them; they're rowdy and difficult to manage when they get home" or "Joint custody just isn't working, and I want primary custody; the children won't listen to me when they come back from your house."

I have seen couples reach an impasse because the problem has been defined as relating to the custody and visitation schedule. Changing the custody or visitation schedule is just one solution to an as-yet-unclear problem having to do with the children's emotional reactions. The children could be responding to any number of divorce-related stresses: having to say good-bye so often, difficulty making the transition between households, hearing their parents argue over the schedule, or not spending enough time with the noncustodial parent. The way the parent in the example described the problem did not allow room for discovering the true cause behind it, and included a solution that only served to provoke the other parent. As in the previous examples in this chapter, the discussion turns into a who-is-right debate when, in fact, there is a legitimate concern and many reasons for children's uncooperative behavior during the transition from one household to the other. A way to state this issue neutrally is the following: "The children are very difficult to handle when they return from time with you. I would like to discuss this. I don't know what is causing the problem or what to do." A broad factual description of the problem, not who causes it or what to do about it, is the best way to have the kind of informed dialogue that leads to workable solutions for both parties.

REFRAMING: HOW TO USE NEUTRAL LANGUAGE

One of the special skills of mediators is their ability to reframe disputes so that the language is not inflammatory and solutions can be found. Here are examples of how to phrase the major settlement issues in language that is less likely to antagonize your spouse when you bring up these sensitive subjects:

Custody

- How are we going to share/divide the responsibilities and tasks of parenting now that we will be living in two households?
- How will the children be assured that they have the love and involvement of both of us?
- When will the children be with each of us?

Interim Financial Support

- How is the family income going to be allocated to each household to enable both of us to meet our expenses?
- How are we going to finance the separation and take care of our joint responsibilities and debts?
- What amount of money do we each need to meet our monthly expenses?

Spousal Support

- How can the total family income be shared to allow for the transition to more economic independence?
- How should the family income be used to help the unemployed spouse prepare for more self-sufficiency?

Child Support

- How will we share the costs of raising our children?
- What are the expenses relating to the children and how should they equitably be shared?

Property Division

- How can our assets be equitably divided to give us each as much of what we need as is possible?
- How should the marital assets adequately provide for a lifelong homemaker?

You may be thinking that you can't possibly talk like this. It sounds so unnatural. This is true, but the way you introduce a problem either blocks productive discussion or makes it possible to have a successful dialogue. You can either make the other person defensive or encourage open-mindedness. The way you bring up an issue and state the problem is the critical first step. You have to think carefully before you speak. I can't emphasize this enough. Whenever I have to talk to my ex-husband about some touchy issue, I choose my words very carefully and state problems as neutrally as I can, even if I am angry and think he is responsible for the problem. For example, I will say, "Elana leaves her schoolbooks at your house often. How can we deal with this?" What I really want to say is, "I'm tired of doing all the driving when she forgets something important at your house." But stating it that way would only result in an argument about who does the most driving rather than trying to creatively deal with the problem of books that have been left at the other parent's house.

Reframing: An Exercise

It is more difficult than you think to reframe an issue in broad neutral terms without ascribing fault or including a solution, especially in the heat of emotion. Remember the four criteria:

- Be descriptive without attributing fault
- Use the broadest and most general terms
- Use neutral language or the third person
- Don't include a solution with your definition of the problem

Rewrite the statements or complaints below using neutral problem definitions (suggested answers are at the end of the chapter):

1. It is not fair that you have the children so much of the time.

   _____

   _____

2. The children need to stay home on weeknights and get their homework done. _____

   _____

3. I shouldn't have to pay for new appliances and bedroom furniture while you get to keep everything and not put out any money. _____

   _____

Think of several issues between you and your spouse that have come up in the past or that need to be discussed. Write them down as neutral descriptive problem statements that do not ascribe blame or include solutions. Refer to these notes when it is time for a discussion.

1.
2.
3.

The next chapter will take you through the four steps of negotiating to agreement. Before we go on, here is a summary of the fundamentals of win–win negotiating:

Summary of Win–Win Negotiation Principles

1. Attack the problem, not each other.
2. Define the problem in impartial language, without blame.
3. Avoid taking positions.
4. Focus on your real needs and concerns.
5. Recognize your shared and overlapping interests.
6. Make solving the other's problem, your problem too.
7. Look for solutions that meet the needs of both parties.
8. Take the time to evaluate all of the options before deciding on a solution.

Suggested answers to the reframing exercise on 227.

1. I have (or there is) a problem with how time with the children is being shared between households.
2. The children don't seem to be getting their homework completed during the week.
3. How are we going to equitably divide our furniture and finance the costs of setting up a second household?

14

Working Toward a Settlement

Peace is inevitable to those who offer peace.

A COURSE IN MIRACLES

As I state throughout the book, successful conflict resolution is based on recognizing and accepting the interconnectedness of your disputes. Trying to get what you want at the expense of the other only leads to further problems. Addressing the other person's needs and concerns without sacrificing your own self-interests should be the guiding principle. Even though you may disagree with the level of your partner's stated need or its legit-imacy, as in the amount of child or spousal support, you have to be willing to work with the other's concerns.

This chapter is designed to help you negotiate those settle-ment issues you feel that you understand and have the compe-tence to negotiate, whether you are working with your attorneys, a mediator, or on your own. It is not intended to be a comprehen-sive guide to the issues themselves or a guide to your legal rights and entitlement. Go as far as you can on your own. Do not feel discouraged if you are unable to reach agreement on all of the issues. Obviously, the more you can do on your own, the smaller will be your costs in mediation and/or legal fees.

WIN–WIN NEGOTIATING STEPS

Once you have defined the issue neutrally, as described in the previous chapter, you are ready to begin the negotiation process. The fundamentals of win–win negotiating can be broken down into four concrete steps. When a disputed issue is complex, emotionally charged, or at an impasse, it is helpful to go through these steps systematically or to put them in writing. Writing things down helps organize your thoughts and enables you to respond to each other less emotionally. A worksheet is provided for your use at the end of the chapter. The steps in win–win negotiating are:

1. Identify your real needs and concerns.
2. Develop a variety of options and possible solutions.
3. Negotiate the options.
4. Make decisions and implement them.

Step 1. Identify Your Real Needs and Concerns

By identifying the specific needs and interests that are represented in your position, it becomes possible to find solutions that address those interests instead of fighting over opposing positions. Let's go back to the example of Bob and Carol from the previous chapter. They had been married for 16 years and had two school-age children. Bob was a dentist and Carol a homemaker who had helped put Bob through dental school before they had children. When they tried to discuss their disagreements over spousal support, they each took strong positions about what they thought was fair.

Carol's position:

We agreed I would stay home and take care of the kids. Now he expects me to go back to work, full-time. That's baloney after all I've done for him. I'm 40 years old; all I know is being a mother. I gave everything I had to this marriage. I gave and gave and gave. The kids still need me. I don't want a career. I want my life, my friends, my community activities. He is making good money. He owes it to me. I've looked forward to when life would be easier. It's not fair. There is no way I'm working full-time. I want full support until the children graduate from high school.

Bob's position:

I've been a workaholic—with a second business on the side. Working and dental school. I wanted to be a good provider. I wanted to be a success. They've had everything. Now I'm tired, really tired. I ask myself what I missed along the way, what I gave up. What was I trying to prove? The kids are almost gone. The marriage died years ago. I want off the treadmill. I'm not going to break my back so she can stay home and go out to lunch. If she wants this divorce, a new life, and independence, she'll have to work for it, just like I did. I'm cutting back. She can get a job. She has abilities.

Every time they tried to talk about it, they pushed each other into stronger stands, with Carol insisting on her rights to full support and Bob threatening to quit his practice before he'd support her for the rest of his life.

If we were to examine Bob's underlying concerns about the spousal support issue and Carol's underlying needs and concerns, their lists might look like this:

Bob's List of Needs and Concerns

1. Reduce stress and pressure.
2. Work fewer hours.
3. Spend more time with the children.
4. Allow more time for recreation.
5. Reduce demands on my time.
6. Assure money for children's college education.
7. Cut as many ties as possible with Carol.

Carol's List of Needs and Concerns

1. Ensure long-range financial security.
2. Maintain continuity of friends and activities.
3. Have security of keeping the house.

4. Be available to the children.
5. Avoid job pressures until I can get my feet on the ground.
6. Relax and start to have some fun in life.
7. Know that the children's college education is provided for.

It is helpful to prioritize your needs and concerns so that when you begin negotiating you can see the areas in which it will be easiest for you to make concessions. Here is how Bob and Carol prioritized their lists:

Bob's Prioritized List of Needs and Concerns

Reduce stress and pressure.
Spend more time with the children.
Work fewer hours.
Assure money for children's college education.
Reduce demands on my time.
Cut as many ties as possible with Carol.
Allow more time for recreation.

Carol's Prioritized List of Needs and Concerns

Ensure long-range financial security.
Be available to the children.
Have security of keeping the house.
Know that the children's college education is provided for.
Avoid job pressures until I can get my feet on the ground.
Relax and start to have some fun in life.
Maintain continuity of friends and activities.

Look at Common Interests and Concerns

In the midst of a dispute, we are intensely aware of our differences. Common ground seems to fall away. However, when you identify your shared concerns and areas of agreement, your differences narrow and become easier to resolve because your real needs no longer seem so very far apart. Bob and Carol, for example, share the desire to reduce their level of stress and not have financial pressures for the next year. They both want to make sure the children have enough money for college. They both want quality time with the children and greater enjoyment in life. Their differences lie in the ways they see spousal support in relation to the achievement of these goals.

In any kind of negotiation shared goals or concerns are a strong impetus for continuing to negotiate. In divorce, you almost always have a shared interest in avoiding the emotional and financial costs of going to court. If there are children, you share concerns about their well-being and about how the impact of the divorce will affect their lives. You may not agree about what the children need, but you do have certain basic goals for them in common. In a sense, your mutual commitment to protect the children and to avoid a court battle become superordinate goals.

Write down what you see as your common concerns, important mutual goals, and issues on which there is already agreement between the two of you. This will be a reminder to you when you feel like throwing up your hands that, in fact, there are some points on which you agree. Professional mediators always remind the disputants of their common interests as an incentive to continue negotiating when discussions get bogged down. Keep this list handy at all negotiation meetings.

What Are the Fears and Anxieties Represented in a Position?

We take positions that intuitively address our fears and anxieties. Deutsch states that conflicts that are based on fear and anxiety are more difficult to resolve than conflicts based on opposing desires.[1] The more you are able to get the fears and anxieties out in the open and worked on supportively rather than antagonistically, the more likely you will achieve agreements.

Sometimes an unconscious catastrophic fear underlies a position, particularly a rigid, unyielding one. The likelihood of "worst fears" occurring is remote, but because they usually have not been examined rationally in the light of day, they hang in the corner of your consciousness as vague but looming possibilities. If not recognized, they impede the free give-and-take that is so necessary for successful negotiation.

Catastrophic fears usually have to do with abandonment and survival. In divorce they tend to be about such things as: "My ex-spouse will turn on me, move, and take the children, and I will never see them again"; "I will lose my job, become destitute, and be forced to live on the street."

I had a client, an attractive woman with a lovely house and a significant cushion of stocks and bonds, who was terrified that when the spousal support terminated she would become a bag lady. She had never supported herself and as a child had seen her own mother suffer terrible financial hardship when her father abandoned the family. Even though her adult mind recognized that with $100,000 in the bank and a house that was nearly mortgage-free she would not wind up destitute and on the street, the child inside her, who felt helpless when her own father left, still felt helpless and afraid. Instead of attacking her for her excessive demands for spousal support, the husband (with the help of a mediator) was able to review her financial resources step-by-step and plan for the contingencies she feared.

If you sense any catastrophic fears hiding in the back of your mind, here is an exercise that may help you get a handle on them.

CATASTROPHIC FEAR EXERCISE

1. Write down your worst fears about your divorce. Let your mind wander, and don't worry if they don't sound rational.
2. List all of the things that would have to happen in order for any one of these catastrophes to occur. On a scale of 1 to 5 rate how likely it is that any of these things would occur.
3. Describe what you would do if *any* of these fears did materialize (i.e., have a game plan just in case).
4. Last, write down your realistic fears and anxieties about the divorce. Then list what you think your spouse's fears and anxieties are.

Step 2. Develop a Variety of Options and Possible Solutions

After having a clear sense of your needs and concerns, you can begin to look for different ways of addressing them. The process of searching for solutions consists of four steps: (1) brainstorming a variety of options before deciding; (2) creating solutions for mutual gain; (3) evaluating the options; and (4) making proposals.

Begin by brainstorming. Brainstorm some ideas for meeting the needs on your list as well as your spouse's list. When you brainstorm you write down any and all ideas, no matter how unfeasible they may sound. You don't edit your ideas, and only later on do you evaluate them. Here are the ideas Bob and Carol came up with for themselves and each other:

Bob's Brainstorm List of Options for Himself

Sell or dissolve denture business.
Reduce my living expenses to decrease pressure for income.
Get out of town more often for leisure.
Have blocks of time when each is fully involved as parent and blocks of time "off duty."
Create a college fund to which we both contribute in proportion to income.
Keep dental practice and use equity to finance loans for college.
Take a sabbatical.
Sell dental practice, teach, travel, and give Carol a lump sum.

Bob's Brainstorm List of Options for Carol

Keep family house and all equity as future security.
Refinance house to reduce payments and expenses to be able to work part-time.
Take in a roommate to reduce expenses.
Have one year full spousal support with no job pressure.
Reduce spousal support second and third years in proportion to Carol's income.

See if any of the community and volunteer activities could lead
    to a job; put the word out that she is looking for a job.
Go back to graduate school.
Transfer all IRAs and half my pension to Carol.
Have all medical and dental expenses for the kids come directly
    to me.
Keep Carol as beneficiary of my life insurance as long as the
    children are minors or in college.

Carol's Brainstorm List of Options for Herself

Ask for full spousal support for 5 years, then half that amount
    until the kids graduate from high school.
Keep the house and pay Bob's share of the equity after the kids
    graduate from college.
Have Bob pay for special recreational expenses and medical bills
    for the children.
Get cash settlement from the dental practice for my retirement.
Go back to graduate school next year for master's degree in
    teaching, then work part-time.
Get away from it all: lease the house, look for a job teaching
    English as a second language in Japan, and take the children
    to Japan for a year.

Carol's Brainstorm List of Options for Bob

Work a half day on Friday before his weekend with the children.
Become a soccer coach to have more regular involvement with the
    children.
Take the children to dinner one at a time each week.
Allocate two nights a week when the children stay over.
Hire a better administrator at clinic so he doesn't have to do
    so much himself.
Let his accountant do more.
Have a partner buy into his practice and use the cash to buy
    me out.
See a therapist for depression.

Evaluate the Options

Study each other's lists of options. Your spouse may have come up with an idea for you that is worth considering. After reviewing what each of you has written, check off the most promising ideas and begin to discuss their feasibility. Are there ways that any of the ideas could be improved or modified to be more acceptable or workable? After you have reduced the list to the best possibilities, see if there is additional information or data that is needed, like the current value of stocks, bonds, or house equity, the cost or penalty of transferring or liquidating an asset, the cost of purchasing separate health insurance, the cost of day care, and so on. If you are negotiating financial issues, have current information available and agree on specific values before making final agreements.

Compare the earlier lists of your prioritized needs and concerns with the lists of options. You can determine your "give" on an issue by thinking about how strongly you feel about it. Try to see what matters most to you and what you would be willing to trade off for something you want more. Photocopy all of these lists so you can review them on your own and develop proposals for the next meeting.

Developing Proposals

Looking at both the needs and the options lists, begin to formulate a comprehensive proposal that seems workable. You can do this apart, together, or in consultation with a mediator or your attorney. Make sure that the proposals you advance also address the needs and concerns of your spouse. If they are too one-sided, they will be automatically rejected as unfair and could undermine any feeling of goodwill. If you develop proposals separately, write down two to three proposals that you can live with so that when you begin to negotiate you have a wider range of acceptable solutions.

Let's say that Bob and Carol have considered the most feasible ideas in light of their individual needs and goals and have come up with proposals. Bob's basic concerns were reducing stress, having more time to enjoy life, and spending time with the children. Carol's were having the security of keeping the house and avoiding the pressure to reenter the job market for a while.

Bob's proposal was that he sell his denture business for about $30,000 and give Carol the entire amount in cash in lieu of one year of spousal support. That would be an extra $15,000, the equivalent of a year's spousal support at $1,250 per month. He would also give her the $10,000 cash in the bank. After the first year, he would pay $600 per month spousal support for 4 more years. He would pay child support according to the formula used by the court. Carol would have the house and would pay him 40% of the $125,000 equity if she remarried, sold the house, or when the children graduated from college, whichever occurred first. Bob would keep the dental practice, valued between $40,000 and $50,000, but he would pay for college expenses by borrowing against it. They would divide all stocks and retirement accounts, with Carol receiving 60 percent.

Carol's proposal was for Bob to keep all the equity in the denture business and 70% of the retirement funds in exchange for her receiving all of the equity in the house. In consideration of the 10 years she had been out of the work force, she felt she needed $900 per month spousal support for 2 years, $700 per month for 2 years after that, and $600 per month for the next 4 years. She was willing to let Bob keep any value in the dental practice if he paid for all educational expenses for the children and provided her with long-term support. Their other investment accounts would be divided fifty-fifty. Child support would be calculated according to the state guidelines.

Bob and Carol's proposals were not that far apart from each other. Carol had made the decision that she was willing to work part-time and not ask for full spousal support in exchange for all the equity in the house and longer-term support. Bob felt that by liquidating the second business and giving Carol all the cash and more than 50 percent of the house equity and investment accounts, he would have less financial pressure. Through further negotiation, bargaining, and compromises, they were able to modify the details of their proposals until they came up with one that was acceptable to both.

Step 3. Negotiate the Options

After you have developed proposals, it is time for the actual bargaining and negotiating to begin. This is when you try to create compromises, trade-offs, or develop new options in order to reach final agreement. It is the rare couple who can do this all on their own, so don't be discouraged if you need the help of a neutral third party mediator or if you prefer your attorneys to do the final negotiations. Remember, negotiating means a give-and-take to get what you need. You must be prepared to accept that you will *not* get everything you want. Some people come into mediation thinking that it is just a nice way to get what they want. This is a mistake. You have to enter negotiation with a willingness to give as well as take.

Bargaining Strategies

Here are some useful bargaining strategies based on the principles in the book *Getting to Yes* by Fisher and Ury:[2]

1. When you both want the same thing, try to come up with additional ideas rather than try to convince your partner of why you should get what you want. I had clients who were locked in a battle about who deserved the antique oak dining set. They argued over who found it, who did more of the refinishing, who repaired it, and so on. This approach got them nowhere. What worked better was when the husband decided to offer the wife other household items she really wanted but that were also disputed and also offered to repair her car. In negotiation language this is called "sweetening the pie."

2. Another variation on "sweetening the pie" is to look for ways to offer something your spouse would want that is of little importance or cost to you. A mother, for example, can offer the

father extra time with the children after he has been out of town. A husband can offer as part of the settlement to provide the labor to build a fence, paint a room, or repair a roof so that the wife doesn't have to pay to have it done. A wife with lower income can offer the husband the children's tax dependency exemptions. These "extras" tend to make your offer look more attractive or at least make your spouse more open to considering it because you are acting in the spirit of generosity. It is not dissimilar to the salesman who says if you buy this washer and dryer, he will throw in a free toaster oven and white bread for life.

3. Another technique is to broaden the choices, rather than just compromise down the middle. See if you can find some *new* solutions that are advantageous to both. Let's take the case of a couple who are $200 per month apart on their agreement on child support. The mother's concerns are that extra expenses always arise and her budget is tight; she worries about how she will pay for unexpected things. The father wants to be sure that the money is spent on the children. He feels like he is paying all this money but doesn't have much involvement in or influence over their lives. One option for the sake of agreement is to simply split the difference and increase support $100 per month. There is nothing wrong with doing this. However, you could also look for additional ways to satisfy each person's concerns. The father could assume direct expenses like giving the children their allowance, purchasing clothing for school in the fall, or arranging and paying for the extracurricular activities. This relieves the mother of the worry that the children will be denied something because she doesn't have enough money. It also gives the father the opportunity to be more involved in his children's lives and assures him that his money is going directly to the children.

4. Try to think of creative ways to meet the other person's needs. You can actually advance your case if you take care of your spouse's interests. In the Bob-and-Carol example, Carol offered a variety of proposals that addressed Bob's concern about reducing his immediate work and stress level. She offered to take reduced spousal support and was willing to go to work part-time, which

she saw as a major concession. In exchange, she was able to negotiate for longer-term financial security, which she felt was more important than what she had given up.

5. Sometimes an impasse can be resolved if you examine more specifically what each party wants. This may reveal that what is actually most important to each about a disputed issue does not conflict. Let's say a couple has a disagreement about whose turn it is to have the children for Christmas. They both have plans with their respective families, who will be visiting from out of town. They begin arguing about whose turn it is when, upon closer examination, they discover that the times they each want the children *the most* do not conflict. One family is having the big dinner Christmas Eve, and the other Christmas afternoon. The children's participation at these times is the overriding issue for each. It is like the common example of two people fighting over an orange until they discover that one person only wants the peel for baking and the other only needs the juice. When you have a dispute, try to break it down to discover what aspects are most important to each; then create compromises. In negotiation language this is called "dovetailing interests." It takes an issue out of the "fixed-sum" dispute of having to divide a set number of days a month or a fixed number of dollars.

6. Sometimes a test of whether a particular solution is fair is to ask whether each party would be willing to take either half. Even as a hypothetical exercise, this question can give a new perspective on what you each have.

7. If you can't reach final agreement, there are a variety of ways to consider partial or provisional agreements:

- You can agree to try it one person's way for a given period of time, then the other's. This is often a good solution when there is an impasse over the schedule of sharing time with the children.
- You can agree in principle, if not in procedure. You can agree that you want the children to stay in the family residence but not agree on the financial arrangements.

- If you can't agree on substance, you can agree on what the next step should be, for example, getting more information on consulting an outside adviser like an accountant, financial adviser, child psychologist, or mediator.
- You can make the conditional agreement based on whether other provisions are satisfied or not. For example, if the schedule is kept and agreements are not broken, then time with the children in the nonresidential home can be increased.

8. Don't go into negotiations with a rigid bottom line. For instance, suppose a husband, after talking to his attorney and friends, has a bottom of line of no more than $500 per month spousal support for 2 years. The wife, who has similar sources of advice, has a bottom line of $700 per month for 5 years. Holding to a rigid bottom line can create a premature stalemate. Sometimes the information on which a bottom line is based is not accurate or complete. You need to be open to information that becomes available during negotiations.

9. Evaluate proposals against what Ury and Fisher describe in *Getting to Yes* as your "Best Alternative to Negotiated Agreement" or BATNA, that is, the alternatives available to you if you are unable to reach agreement. What are your choices if, for example, you are not able to keep the family home, the family business, or get tuition for school? Do you have other options and do they appeal to you? The better your alternatives, the greater your negotiating power. You don't have to settle for bad terms just to keep the business or the house.

Step 4. Make Decisions and Implement Them

Write down all of your agreements and decisions. Be specific about how the plan will work. Specify who will be responsible for what, when the plan is to begin, whether it is long-term or short-term, and, if appropriate, what the contingencies are.

Give yourself time to think about your decisions. Be sure that you were not pressured. Don't say yes when you have serious reservations and suspect that you will change your mind. If you are uncomfortable with a decision, it is better to reserve approval and think about it or make a provisional agreement to be reviewed within a specific time period than to adopt a course of action and change your mind later.

The financial settlement in divorce can be extremely complex. Tax considerations affect final settlement figures. Assets like real estate, professional practices, and businesses require appraisals, and the appraisals themselves may be disputed. Defining "community property" is often a disputed issue in community property states. The evaluation of retirement plans, often the most significant asset next to the family home, has evolved into a specialized area of professional expertise. In my experience it is difficult for couples to negotiate all these complicated issues without professional assistance, especially when significant assets are involved. As I stated earlier, my purpose is to help you to negotiate the issues that you feel you understand and to provide you with the fundamentals of a win–win negotiation process so that you can work more effectively with your attorney or mediator. Use the experts you need, and work with your spouse where you can. Chapter 16 will give you an overview of the legal issues in a divorce and show you how to work with an attorney to minimize the risks of escalation.

What follows is a summary of the win–win negotiating steps and a worksheet to guide you through a negotiation session. While working on the settlement terms of your divorce, whether financial or parental, follow the steps in the outline. These steps can be streamlined when negotiating practical matters and arrangements whereas following the entire sequence will be useful when you find yourselves locked in a dispute over more substantive issues.

SUMMARY OF WIN–WIN NEGOTIATION STEPS

I. Identify the issues clearly:
   A. Clarify your concerns, needs, and goals before bringing up an issue.
   B. List what you anticipate to be the major areas of disagreement, including any red-flag issues that you know will inflame your partner.
   C. State the problem neutrally without blame and without including a solution.

II. What are the needs, concerns, or fears represented in the dispute or position taken?
   A. List your needs, concerns, and/or fears.
   B. List your spouse's needs, concerns, and/or fears.
   C. List your common interests, common goals, and areas of agreement.
   D. Prioritize your needs or goals.

III. Information gathering and data collection:
   A. Get accurate values, appraisals, and information on issues under discussion.
   B. When you disagree, use an outside expert (e.g., accountant, appraiser, psychologist).

IV. Search for solutions:
   A. Brainstorm possible solutions; create a variety of ideas before making any decisions.
   B. Consider all ideas openly and don't prejudge; check off the most promising options.
   C. Develop proposals that address the concerns of *both* parties.

V. Bargaining and negotiating:
   A. Find compromises, make trade-offs, come up with ways to "sweeten the pie," and work to find ways to come to an agreement.

VI. Reaching agreement:
   A. Give yourself time to think about the agreement.
   B. Put decisions or agreements in writing, with specifics of implementation (i.e., how, when, who will do what).

NEGOTIATION SESSION WORKSHEET

1. Describe the problem in neutral language:

2. List your (prioritized) needs and concerns:

3. List your spouse's (prioritized) needs and concerns:

4. What are your common goals and areas of agreement?

5. What are each person's major anxieties or fears?

6. Brainstorm all possible options (check off the most promising):
   a.

   b.

   c.

7. List several proposals:
   a.

   b.

   c.

8. Final decisions:

9. Plan for implementation (how, when, who will be responsible for what; be specific):

15

Mediation

He catches the best fish who angles with a golden hook.

LATIN PROVERB

Many couples have difficulty negotiating a divorce settlement on their own because they get defensive and start to argue the moment they disagree. Open communication breaks down and deteriorates into accusations and counteraccusations. The couple get sidetracked into arguing over whose fault it is, often losing sight of the problem at hand. Mediators are a bit like traffic cops: they direct the flow of dialogue to control angry outbursts, interruptions, accusations, and inflammatory remarks. By enforcing ground rules and bringing structure to the discussions, by paraphrasing contentious remarks, and by permitting one person to speak at a time, the mediator steers parties on a positive course. The mediator's ability to successfully control destructive and hurtful communication is crucial. Disputants are more willing to listen to each other when they are not under attack. When they listen to each other, understanding is increased; with more understanding comes less blaming; with less blaming comes more of a willingness to be fair; and with a willingness to be fair comes the possibility of rational and creative solutions. The mediator helps people talk to each other without letting all of the emotional baggage get in the way.

WHAT TO EXPECT FROM THE MEDIATION PROCESS

One way to look at the mediation process is in terms of stages. The first meeting is an orientation session, where the mediation process is explained, problems are aired, and the disputed issues are clearly defined. Each side hears the other one out. The mediator controls the dialogue by helping parties express their concerns in more neutral language. When both parties can speak their mind and air their grievances and anxieties in a constructive manner, the level of anger diminishes and it becomes possible to focus on the problem at hand like rational adults. The communication that the mediator facilitates in the initial session often diffuses a lot of existing tension and hostility.

Next, the parties must agree on how they are going to establish the value of their assets and properties. The mediator will ask each of you to prepare full financial statements. Full disclosure of all assets is required; otherwise, the settlement can be set aside by the court. A mutually agreed data base is necessary before real negotiation can begin. You must not only agree on the value of the assets of the marriage, but where value must be determined independently—as in the case of a business, a professional corporation, a pension, or the family residence—you must agree on how that value will be determined. Mediation generally has more flexibility in this regard than the traditional adversarial approach because parties can agree to use one appraiser, can agree to set the value themselves, or can decide to use approximate values, trading off high and low value on different properties. You will also need to prepare budget and income information for computing and negotiating child and/or spousal support. Many states have child support schedules, which are mathematical calculations based on income ratios.

Once the assets are inventoried and valued, the process of negotiating and developing concrete proposals takes place. Mediators usually ask the parties to identify their goals and priorities, as described in chapter 14, so that the proposals they eventually develop address their real needs and concerns. Wherever you disagree, the mediator will help you come up with creative options, find acceptable compromises, and steer you away from hopeless impasses. Creative settlements can be developed based on what is most important to each person. You can trade "intangibles" for dollar value, for example, rental houses with growth potential but a headache to manage, for CDs that are perhaps valued at a lesser amount but represent a secure income. Other trade-offs might include a wife receiving all of the equity in the family residence in exchange for reduced spousal support, or a husband being able to keep a much loved but expensive boat because his wife is willing to accept reduced support payments but over a longer period of time, thus enabling the husband to afford moorage payments. By focusing on what is most important to you and negotiating directly with your spouse, you can spend your energy looking for creative solutions rather than playing games to force the other person into giving you what you want.

In addition to the financial issues, a mediator will help you formulate a parenting plan, as discussed in chapter 7, and help you establish the ground rules for a working relationship as divorced parents.

When agreements are reached covering whatever issues you have chosen to mediate, the mediator will draft a written memorandum outlining your agreements. This agreement is reviewed by your respective attorneys and then brought back to mediation for final negotiations, if necessary. One of the attorneys then incorporates the mediated agreement into the final decree to be filed with the court. In many states it is not necessary to appear before a judge when a divorce decree is entered by a stipulated agreement.

Sometimes couples terminate mediation before resolving all of the issues. There may be one issue that simply has to be resolved by the parties' attorneys, although sometimes parties who not were able to "give" on a certain issue at the time of mediation are later willing to compromise in order to conclude the divorce. Sometimes the financial issues turn out to be so complex that one party, often the wife, is overwhelmed and feels incapable of continuing to negotiate on her own. Sometimes it becomes apparent that a spouse is not being honest, is not operating in good faith, or is simply not ready to deal with the issues in a reasonable manner.

It should not be considered a failure if all of the issues are not resolved in mediation. Generally, couples receive some benefit from the experience. Anger is frequently reduced, and the face-to-face dialogue usually increases the parties' understanding of the issues and each other's positions, setting the tone for a less adversarial settlement of those issues that are left unresolved in mediation.

HOW TO WORK WITH AN ATTORNEY WHILE IN MEDIATION

The role of an attorney varies considerably when you use the services of a mediator. Some couples retain attorneys before entering mediation and consult with their respective attorneys throughout the mediation process. Others don't meet with an attorney until it is time for the agreement to be reviewed at the conclusion of mediation. There is no right or wrong way to work with an attorney. It depends on your situation, what role you want an attorney to have, and what your attorney advises.

With respect to the mediation process, your attorney may be concerned about whether you can effectively represent your own interests in negotiating with your spouse, whether there will really be a full disclosure of all assets, whether there is a danger of establishing precedents that may ultimately go against your interests in the event of litigation, and whether you will be protected from signing an ill-advised agreement. Christine Leick, an attorney in Minnesota who frequently works with clients in mediation, described in an article in *Mediation Quarterly* (1989)[1] what she sees as the purpose of attorney consultation *before* mediation begins:

- To review the parties' financial situation and to determine whether the client has an adequate grasp of it

- To review with the client all the issues that will need to be addressed in mediation and to describe the range of potential outcomes and how the law applies to the client's particular situation
- To provide a written summary of these issues for the client to use in mediation
- To emphasize what the attorney thinks would be a fair and equitable settlement, in order to set the stage for mediation
- To obtain a list of important documents that might need to be reviewed and to advise the client of the right to formal discovery (whereby the other party is required under oath to provide documentation regarding income and assets)
- To help evaluate the appropriateness of mediation and the power differential that may exist between the spouses
- To determine whether legal orders, such as freezing assets or accounts, needs to supplement mediation
- To avoid finding serious flaws in the agreement after the parties have completed negotiations and thus "upset the applecart."

Many couples feel comfortable enough with each other and knowledgeable enough about their situation that they simply don't feel they need an attorney's assistance during mediation. Other couples have complex assets and properties, making independent legal counsel advisable.

ADVANTAGES OF MEDIATION

While it is not a panacea and is still hard work, mediation does have many advantages over traditional adversarial approaches. Parties are more likely to live up to the terms of an agreement they have fashioned from hard work and good faith than a settlement imposed by a court. Mediation tends to build cooperation and open up the lines of communication, and the participants are able to create individually tailored agreements that meet the unique needs of their own family. In mediation, parties are able to consider mutually agreed standards of fairness as well as the legal ones. This has been referred to as "private ordering." Mediation is less costly in time, money, and emotional turmoil, and the parties have more direct control over decisions. Mediation is available and accessible on short notice. You can avoid the long and costly delays in getting court dates. Perhaps most importantly, the mediation process avoids the winner/loser syndrome—which doesn't really end hostilities because the loser often waits until conditions are more favorable to redress his or her losses.

While the research on mediation has not been extensive, there are some interesting findings: almost 80 percent of the people who used mediation recommend it, whether or not they themselves reached a full agreement.[2] Couples who mediate are more satisfied with the process and spend almost half as much money as those who use the traditional adversarial process; and mediation seems to significantly lower the levels of conflict during and immediately after divorce.[3] Ultimately, what concerns most people is whether or not they will get as good a settlement through mediation as through the traditional adversarial process. The two major studies comparing mediated and traditional adversarial divorce found no significant difference between them in either spousal support or overall economic settlement.[3] The major difference between couples who chose mediation and those who worked traditionally with their lawyers was that the couples in mediation believed that their spouses were basically honest and fair-minded. Both groups had similar levels of anger, conflict, and communication problems. After divorce, couples who mediated were twice as likely to try to talk and work out disagreements as those who used the adversarial process.[5]

WHEN YOU SHOULDN'T MEDIATE

There are no hard-and-fast rules about whether or not you should mediate. However, there may be obstacles to and cautions against it when certain conditions exist, for example, when one party strongly resists the divorce, when one party clearly dominates the other, when one person is not capable of rationally approaching the issues, when one party is unwilling to be fair-minded, or when there is evidence of bad faith negotiating behavior or a history of family violence. These factors do not always mean that you can't successfully mediate some or all of the issues. But it does mean that mediation may take longer or that certain protective measures or safeguards must be built into the mediation process. Before you decide that it is impossible for you to mediate, remember that any protection you can obtain from the formal legal process can be applied and built into mediation too. For instance, if you don't trust your spouse in terms of financial disclosures, formal depositions can still be taken while in mediation.

One of the most controversial issues in the mediation field is whether mediation is appropriate where there has been family violence. Some argue that mediation jeopardizes abused women and their children and that violence and threats of violence must be treated as criminal acts. Other mediators believe that with proper screening, assessment, protective orders, and ground rules, mediation can be effective without jeopardizing the safety or negotiating power of the abused spouse.[6] Consult with the appropriate professionals to help you make this determination if you are in this kind of situation.

HOW TO FIND A MEDIATOR

As of this writing, there is almost no regulation or credentialing of mediators. Most mediators are either attorneys or mental health professionals with specialized training in mediation. The best way to find a mediator is to ask a friend or your attorney to recommend one or to call your State Mediation Council. Most counties have Family Court Services or similar agencies that provide mediation of custody and visitation matters. The Academy of Family Mediators, a national organization of professional mediators based in Eugene, Oregon, has a referral list of mediators in your area who meet minimum standards of training. The International Association of Family Conciliation Courts in Madison, Wisconsin, has a national list of court-connected mediation services.

Mediators in private practice tend to mediate both financial and parenting issues whereas court-connected services primarily mediate parenting issues. Most of the court-connected services are free or have sliding-scale fees. Some mediation services in the private sector offer a team approach, usually an attorney and mental health professional. While the fees may be higher than for a single mediator, the team model can be the most effective if your estate is large and complex or if there are high levels of conflict. Whether you choose a mediator with a legal education or with a mental health background depends on what you feel your situation requires. Again, if your assets are complex, you may be more comfortable with a mediator with a legal education. If your primary concern is parenting issues, you may be more comfortable with a mediator with a mental health background. Because there is no certification of mediators, be sure to ask any mediator, whether an attorney or a mental health professional, how much experience he or she has had mediating divorce cases and what his or her education and training has been.

Many people are not sure if they are doing the right thing by using mediation. It all seems so overwhelming. It feels as if it would be so much easier to let a lawyer handle it. Mediation is hard work. It is difficult to treat the division of dreams as a business deal. It is difficult to talk calmly and rationally about things that continually remind you of what might have been.

While mediation is not a panacea, for those who measure the success of a divorce settlement on a human as well as economic scale and who want to dignify the severing of a profound bond, mediation offers a most welcome alternative to the traditional adversarial process.

16

Lawyers and the Legal Process

What to Expect and How to Reduce the Escalation of Conflict

> It is not what a lawyer tells me I *may* do; but what humanity, reason, and justice tell me I ought to do.
>
> EDMUND BURKE

Throughout the book, I have spoken of divorce as a period of transition for the family. When there are children, you and your former spouse still have legal, economic, and emotional ties to each other. In the book *Divorcing Families* Connie Ahrons states that you uncouple, you don't "unfamily." Many separated couples work hard to create a decent relationship with the other parent. Yet we are all aware of how stresses can intensify and conflicts can escalate when you begin to deal with legal matters. Once a personal matter becomes "legalized," the description of the issues is often translated—literally—into a foreign language. The divorce process is lost in the thicket of "pleadings," "interrogatories," and "depositions." When decisions need to be funneled through the bureaucracies of attorneys' offices, the completeness and accuracy of the communications from client to lawyer and lawyer to lawyer and spouse to spouse may become the first casualties.

This chapter presents an overview of the legal issues in divorce and suggests ways of dealing with attorneys that can reduce the adversarial atmosphere and prevent the breakdown of communication. It has been written in collaboration with family law attorneys and shows you how to work with an attorney as constructively as possible and understand the options you have at various points in the legal process.[1]

INTERVIEWING AND CHOOSING A LAWYER

Choosing attorneys is one of the most important decisions you and your spouse will make. The attorneys' styles will have a direct bearing on the whole divorce process, not just the settlement you get. In fact, a colleague of mine who is an attorney says that what makes the most difference in whether his cases are settled reasonably is who the attorney is on the other side. Interestingly, in a study of New Jersey attorneys, 41 percent cited the inappropriate behavior of opposing counsel as the most significant problem with the legal system in divorce.[2] While you don't have control over the attorney your spouse retains, you can make a careful selection in your own situation.

In choosing an attorney, think about the expertise you feel your situation requires and what you see as your personal needs for guidance or counsel. Attorneys fall all along the continuum from aggressive advocates to "counselors."[3] The more "psychologically aware" and family-minded attorneys see their role as one which incudes such nonlegal elements of divorce as helping women who have been homemakers develop a plan for reentering the job market or helping men who have not actively cared for their children develop a plan to become a more involved parent. They are concerned about your future as well as the welfare of your children, and are oriented toward achieving a negotiated settlement and working cooperatively with the other side. The aggressive advocates, on the other hand, tend to emphasize the mechanistic legal aspects of representation and "winning." Often they want to take control and "go for the max." Don't assume that just because you have a tough-sounding lawyer you are better protected. Remember, after the divorce the lawyer will not have to live with the settlement—you will.

Choosing a Lawyer

First and foremost, your comfort level with the attorney is of vital importance. Don't be afraid to interview more than one lawyer. Assess how well they explain issues and whether they strive to make you part of the process. Remember, attorneys work for you, not you for them. Find out where the attorney stands on controversial issues that are important to you, such as joint custody or mediation. Some attorneys support joint custody while others are very wary of it. Some attorneys support mediation and alternate dispute resolution procedures, and others don't. Ask the attorneys you are interviewing how they feel about these issues. You may be able to work with an attorney regardless of his or her views, but you should know these things before you actually retain the attorney.

Another consideration in choosing an attorney is whether you want an attorney who keeps you informed, explains legal procedures, and presents you with options about how to proceed. Or do you prefer the "I'll-handle-everything" approach? While you may just want to get it all over with because you don't have the energy or emotional reserves to pay attention to every step of the process, by not participating you risk losing control over important decisions that may affect you the rest of your life. And the divorce will cost a lot more because you are having the attorney handle everything. Furthermore, the attorney may do something, unintentionally or as a routine procedure, that unnecessarily inflames your spouse and increases the level of hostility between the two of you.

If you are looking for a mutually fair outcome rather than getting as much as you possibly can from the settlement, then choosing an attorney who will help you develop realistic expectations and a perspective on what is fair will pave the way for more reasonable negotiations with your spouse. When attorneys give you realistic information about what you can expect and it does not conform to your expectations, try not to confuse their advice with a lack of support for your welfare. Often what you think you deserve does not correspond to your legal rights. Better attorneys will help you set realistic goals. If you still strongly question the attorney's advice, get a second opinion.

While you may want an attorney who is wiling to act in a strong advocacy role for you, especially if the other side appears arbitrary and uncooperative, watch out for the "barracuda" types. Some attorneys "fan the flames" or overidentify with your situation because of their own divorce experience. Others want to present an inflated proposal as an opening bargaining strategy. But remember, the other side will usually respond with an equally excessive position. Be aware that choosing the most aggressive attorney encourages your spouse to make a similar choice. Interestingly, one study reports that cooperation-oriented attorneys are rated twice as effective by their peers as competition-oriented attorneys.[4]

Ideally, you want an attorney who is not only concerned with advancing your interests but who also considers the impact of decisions on your children and the whole family system. He or she should help you focus on how you will fare after the divorce, what you will need to rebuild your life, and what is best for your children. Your attorney should encourage the use of mediation or face-to-face negotiations with your spouse wherever feasible and should be sensitive to keeping the hostility and costs down.

In some complex cases you may need an attorney with special expertise. Most attorneys who specialize in divorce can give you general guidance in business matters. However, do not expect most attorneys to have special expertise in complex areas such as tax law or highly technical business transactions. Your attorney is not a substitute for an accountant or financial planner.

Look for an experienced attorney with a specialization in family law, rather than one who occasionally handles divorces.

You will be better advised by someone who deals regularly with divorce matters and the courts. Be sure you and your attorney are in philosophical agreement about your goals and priorities and how you want the case to be handled. If your attorney meets your basic criteria, trust your personal reaction to determine if you feel comfortable with him or her. You need to feel that your lawyer understands your needs and is accessible, and that the two of you can communicate.

Interviewing a Lawyer

When interviewing attorneys, you want to be sure that they are being candid about their approach and feel comfortable referring you to someone else if they do not meet your requirements. Here is a list of questions that will help you in making your final decision. You can ask some of these questions on the phone in order to narrow down your list.

1. What percentage of the attorney's practice is divorce? How long has he or she been in practice?
2. Does the attorney have trial experience and the capability of going to court if the case cannot be settled?
3. What is the attorney's philosophy in working with divorce cases?
4. What is the basis on which the attorney charges for services? What are the anticipated costs for your case?
5. Does the attorney have any suggestions for reducing the adversarial nature of the legal proceedings?
6. How does the attorney feel about shared parenting and joint custody? What are his or her personal or professional biases?
7. How does the attorney feel about mediation or other methods of dispute resolution?
8. How does the attorney feel about you directly negotiating with your spouse?
9. What is the office policy for returning phone calls and handling emergencies?

Legal Fees and Retainer Agreement

One of the biggest sources of friction between lawyers and clients is attorney's fees. Divorces often end up costing far more than either party intended, especially if they are complex and full of conflict and animosity. Seldom are clients satisfied enough with the result that they willingly agree to pay the fees charged. If you are not careful, the money for your children's college education can be spent on lawyers' fees. Discuss fees openly and early in your interview with an attorney. Better attorneys generally have a written retainer agreement that describes what services the attorney will provide, the billing arrangements, and the initial retainer. If they do not have a written agreement, find out why, and if they won't prepare one, be cautious. Don't be lulled into assuming that your spouse will necessarily pay all of the attorney's fees and that you need not be concerned. There are few cases where one party is ordered to pay for both attorneys, especially when both parties are employed. Even if the court were to make such an order, it is likely to be taken into account in the overall settlement, which may mean that you will get less of the marital assets. Here is a list of questions you should have in mind about legal fees as you interview attorneys:

1. What is the attorney's hourly rate for services? Is that rate high, low, or average for your geographical area?
2. Does the attorney bill for telephone calls? Most do (all attorneys have to sell is their time).
3. What is the initial retainer? Is it nonrefundable and are hours spent counted against the retainer, or will you be billed for each hour of the attorney's time spent on your behalf in addition to the initial retainer?
4. How does the attorney keep track of the time spent on your case? Can you see the time records? Will you be sent an itemized bill?
5. Can you discuss money straightforwardly with the attorney or does that threaten him or her?

6. How can you participate in preparing your case so as to keep attorney's fees to a minimum?

Remember, attorneys deserve to be paid for their time and effort on your behalf and there may be time spent on your case out of your view. However, you deserve to know and need to keep an eye on the attorney's fees as they accumulate. Too often, you can get $5,000 more in the divorce settlement—but discover that you have spent $7,500 to do so. Finally, don't be penny-wise and pound-foolish: if you fail to contact your attorney on an important matter in order to save money, you may end up paying more in the long run.

THE LEGAL ISSUES

The basic legal issues to be resolved in a dissolution of marriage can be grouped as follows: (1) parenting responsibilities, including time with the children, decision making, and legal custody; (2) financial responsibilities, including child support and maintenance or alimony; and (3) property division.

Parenting Responsibilities

This is the area most lawyers refer to as "custody and visitation." The phrase *parenting responsibilities* suggests that both parents will continue to be involved and take part in their children's lives. While custody needs to be decided in the end, the more important issue will be how the children can spend time with each parent and how both parents can be involved in making decisions about the children.

Custody

In most states the decree of dissolution requires that you specify whether custody of the children will be joint or sole and, in either case, which parent is to have physical custody of the children at which times. Some jurisdictions recognize a distinction between joint physical and joint legal custody. As stated earlier, joint physical custody implies a shared parenting arrangement in which each parent has physical custody of the children for a substantial period of time. Joint legal custody means that both parents will continue to be responsible for making the major decisions about a child, regardless of residential arrangements. Such decisions include religious and cultural upbringing, schooling, elective medical procedures, and marriage before the age of consent. A decree should also include provisions regarding when a custodial parent can move out of state or out of the area in which the child is currently residing. Some states have laws that do not allow a parent to permanently move out of the state with the children without the court's approval or the other parent's consent.

Visitation

Parenting plans often require considerable detail about when the children will be with the nonresidential parent. While relatively amicable parents need very little detail, embattled couples may demand a detailed agreement covering such issues as frequency of visitation, special events, holiday and vacation schedules; how, when, and where the children may be picked up or dropped off; procedures for notification of changes in schedule; and restraints on third party contacts, detrimental activities, or telephone contacts. If the parties are geographically separated, a decree should also cover responsibility for transportation costs and travel arrangements.

Financial Responsibilities

The divorce decree should provide for how the parties are going to allocate their responsibilities to support their separate households in the future. Specifically, the main concerns are child support and spousal maintenance or alimony. Other issues that need to be addressed as well are insurance, health care costs, college, and special events like weddings and confirmations. The first task will be to decide who should pay whom how much, so that both parties can have adequate income to meet expenses. This does not necessarily mean that the income of both households will be the same, but neither party should feel taken advantage of. The financial responsibility issues are:

1. Child support
2. Spousal maintenance
3. Life insurance to protect child support and/or spousal maintenance and college costs
4. Health and medical insurance and nonreimbursed health care costs
5. College education or vocational training costs and expenses
6. Special events, such as weddings or confirmations
7. Payment of outstanding debts
8. How and when amounts are to be paid
9. How and when financial responsibilities should be reviewed and/or modified
10. What the tax considerations of the plan are, including the child dependency exemption, maintenance or alimony deduction, head-of-household status, and child care credits

Child support and spousal maintenance require special mention. Federal law has required that every state adopt child support guidelines and schedules setting a standard for the determination of amounts to be paid. In every state child support is payable until a child reaches age 18, although many states have provisions for the extension of child support while a child attends college, vocational training, or has special needs or disabilities. This is a specific area you need to check into with your attorney. Some controversy exists over whether or not you and your spouse can agree to amounts of child support that are different from the child support guidelines. The answer varies depending on the state and the view of the court or judge in your community.

Maintenance and *alimony* are both terms used with reference to spousal maintenance, the amount one party could be ordered or might agree to pay the other party for his or her support, separate from child support. Few states have schedules for establishing maintenance, and states and judges vary widely as to whether maintenance is even allowed or how much maintenance will be awarded and for how long.

The determination of the amount and duration of maintenance is one of the most complex aspects of a divorce settlement. Courts will frequently consider numerous factors, including but not limited to: length of marriage; age, physical, and mental health of the parties; contribution by one spouse to the education and training of the other spouse; earning capacity of each party, including educational background, training, employment skills, work experience, and the need for further education; impairment of earning capacity due to a party's absence from the job market; ages of the children and parenting provisions; the tax liabilities to each party; the long-term financial obligations of each party; costs of health care; and the standard of living establishing during the marriage. The advice of an attorney is essential in negotiating and deciding on the appropriate level and duration of spousal support. Very little in this area is clear-cut.

Property Division

Property division generally concerns the division of the assets and property the parties have accumulated up to the time of the divorce. Property division is subject to complex rules, which vary from state to state. The definition of marital and nonmarital property, in particular, is a thorny area of divorce law. Even when discussing this with your respective attorneys, you and your spouse are likely to get different opinions about such things as the distribution of inherited property or assets accumulated prior to the marriage. The divorce decree should address the distribution of all of the property owned by either party, whether acquired during the course of the marriage or not.

Among the most difficult problems in many divorces is the correct valuation of such complex assets as professional practices, corporations, commercial properties, and retirement assets. Many disputes erupt over the determination of value. Even with professional appraisals, judges often have difficulty valuing complex properties at trial. Value will often need to be negotiated. If you have complex or extensive holdings, there will be a number of decisions you will have to make along the way about how much you need to know in order to determine the value of your assets and make an informed decision. Oftentimes this depends on how much money you want to spend and are able to afford on appraisals and on how much information your attorney thinks it is necessary to obtain. Don't be afraid to ask your attorney if more informal processes can be used to establish the value of your assets.

Finally, as you think about the mechanics of the division of assets and how and when one party will pay the other for their interest in marital property, remember that all monies do not necessarily need to be paid on the day of the divorce. This is an area where there is room for negotiation. You can agree that monies will be paid out over time, even years after the divorce. However, if monies are to be paid in the future, you need to consider interest rates and how to protect your share of the asset. For example, payment of one spouse's share of the equity in the family residence is frequently deferred and secured by a lien against the house.

A basic checklist of property assets and issues to be considered includes:

1. Personal property: cars, boats, vehicles, and household items; art and other kinds of collections
2. Bank accounts and certificates of deposit; stocks, bonds, and whole life or universal life insurance policies with cash value

3. Real property: family residence, other real estate
4. Retirement/deferred compensation assets: IRAs, pensions, 401(k) plans, annuities, Keoghs, profit-sharing plans
5. Business interests: ownership or partnership of a business or professional practice
6. Debts (affect both financial responsibility issues and the overall value of property)
7. Tax considerations: capital gains taxes, penalties for withdrawal of retirement assets, etc.

THE LEGAL PROCESS

At various points in the legal process you will be faced with choices in the procedures that could be followed. More formal or aggressive approaches as well as less formal, more conciliatory approaches are almost always available. Your attorney should be able to describe all the options to you so that you can make a choice that is appropriate to your particular situation. The risk in not discussing such matters with your attorney is that your attorney may simply follow the procedure with which he or she is most comfortable. This may have the result of needlessly inflaming the situation. Various options exist particularly with regard to filing a petition for divorce, fact finding, and settling a case. If you are well informed about some of these legal procedures, you may be able to reduce the risks of conflict escalation.

Service of the Petition

Divorce proceedings start with a petition or complaint filed with the court by the person who is initiating the divorce. This is commonly called "filing for divorce." The petition must be "served" on the spouse, providing notice that divorce proceedings have been initiated. The other spouse must have time to file an "answer" or "response" to the petition. Serving the petition can be done formally, that is, by a sheriff or process server, usually at the spouse's place of employment. Spouses who are served with divorce petitions are faced with the embarrassment of having a process server arrive at their place of employment and personally notify them of a lawsuit in front of coworkers. A much less inflammatory method is to ask the spouse to accept service of the petition that has been filed by signing a short document called an "acceptance of service" in front of a notary public. This document is then filed with the court to show that the opposing spouse received notice of the case. This method is private and more courteous than a formal serving of the petition and tends to preserve the opposing spouse's dignity.

Discovery

Discovery is the fact-gathering and investigation stage of a legal case. It includes inventorying and valuing assets and ascertaining income and expenses. Discovery can also be approached in a formal or informal manner. In formal discovery, attorneys may file interrogatories—pages of questions about a party's circumstances, which are answered in writing under oath by that party; take depositions—out-of-court formal questioning of the other party in the presence of a court reporter; or file motions to produce documents like tax returns or canceled checks if requests for documents have met with resistance. Formal discovery can often be very expensive. It may be necessary, however, when the assets are complex and the parties are especially distrustful of each other. Even in less complex cases attorneys, left to their own devices, may encourage formal discovery because they are always concerned about missing something and will tend to cast the broadest possible net unless instructed otherwise. Keep in mind that a spouse can become quite angry at having to produce copious amounts of marginally relevant data.

In contrast, you may prefer to take a more informal approach to discovery and hold off on the formal procedures unless or until you feel that you are not being given necessary information.

Attorneys will frequently just agree that both parties are entitled to all information. Consider with your attorney what information is actually needed in order to make informed decisions for settlement. By tailoring your request for documents and by asking for them in an informal manner, you may be able to obtain all necessary information and preserve goodwill at the same time.

Good common and business sense require that certain information about your financial situation be disclosed, documented, and corroborated. However, this does not have to be an onerous task. At the very minimum, each party should have copies of the following:

1. Personal federal tax returns for the previous 3 to 5 years.
2. Business partnership or corporate tax returns, where applicable.
3. Bank or formal statements of accounts, stocks and bonds, life insurance policies, IRAs, and so on.
4. Employer statements of employee benefits, including pensions and profit-sharing plans.
5. Most courts require completion of financial statements, which include statements of property, income, and expenses.

Almost all financial information is "discoverable," that is, a court will order it to be produced if requested. Little is gained and unnecessary attorneys' fees are incurred by resisting requests for information. The matter of information and documentation needs to be framed as a business issue, not a trust issue. This avoids construing requests for information as harassment. Many attorneys are willing to provide basic information informally if they are offered the same in return.

After the basic and, if necessary, special information (e.g., profit-and-loss statements of a business) has been obtained, an informal meeting of attorneys *and* clients can be helpful, especially in complex asset cases, to discuss and make sure the parties and clients understand the assets. At this time the attorneys and clients can ask each other further questions.

DISPUTE RESOLUTION OPTIONS: WAYS TO SETTLE YOUR CASE

You have various options for settling your divorce case throughout the process. Face-to-face dialogue and negotiation have been emphasized throughout this book, and mediation has been suggested as an effective method to resolve your disputes. However, mediation is not the only alternative. Another way to think about the legal settlement process is in terms of what can be called a "dispute resolution continuum." As you can see from the figure below, on one end of the continuum decisions are made and conflict is resolved at a very informal level; the parties communicate directly with each other, presumably with their attorneys in the background as consultants. On the other end of the continuum decisions are made formally by a judge following a trial. In between, as you move from informal to more formal methods of resolving the issues, the attorneys' role becomes more active. Thus, during the divorce settlement process you and your spouse could negotiate with a mediator; have a settlement conference with the lawyers; have lawyers assisted by a mediator negotiate the settlement with both of you present; have a settlement conference with the judge; or sometimes you can arbitrate part or all of the case. As a general rule, don't use a more formalized mode of conflict management when a less formal process will do. Often, once a conflict has moved into a more formal arena, the divorcing parties and attorneys lose sight of the value of the informal processes which are still available.

Dispute Resolution Continuum

Direct ➤ Mediation➤ Attorney ──➤ Settlement ➤ Arbitration➤ Reference ➤ Trial
talks   Negotiations   Conference   Judge

Mediation

If direct informal discussions are not advisable or have been unsuccessful, you can meet with a mediator who will facilitate discussions and negotiations. Usually, attorneys remain in the background, and settlement options are reviewed with them outside of the mediation sessions. In some jurisdictions mediation of parenting responsibility issues is required before the parties have access to a judge, except in an emergency. Mediation has been covered more fully in the previous chapter.

Attorney Negotiations

Many models are available for a roundtable or four-way discussion, in which both the attorneys and their clients jointly work out a settlement. Litigation is always an available course, but settlement options can still be explored in a nonadversarial fashion if the attorneys are supportive of such alternative dispute-resolution models.

Settlement Conference

Many courts have instituted programs, some voluntary and some mandatory, in which the attorneys, and sometimes even the parties, meet with a judge to review their respective positions and negotiations. The judge may function as a mediator to help the parties settle, or he may simply tell the parties how he would likely rule if he should hear the case. Against this backdrop, the parties will have more information with which to make decisions. Obviously, judges have great latitude and no one would presume to predict what any one judge might do with a litigated case, but input from a judge can be very effective assistance.

Arbitration

Failing resolution by less formal means, you still have other options as you move along the continuum. An arbitrator, usually a lawyer, can be retained to decide some or all of the issues. In some jurisdictions there are formal arbitration programs that may be mandatory in cases that do not involve children or where the amount of money involved is less than a certain figure. There is usually a method for requesting a hearing before a judge if one party is unhappy with the result of the arbitration. But remember, the arbitrator is essentially a judge who will decide for you, not with you.

Reference Judge

You may also retain the services of what is called in some jurisdictions a "reference judge" (rent-a-judge). Former judges or specially designated attorneys who sit as judges on a case-by-case basis may be retained by mutual agreement. These judges have the full authority of a regular judge; their decisions are reviewable by the appellate courts. The advantages of using a reference judge are that you can control the scheduling of the case and are selecting a person with known expertise in this area of the law.

There is no right or wrong place to be on the continuum; each case is unique. Settlement conferences involving your attorneys may be considerably more expensive than mediation since both attorneys are billing time at these meetings. A lot depends on your willingness to be involved in the settlement process, the level of cooperation and communication between you and your spouse, and whether you are deadlocked on some or all of the issues. Think about alternative ways you might be able to proceed rather than assume you must necessarily go to trial just because you and your spouse have not been able to reach an agreement.

HEADING OFF POTENTIAL PROBLEMS

We all know that the atmosphere can become more adversarial as you deal with the legal system. If you anticipate some of the problems, you will be able to respond more effectively and reduce the risks of spiraling conflict. Here are some of the most common problems you will encounter:

The Grapevine Syndrome

Miscommunication often occurs, especially when lawyers act as intermediaries for spouses who are not speaking to each other.

Each party gives their attorney a different account of an incident that is then relayed back and forth. Your attorney tells you what the other lawyer said that your spouse said you said and your reaction is, "I never said that, or at least that's not what I meant." Or a wife's attorney reports to her that her husband's attorney told him that the husband wants the equity from the house. The wife panics and gets all worked up because her husband told her that she could stay in the house. She assumes that her husband's wanting his equity from the house means that she is going to have to move—when that may not have been his intention at all. When there is little direct communication between the principal parties, misinformation, misunderstandings, and counterresponses based on these are common occurrences. *Expect some of the information you receive to be faulty and incomplete.* Check out all information that is confusing or contradicts previous understandings. Be especially careful of hearsay and don't jump to conclusions when you hear something until you understand what was said and the context in which it was said.

The Paper Chase and "Boilerplate" Language

Documents are the primary way in which attorneys move the legal process forward. Paperwork is so automatic that attorneys rarely think about this aspect of divorce. Spouses can become quite angry because they think that the other side is burying them in paper for no particular reason. In addition, documents often contain "boilerplate" language—that is, standard legal forms stored in a word processor. The language in these forms, words like *demand* or *award of custody*, while understood by lawyers, are seen by clients as inflammatory. Explanatory cover letters—or, at least, the realization that many of these documents are computer-generated and shouldn't be taken personally—might avoid some of the anger this paperwork generates.

Attorneys use documents to confirm agreements and to make formal demands for things like requests to produce material or schedule depositions. One reason for so much documentation is to create a record to support later claims for attorney's fees if the other side has been obstructionistic and wasted time and expense. The best way to avoid this circumstance is to encourage face-to-face meetings with the other side as much as possible. Don't let your attorney just write "demand" letters. They generally only make matters worse. The other side will almost always view the "demand" as a hard-and-fast position and close down negotiations—even if that wasn't your intention. For instance, if your attorney's letter to your spouse says you "want custody," there will be whole range of possible arrangements that will be overlooked because your spouse's attorney is likely to respond with an equally strong position.

The Paranoia Syndrome

Part of an attorney's job is to make sure that you understand the worst possible scenario so that you are informed about all risks. This may have the effect of raising your apprehensions about how much you should trust or cooperate with your spouse and can start you thinking about using more formal, rather than less formal, methods of proceeding. Your attorney can't really tell you whether or how much to trust your spouse. However, he can tell you what the risks are and what you should do if you want to be protected. Unlike mediators, attorneys have seen the divorce agreements that break down, that is, when people refuse to pay support, clean out checking accounts, make ridiculous demands, or deny visitation rights. To some extent, they view the universe of divorce through the prism of failed communication and cooperation. They don't want you to be exposed to these risks. They are likely to advise more legal protection rather than less. When both parties are being advised about these risks by their respective attorneys, they are likely to be more cautious in discussing things directly with each other, and this increases feelings of mistrust. As one client put it:

We were getting along just fine—trying to work things out ourselves. After she spoke to an attorney, she was like a different
person. She changed her mind about all previous agreements. She
wanted to do things by the book. I couldn't talk to her anymore.
What the hell was I supposed to do after that?

BOB, *separated 6 months*

There is a risk that with each legal maneuver you use to
strengthen your position, your spouse will take equally strong
measures to strengthen his or her position. This is especially
dangerous when what your lawyer advises may not be in the best
interests of the children or the family. The most common examples
of this kind of advice would be to limit the other parent's contact
with a child to strengthen your position as the "primary parent"
or not taking a job until after the divorce because it might reduce
the spousal support award.

There are always risks in divorce, both in cooperating and in
formalizing the process. Remember to keep your perspective.
When an attorney advises you about the worse case scenario,
assess how likely it is to occur in your case. The best predictor
of behavior is probably what your spouse has done in the past. If
your spouse has not hidden money or assets before, he or she is
not likely to do so now. People get frustrated and angry during
divorce and often threaten things they don't mean or couldn't do
even if they wanted to. Ultimately, you need to find the right
balance between what your attorney advises and the level of
cooperation and openness you feel you will be able to maintain
with your spouse.

TIPS TO REDUCE THE ADVERSARIAL ATMOSPHERE AND THE ESCALATION OF CONFLICT DURING THE LEGAL PROCESS

The basic issue in handling legal proceedings is to remember
that you have choices—choices in the attorney you select, pro-
cedural choices, and choices in following your attorney's recom-

mendations. Legal matters don't have to turn into a battleground if you are careful and your attorney understands your needs and concerns.

1. *Try to ensure that nothing inflammatory leaves your attorney's office.* Written communications should be neutralized. Standard legal forms and court documents contain boilerplate language that undermines trust and can destroy goodwill, especially when the other person doesn't understand these documents. Most of the time that language is unnecessary. Ask your attorney not to use words like *demand* and *award* and to use conciliatory language that emphasizes the desire for a fair settlement despite the formality of the legal process or documents. If you feel that your spouse will be angry about an issue, ask your attorney to write a cover letter reiterating your desire for a mutually satisfactory resolution. You can also forewarn your spouse of letters from your attorney's office (like requests for information) and their purpose so that they will not be misinterpreted. Restate that the legal procedures do not mean you are no longer interested in negotiating. Write a short note if you cannot communicate this verbally.

2. *Anticipate the hard issues.* Discuss with your attorney in advance those issues that you believe are going to be highly charged (e.g., the inheritance, the value of a professional practice, or spousal support). Even if you believe your position is justified and your spouse has no right to react, it is to your advantage to handle these matters delicately. Have your attorney initiate discussion of these matters in a way that respects your spouse's feelings and anticipates objections.

3. *Anticipate your spouse's reactions.* You can't expect your attorney to forewarn you of the possible impact of each procedure on your spouse. It is up to you to discuss options with your attorney about whether or how to go ahead with some procedure or request for documentation. Then, make an intelligent decision based on how you expect your spouse will react.

4. *Use legal tactics as a means of bringing your spouse to the negotiating table.* You can bring legal pressure to bear while still keeping the door open for a negotiated settlement. Assess what kind of leverage you have. For example, if the other attorney won't meet informally, set a deposition that will force the attorneys and parties to meet in person. This may provide an opportunity for a four-way settlement discussion. A client whose ex-wife refused to go to mediation over ongoing visitation disputes remained stubborn until she received a letter from her ex's attorney presenting her with the choice of mediation or further legal action as her only two options. When she saw that she couldn't ignore it anymore, she chose mediation over hiring a lawyer.

5. *Don't underestimate the role of acknowledgment or apology.* Sometimes an acknowledgment or an apology is the key to changing the atmosphere and finally achieving a settlement. As one woman said to her soon-to-be former husband, "I just want you to acknowledge that I am not choosing to ask for spousal maintenance even though under the law I am entitled to it; then I would be willing to discuss the other things." Think about whether there is an emotional issue blocking final settlement and what you might be able to say to your spouse that might acknowledge it or ease the feelings he or she may have.

6. *Be willing to negotiate.* Identify those assets that you can offer in return for what you want. Think systematically about your negotiation strategy. Identify what you want ideally, what your fall-back position is, and what you are willing to live with.

7. *Keep in mind the noneconomic benefits to be gained from negotiation.* You may make a major concession, but in the process buy goodwill. An example might be not asking for half of your spouse's inheritance. An aggressive attorney would say you are entitled to half and you should go after it. This might buy you years of dealing with an embittered spouse. This is a tricky issue because you don't want to go to the other extreme of giving too

much away in order to gain peace or because you feel guilty about leaving the marriage. Explore these kinds of decisions with your attorney and carefully weigh the consequences of each alternative.

CONCLUSION: THE MYTH OF JUSTICE

What seems to be hardest for most people to come to terms with when dealing with lawyers and courts in legal conflicts is the "myth of justice." A myth isn't a lie, but it isn't entirely accurate either. A myth is part real and part what we want or need to believe to have the world make sense. The myth of justice is what people want or need to believe about what happens in courts. Most people believe the judge will listen carefully to both sides of a dispute and, with special wisdom, will determine the right answer. Most people believe that when the judge hears their side of the story, he or she will find that they are right. In fact, justice is defined as you leave the courtroom: if the judge found in your favor, you call it a fair decision; if not, you say it is not justice.

There is a big gap between what really happens in courts and what most people expect to happen. That is true for most legal conflicts and especially for divorce and family conflicts. The myth of justice runs very deep in our culture; we are encouraged to believe that people get what they deserve, that the legal system works to discover the truth, and that justice is served. Our legal system may be the best we can possibly have to settle disputes if we can't do that for ourselves, but it is very seldom that people who have gone to court feel that justice has been served. Judges who are candid will frequently comment that they have done a good day's work when they have dissatisfied *both* parties. That is not as callous or as mean-spirited as it sounds. What judges have come to understand is that it is seldom clear who is right or wrong in a divorce. Judges know that it is very unlikely that they can make a decision that will satisfy both parties; it makes little sense to make a big winner and a big loser because that will only encourage more conflict. So the best alternative is to dissatisfy both parties.

Judges don't want to decide how other people should divide their property and parent their children. They know that the best people to make those decisions are the people themselves and that the agreements that result from those decisions are the ones that will most likely be followed, not decrees issued by the court or forced by attorneys.

As with other aspects of the divorce experience, there are things you can control and things you can't control. By realizing what you can influence in the legal process—selecting the attorney, discussing how the case will be handled, being aware of the paperwork from your attorney's office, and anticipating and taking into consideration your spouse's reactions—you can, in fact, have a role in reducing the adversary nature of the legal proceedings, which so often spin out of control.

V

MOVING FORWARD

Part V examines how to loosen those ties that bind. The process of emotional divorce often begins long before separation and can continue well after legal divorce. Here you are helped to understand the nature of these continuing emotional ties and their role in the conflicts after divorce. I describe rituals to help you let go of the past and get hold of your own future. The book concludes with suggestions for dealing with difficult spouses or ex's who continue to create problems and ways to improve your relationship with your ex and make life more peaceful.

Conflicts After Divorce

Are You Emotionally Divorced?

> When one door of happiness closes, another one opens.
> But often we look so long at the closed door that
> we do not see the one that has been opened for us.
>
> HELEN KELLER

For two years after we were divorced he was still right in the middle of my life. We fought over schedules, money, jackets, and boots. I still cried on friends' shoulders about what he had just said or done to me. He was the bad guy. I was the long suffering victim. Now I can see that attitude hurt me as much as him. I still don't like him, but there is no point giving him the power to make me miserable either.

BARB, *divorced 3 years*

The failure to get an emotional divorce is at the root of much postdivorce conflict. Couples who find themselves embroiled in continuing conflicts after divorce are often not even aware of the level of emotional involvement they have with each other. Even though the issues in dispute always seem justified, they become the forum to play out the unfinished business of the marriage. There is still a version going on of "You can't control me, I'll show you"; "You'll pay for this"; "You'll never do this to me again"; and so on. These issues die hard.

The process of emotional divorce begins long before separation and rarely ends with the signing of legal papers. Legal divorce frequently occurs in the absence of emotional divorce. Most experts say it takes 2 years for life to restabilize after divorce. The continuing interactions surrounding the children are occasions to disagree, feel rejected or jealous, and restimulate all the feelings from the past. It is not easy to get over a divorce when you have to regularly face your former mate.

This chapter helps you understand some of the dynamics of postdivorce conflict and shows you what you can do to improve the situation and release yourself from the hold your divorce or your former mate may have on you. While the context for this chapter is the time following the legal divorce, these dynamics are issues you will grapple with and work toward resolving throughout the separation period as well.

Cold War Is Still War

Hunt and Ellen had been divorced for 2 years. Communication was strained, and while there were occasional blowups and tension over schedules, they had managed to keep their relationship relatively civil. But when Hunt remarried, he started to press Ellen for more time with their daughter, Jessica. He saw his chance to recreate the family he had lost and to get out from under Ellen's thumb. She had had control of the visitation up till then, and he was tired of being told what he could and couldn't do. Ellen bristled under the pressure for extended visits. She had practically raised the child by herself, and she wasn't going to change everything to please Hunt just because now, all of a sudden, he wanted to be a father. She felt that she had catered to his work and his needs for 12 years. She had read the books on codependency. She felt she had to draw the line.

When Ellen refused Hunt's demands for increased time with their daughter, he suggested that Jessica live with him, since he could offer more of a family life. Ellen was outraged to the core; why, Hunt didn't even know the name of Jessica's teacher or pediatrician! She couldn't believe he was doing this. There were icy stares when Hunt came to pick up Jessica on his weekends. His longtime feelings about his ex being a "controlling bitch" intensified as their arguments about who had the right to run things escalated. He began to see Ellen as overinvolved, overprotective, and not encouraging Jessica to try new things. The more he looked, the more he saw Ellen's faults. He and his new wife became convinced that Jessica would be better off with her new stepsisters in their family. Hunt called his lawyer to talk about changing custody, but the lawyer said that he would have to show fairly serious parental inadequacy in order to get a change of custody. The lawyer recommended mediation.

Hunt and Ellen fell into the traps that often ensnare divorced parents. While they were able to be civil a good deal of the time, beneath the surface the cold war and power struggles of the marriage were being played out in their negotiations about parenting arrangements. Each took unyielding positions at various times and refused to accommodate even reasonable requests. Hunt was unconsciously invested in his image of Ellen as a controlling bitch. He collected grievances and catalogued the times she denied his requests or tried to tell him how to take care of Jessica. Even though he was happily remarried, his anger kept him emotionally tied to Ellen.

Ellen, for her part, was determined to be compensated for all of the accommodations she had made in the past and was thus unable to evaluate Hunt's requests with an objective eye. It was hard to admit that she was still deeply hurt by Hunt's lack of involvement with the family during their marriage. It was especially painful for her to watch him be with another family in ways that he had not been there for her. She focused her anger by rarely going out of her way to accommodate anything he asked for, and she certainly wasn't going to let him use "her" daughter to have this nice little family that he never had with her.

Neither Hunt nor Ellen could look at the present situation practically. Even though their disputes were couched in terms of what was best for Jessica, the struggle over who was controlling whom was really what determined all of their parenting decisions. They were not even aware of how emotionally involved they were with each other and how their escalating hostilities were beginning to affect Jessica. Neither was seeing Jessica's need to be part of both families or taking into account her feelings for her new sisters or stepmom.

Anger is a normal and healthy response to loss and pain. Focusing on your anger and your spouse's deficiencies is a way of separating yourself emotionally. The paradox is that the same anger that helps you distance yourself emotionally keeps you emotionally tied to your former spouse if it is not resolved. When you are angry at someone, you remain emotionally invested in that person. You actively think about what the person did to you and what you will do in return. It eats away at you. Like Hunt and Ellen, often you don't even realize how emotionally involved you are with your ex.

Most recurrent custody and visitation disputes, during divorce and afterward, are not really about the children but about the relationship between the parents. Couched in terms of the children's needs, these conflicts mask fears of being alone, ambivalence about the divorce, continuing emotional dependencies and attachments, and efforts to assuage wounded pride and punish a spouse. For some, keeping the anger stirred up staves off the temptation to get back together or wards off terrible feelings of emptiness. *Concentrating on the faults of or fights with your ex is a good excuse not to look at yourself.*

THE PSYCHOLOGY OF POSTDIVORCE CONFLICT

In their book *The Impasses of Divorce* researchers Janet Johnston and Linda Campbell identified several underlying dynamics found in couples who were entrenched in continuing disputes.[1] While their research focused on that small percentage of the divorcing population who keep returning to or threatening to go back to court, the issues that drive these disputes, to varying degrees,

exist in all divorces. What follows is a summary of the d
found by these researchers to contribute to persistent cont
if the following themes underlie, to any degree, the dift ̲ ̲uɩɩes
you may be having getting along with your ex or if they contribute
to your continued emotional involvement with your former spouse.

Totally Negative View of the Spouse ("My ex is an absolute bastard/bitch")

For people who had unrealistically high expectations and
hopes riding on their marriage based on the fantasy of what the
partner was supposed to be, the marriage's end is experienced as
a profound betrayal. The spouse who was supposed to save them,
help them escape from an unhappy situation or be the answer to
all their problems now becomes the embodiment of lost hope and
disappointment and is hated intensely. It is as if history were
rewritten, and a very negative view of the spouse is constructed.
The spouse is thought of as crazy, no good, a real cad, a liar, not
caring at all about other people, and so on. Many couples feel this
way when they separate. They feel they don't know this person
anymore: "If she could do this to me, what else could she do?"
Instead of developing perspective and understanding, some people continue to maintain such a completely negative view of their
spouse that they interpret everything that happens as further
evidence of the spouse's total unworthiness.

If you are utterly convinced that your spouse is the bad guy
and you are unable to develop a more balanced perspective, you
will never be free.

Exercise: Ask yourself why it is so important for you to view
your ex so negatively. What are you getting out of it? Write down
the first three things that come to mind.

If your former spouse still hates you, think about whether
there is anything you can or want to do to try to change this
perception. You might act inconsistently with your ex's view of
you: if you are accused of being late, be early; if a no is expected,
say yes. Behave in positive ways that are not expected. Be more

cooperative, even if your ex is not. Even if this doesn't change anything, don't retaliate. Let your spouse's hate be his or her problem. Don't let it destroy you.

Ambivalence About the Divorce ("Maybe we'll get back together")

You must ask yourself whether you have really accepted the fact that the marriage is over. Do you have hopes of reconciliation in the back of your mind? When a relationship is left open or unresolved or if you are still ambivalent about your decision, you remain emotionally vulnerable to the other person and can be hurt. It is easy to let doused hopes and disappointments affect your decisions about parenting arrangements. You have to be careful to keep your parenting decisions separate from the ups and downs of your relationship. Don't refuse to accommodate the other parent or deny a request because you feel rejected.

Even if you are sure that you no longer want the marriage, you may still be vulnerable to your former spouse. If you are trying to prove you are as good as your ex, want to show him or her what a mistake it was to divorce you, or are seeking approval or friendship, you are leaving yourself open to disappointments that could spill over into the parenting arena. It is best to try not to have any emotional expectations in regard to a former mate—unless you are one of the rare couples who have a friendship that is truly reciprocal.

Exercise: Write down any ways you still seek attention, approval, or validation from your ex. Ask yourself why you still care what your ex thinks of you. Can you make your ex's opinion matter less?

Wounded Ego: Saving Face

Most people's self-esteem suffers when a marriage breaks up. Some individuals have a fragile ego, which they protect by insisting others see them in a positive light and by faulting them when they do not. The problem is always someone else, and these

individuals have great difficulty accepting responsibility for
their part of a problem. In divorce, they try to save face by blaming
the other parent or turning to court to "prove" that they are not
failures as parents. They create conflict by overreacting to comments and behaviors that are often misinterpreted as criticism.
They turn minor problems into major issues as they try to save face
and bolster a damaged sense of self-esteem.

All people tend to be more cooperative when they feel valued.
Individuals with deeply wounded egos especially need to be
shown some appreciation for *whatever* positive contributions they
make. Unfortunately, the hostility these people provoke leaves
little room for respect or positive comments. It is easier not to
become defensive yourself if you realize that their behavior stems
from their own weakness. Try to see the anger and antagonism as
your spouse's problem rather than as a reflection on you, and let
the provocations go by you as much as you can. See if you can
make occasional appreciative comments about something your
former spouse has done as a parent or go out of your way to thank
your ex for things you might otherwise take for granted; for
example: "Johnny appreciated your taking him to baseball practice. He was very proud when you stayed and watched for a while."

Perhaps your own self-esteem has been shaken and you are
trying to prove to your spouse that you are as good as he or she is.
Ask yourself if you might in any way be compensating for feelings
of failure or not feeling good about yourself by trying to prove
that you are a good parent or better than your former spouse? If
this is true, try to focus on what you think is good about *your*
relationship with the children and what you think are your good
points as a parent. Look inside and start to notice your strengths
instead of trying to prove them to other people or using your
former spouse as your standard. (Use the questionnaire in chapter
8 to review your parenting strengths.)

Previous Traumatic Losses

Old scars can be split open when a marriage ends. The losses
of divorce can reawaken very painful feelings about previous

losses. Sometimes being faced with another loss is truly unbear-
able; it is one more black hole. Keeping conflicts stirred up
forestalls letting go of the relationship and is sometimes an unconscious psychological defense against reexperiencing the pain of
the past. Having problems with an ex is better than having
nothing. Therapy or a support group are more likely to help you
heal and become strong again than continuing in a destructive
pattern with your former mate.

If there was a divorce in your family in which you were placed
in the middle of parental hostilities or if you lost access to a parent or were left without much money or if you lost a child in a
previous divorce, you are likely to worry about these things
happening again in this divorce. History doesn't always repeat
itself, but the anxiety that it will can be strong. If your fears are not
understood, a spouse or ex is likely to feel threatened by the
demands or attempts to control that your fear generates. Think
about whether anxieties over past losses for either of you might be
contributing to present difficulties.

Fear of Being Alone

If you have never lived alone, never completely relied on
yourself, made your spouse the center of your universe, or defined
yourself around your spouse's identity instead of establishing or
maintaining your own, then the crisis of divorce is for you also a
crisis of identity and dependency. If your sense of self has been
tied to your spouse's, the separation may leave you feeling panicky,
hollow, or dead inside. Clinging to or blaming a spouse can ward
off terrible feelings of emptiness. Fighting is better than nothing
and certainly better than facing a deep void in your life. In the
more extreme cases, this fighting is referred to as negative intimacy, in which couples remain emotionally involved with each
other in unhealthy ways through conflict.

Every divorcing individual has to overcome the fear of being
alone—again or for the first time—and find new and healthy ways
of feeling connected to other people and fulfilled as a human

being. This transition is like a rite of passage, but it can take place at any age.

Conflict can help ward off feelings of loss and fear, it can take away the emptiness and postpone feelings of isolation, and it can be a sign of continued emotional attachment. If you fit any of these profiles and are still struggling with the divorce, you might consider therapy for yourself. Professional help can also help you cope better if your spouse is the one who has not let go.

THE LENS FROM THE PAST: WHAT COLOR IS YOUR FILTER?

We all see the world through the lens of our experiences and beliefs. We assign our own meaning to what we see. Our beliefs shape our experience and our experience shapes our beliefs. When something has been particularly significant, deeply hurtful, or a recurrent experience in our lives, it deeply affects our beliefs about the world. For example, young children who are repeatedly disappointed and let down by a parent will grow up believing that they can't count on *anyone*. Similarly, our attitudes about our ex-spouses are shaped by how they wounded us. While your perception of your ex may have some accuracy, it becomes a problem when it is taken as an absolute and everything that occurs is interpreted through this mind-set. Like Hunt, earlier in this chapter, whose lens was the view that his ex-wife was a "controlling bitch," you will find it difficult to see things from a different perspective. Problems are created because you jump to conclusions without being able to objectively evaluate what is going on.

Think about whether you have a mind-set about your ex through which you interpret negative interactions. Write down what this might be. Some common beliefs are expressed in the following familiar quotes: "She is trying to take advantage of me"; "She is trying to take me to the cleaners"; "She is trying to deny me my rights as a father"; "He doesn't care about the kids"; "He is trying to punish me"; "He has it so much easier." As an experiment imagine that you didn't have this mind-set. Take this filter off when you encounter your ex over the next few weeks, just to see what the world looks like without it. When you interpret the cause of a problem differently, new solutions present themselves.

FOUR DEADLY ATTITUDES: LINKS TO THE PAST

Particular attitudes or things we say to ourselves can keep us tied to the past. Frequently, we don't even realize the tremendous impact these attitudes are having on our lives. Mel Krantzler, in his book *Divorcing*, suggests that when you view your misfortunes through an "altering eye"—that is, when you look for something positive in each situation that appears dismal—you will see possibilities heretofore unnoticed. Every ending is also a beginning. If you are still grieving or angry about the ending, you will miss the next beginning. As I discuss common self-defeating attitudes and how they can be changed, see if any of them make up part of your thinking.

"It's Your Fault"

"It's your fault I'm in this mess. If it weren't for you . . ." Some ex-spouses continue to experience themselves as a victim. They are not remembering what made them unhappy and dissatisfied with the marriage or their role in its breakdown. Continuing to feel sorry for yourself and blaming the other person for your misfortunes prevents you from taking an active role in your own recovery and seeing the choices that are open to you now. You are not paying attention to what *you* want and what is important to you. It is like wearing blinders. You only see in one direction—what was done to you.

"You Have It Better"

"You have it better than I do—more money, a new relationship, a new family; it's just not fair." A sense of injustice is a very common reaction after divorce. From where you sit the other person always has the better deal, more advantages, more choices, and better opportunities. In many cases this is indeed true. Divorce is not fair. Men tend to have more advantages in the marketplace, and women often have a stronger foothold in the parenting arena. A man who doesn't have his children feels this injustice just as keenly as the woman who earns one-fourth the income of her former spouse. These are real differences and vulnerabilities that even the fairest agreements cannot equalize. Even after divorce, your lives may take different turns. A man may remarry quickly and reestablish the family his ex-wife always wanted, while she remains alone, struggling as a single parent trying to find her way back into the job market. A woman may marry into wealth while her ex is still trying to pay off the debts from the marriage and get a down payment together for a little house. Legal remedies are no guarantee of justice either, as many people who have gone through court will testify.

If you continually focus on what is not fair and what the other has, then your energy will be spent on your envy instead of working with what you do have. It accomplishes nothing to continue to compare yourself to your former spouse. Yet we all do this in many ways.

Try to make peace with the differences in your situations. Invest your energies in yourself, even if it is one small step at a time. Even if yours is the tougher road, remember: it is not the path you are given in life but how you choose to walk on it that matters. If you feel the settlement is patently unfair, then you will need to deal with it with your lawyer. Don't allow your unhappiness to fester; try to change it or let it go. *Don't make the divorce your life.*

"I'll Never Forgive You"

"I'll never forgive you for leaving, for what you said, for what your lawyer did, for booting me out of the house with a restraining order, for closing the bank account, for not giving me money . . ."

This thinking comes from the failure to appreciate the mutual contribution to the problems in the marriage or to the confrontations that escalated during the divorce. Many of the terrible actions in nasty divorces are taken in self-protection or retaliation. You may have felt threatened and believed that if you didn't take action, it would be taken against you; your spouse probably felt just as threatened. Aggressive legal maneuvers don't occur in a vacuum. They are part of the risk of our adversarial legal system. Attorneys take their clients' anxieties seriously. They've seen the worse divorce situations, where implied threats are really carried out. They don't want to place their clients in a vulnerable position.

Some spouses are clearly vindictive and try to make life miserable for their former mates. In my experience unprovoked malicious behavior is relatively rare. Even in the scenes of destruction in the film *War of the Roses*, both sides felt justified in their actions. From the outside, we could see how crazy it was; from the inside, they could not. Their hate took over. They were possessed. If your spouse was destructive and hateful, at some point you need to let go of your anger about it and not keep paying him or her back. As bad as some of the actions were, it is over now and it is time to move on.

"If You Really Cared"

"If you really cared about the children, you would do the things I think you should do, be the kind of parent I always hoped you would be . . ." Many divorced people continue to place expectations on their former spouse to be someone he or she is not. You need to learn to tolerate your ex being the parent he or she is, even if in your mind it is not good enough. You can't control what goes on in the other house. You can't influence your former spouse's life anymore. If your ex is not a good listener and intimidates the children, doesn't place the same priority on achievement and discipline, or doesn't spend enough quality time with the children, you have to learn to accept these imperfections and let go of your demand that your spouse be different. Concentrate on your own relationship with the children and teaching them your values.

LETTING GO

Dick was remarried, had a large accounting practice, two preteen daughters, and an ex-wife who was a recovered alcoholic. The affair that precipitated the divorce had hurt him badly. In my opinion, he never fully recovered from it. I met Dick and Helen 2 years after their divorce, when they were embroiled in a bitter battle to change custody. The girls had been living with Helen and seeing Dick on the weekends. Since the divorce they'd had many arguments about money, which caused more bad feelings just as the divorce wounds were beginning to heal.

> DICK: She used me and abused me in every way. The fact is, she is still trying to use me. I can't trust her. I used to forgive her and go on. But she has stabbed me too many times. She didn't stick to agreements. She always wanted more. It was never enough money. The girls had a great time with me this summer. They made new friends and are very connected to the church youth group. I can offer them more at this point.
>
> HELEN: I've been clean and sober for two years. I can't undo the past. I was a very unhappy person. I didn't like myself. I wasn't a very good wife. All I can do now is be a good ex-wife and a good mother. He needs to see me in a bad light. He can't handle that I've changed, that I've succeeded. I don't work full-time so I can be there when the girls get home from school. He is trying to pay me back and he is making the girls the pawns. He can't forgive me.

What was apparent in mediation was that Helen had made her peace with Dick, but Dick had not let go. He was not able to forget about Helen's affair. Even though he was remarried, his anger at Helen was still there. The conflicts over money triggered all of his old feelings of being taken advantage of; the recent dispute over his daughters' change of primary residence was a way for him to finally repay Helen.

Letting go doesn't mean that there will be no more conflicts or disagreements. What it does mean is that they will be about real problems—schedules, costs for the children, and the like—rather than excuses to play out the unfinished business of the marriage.

Every time you can keep an exchange from turning into a fight, you heal yourself. Unresolved conflict adds to the sludge pond that feeds further disputes. Try to let go of each fight when it is over. Don't add it to your pool of resentment. Tell yourself you don't need this aggravation and release it after the incident is over.

As noted earlier, in the years after divorce, the fight with an ex can keep away the emptiness and finality of letting go. Many people need to fight or otherwise remain engaged with their former mate. It serves a psychological purpose, beyond dealing with genuine disagreement. If you sense this may be part of your problem with your former spouse, try the following exercise.

HOLDING ON: AN EXERCISE

In response to the questions below, write down the first thing that comes to your mind, without censoring yourself, even if it doesn't seem to make sense or you don't like what you see. By writing down the first thing that comes to your mind, you can access feelings that may be unconsciously contributing to your struggles.

1. What would your life be like if you didn't have conflict with your ex?
2. What feelings and resentments from the past are you aware of holding on to?
3. What is keeping you from letting go of these conflicts?
4. How will you know when you are ready to let go?
5. What will you need in order to let go?
6. What can you look forward to once you have really let go of the past?
7. What will things be like in 2 years if you don't let go?

RITUALS FOR LETTING GO AND MOVING FORWARD

Knowing that you are holding on to resentments is not the same as being able to let them go. Letting go is partially an act of will and partially an act of release. Sometimes there is no release without a cathartic experience because the feelings are lodged in your body. Rituals are a way of externalizing deeply embedded feelings which are difficult to express verbally. By symbolically enacting your feelings, you extend them outside the body where there can be more release.

A ritual can be a formal, public ceremony that marks a passage or an important life transition. It can be a private act that has personal significance symbolizing the end of one phase of living and the beginning of another. Every culture has rituals or rites of passage that mark the significant life events of birth, puberty, marriage, and death. There are no such rituals for divorce, the death of a relationship. It is a largely private affair with little social support for the grieving. There is no acknowledgment of the loss of the earlier hopes and dreams or of the efforts that went into the union. There is no recognition of the entry into a new phase of life. As one friend said, no one brings you casseroles.

The rituals described in the next several pages are designed to help you move beyond a place where you may somehow feel stuck. Some of these rituals are simple, others have several parts. All are to be carried out ceremoniously. Details need to be worked out ahead of time, including deciding the time and place for the ritual. You might choose a room in your house or a favorite place outdoors, by a river or a mountain, during the day or in the moonlight. If you have been depressed, it is a good idea to discuss the details of your ritual with a therapist before proceeding, since rituals can release potent feelings. Take the time to do the writing and drawing and gathering of symbols that are used in these rituals. The gathering and choosing of symbols is as much a part of the experience as what is done with them in the final act. The idea of a ritual is to live the experience and not pass over it, as happens with so many of our experiences.

The following ritual is adapted from the work of my colleague Stephen Gilligan, author of *Therapeutic Trances: The Cooperation Principle in Ericksonian Hypnotherapy*. His recent interest has been in developing rituals for use in healing trauma.[2] This particular ritual may be carried out over several days or even weeks.

Ritual for Saying Goodbye to the Old and Hello to the New

Think about what or whom you want to say goodbye to.

1. Draw three pictures of this person, experience, or part of yourself you wish to let go of. Get a box of crayons or magic markers and some plain white sheets of paper. Don't worry about how good the drawings are; just let whatever you feel flow. The pictures could be abstract or representative. Title each picture and on the back in no more than three lines write what each picture represents. You may find that one or two drawings is sufficient for you or that you need to do more than three. Or you can do a different drawing on each of three nights. Follow your own feelings.

2. The next night draw three pictures of what you want to say hello to—what you want to be like, the new you without the pain of the past; what you want in your life; or what you want your life to be in the future. Follow the instructions in step 1.

3. Then write a letter to your ex (which you are not going to send) about what happened in the past, how you feel now, and what you want to let go of. Tell your ex everything that you have been carrying around and unable to say.

4. Next, collect symbols that represent the events, feelings, or period in your life you want to let go of. Take a quiet walk by yourself or look around the house, letting your mind wander freely. Trust your intuition about what you will choose. You may even find a symbol while driving your car, going through your belongings, or walking in the woods or at the beach.

5. Do the same thing for finding a symbol that represents what will be new in your life, what you want to say hello to.

6. When you have found the symbols and completed the

drawings and letter, choose the time, place, and manner you wish to honor them. You can choose to bury some, burn them in the fireplace, tear them up, stick pins in them, put them in a special box that you save, or even frame them.

7. Begin the ritual by sitting on the floor with the symbols, drawings, and letter around you. One by one, read aloud and describe the meaning of each drawing about your old life. Then slowly and ceremoniously do whatever you have decided to do with the drawings that represent the past. Do the same thing with the letter and the symbols you gathered that represent the letting go. Allow yourself to truly feel that you are saying good-bye. Let the sorrow and pain flow through you. Let these feelings come into your heart and then let them go. Remember to breathe deeply to help keep you steady. This experience can be quite powerful and can release deeply felt emotions. Recognize your need for support, particularly during this part of the ritual.

8. After taking some time to let the experience move through you, repeat the process with the drawings and symbols that represent your new life. This time, instead of symbolically putting them behind you, find a way to welcome and honor them. They are your private reminders of the birth of something, of a new beginning.

9. After the ceremony, think of three concrete steps you want to take to connect you with other people or your community so that the energy that is freed from the past can be channeled in a way that will continue to move you forward. For instance, you might want to join a club, take up a hobby or sport that has always interested you, participate in promoting a cause you support, or reinvolve yourself in an interest or a friend from the past. Write these three things down and post them on your refrigerator.

10. Finally, have an evening or afternoon of celebration. Do something nurturing or special for yourself. Have a wonderful dinner, get a massage, buy something special, go out of town, take a day off from work, or do something you have always wanted to do.

I had one client who took her drawings of her depressed and

gloomy self and every day for a week reduced them on a photo-copy machine until they were tiny. Then she wore red cowboy boots for the next week to symbolize her bright, gay side. Another client took old photos of her ex-husband, including a 9-by-12 glossy portrait, sat down after work with a fine bottle of wine, and slowly put them through the office shredder.

Rituals can be powerful experiences. You can benefit from doing all or part of them on your own, but maximum benefit comes in a group setting or in therapy. If you are in therapy, talk to your therapist about working with these rituals together. If you are not in therapy, ask a friend to be with you to give you support and provide testimony to what you are doing.

Rituals for Burying the Hatchet

1. Find an object to symbolize the hurt and pain you and your ex have caused each other during the divorce. Write a short eulogy about how this anger and nasty behavior served you and/or how the other person's behavior caused you pain. Find a box to put the symbol in, and choose a time and place to bury it. Ceremoniously prepare the burial site, reading aloud the eulogy, and bury the object. Do this exercise together if you can.

2. There is a Native American ritual in which you dig a hole in the earth and speak into that hole all the things in life that are bothering you—your past anger, regrets, hatred, or frustration. You let them go deep into the earth.[3]

3. Think about a peace offering. Symbolic gestures go a long way in communicating how you feel. In Native American tradition the passing of the peace pipe is a sacred ceremony. Consider how you might ritualize peacemaking with your ex. The gesture has to fit your feelings and convey what you are trying to communicate about new possibilities for the future. For example, as a gesture of goodwill, you can give your spouse some object that you received in the divorce that you think he or she would really appreciate. Or you might get together and exchange something you each know the other would value. Whether you offer a gift or do an

exchange, if you can ceremoniously express your heartfelt feelings, it can be healing.

If symbolic gestures or rituals don't feel comfortable, you might simply ask your ex whether he or she would be willing to bury the hatchet. You can describe your willingness to do so and your hopes for a more positive future.

Rituals to Let Go of Blame

1. Write down everything you blame your spouse for on separate little pieces of paper and why you blame him or her.

2. Write down everything you blame yourself for on separate pieces of paper and why you blame yourself for these things.

3. Choose a time and place for the ritual. Read aloud what is written on each piece of paper, beginning each sentence with "I have blamed you [or myself] for _____ for _____ months or years." End each sentence with "I no longer blame you [or myself] for this." Then tear up the paper into 6 pieces. Repeat this for each piece of paper.

A variation on this ritual is to write all the things you blame yourself and/or your ex for on separate pieces of paper and post them on your bathroom mirror. Read them aloud every morning for a week. Then remove one each morning, reading it aloud and stating, "I will no longer blame you [or myself] for _____."

You can also develop your own ritual or symbolic enactment that represents a commitment to a change, to a letting go of something old and the beginning of something new. I know a woman who threw out all of her old underwear and sheets when the divorce was final and made a ritual out of purchasing new lingerie, linens, and fixtures for her bedroom.

FORGIVING

It would be difficult to talk about letting go and peacemaking without also talking about forgiving. Lewis Smedes, in his book

Forgive and Forget: Healing the Hurts We Don't Deserve, states that hurts that are deep, personal, and unfair create a crisis of forgiving because the only way to truly be healed from this kind of wound is through forgiving. He says, "When you forgive someone for hurting you, you perform spiritual surgery on the soul."[4] In forgiveness there is the recognition that nothing we do to punish the other person will heal us.

Forgiveness is not absolving wrong acts, but it recognizes the fact that others may not have hurt you because they intended to do so but, rather, because they acted out of their own weakness. Forgiveness involves coming to see those who hurt you in a different light, not through the lens of what they did to you but in terms of their own insecurities, vulnerabilities, and pain.

Smedes states that we forgive in four stages. The first reaction is the hurt, which is so deep it can't be forgotten. The second emotion is the hate you feel when you can't shake the memory of what was done to you and you wish your enemy to suffer as much as you have. The third stage is one of healing, when you finally begin to understand the other's perceptions and motivations and are able to view the person who hurt you in his or her human frailty. The fourth and final stage is when you invite the other person back into your life in whatever way that is appropriate for you, even if it is just back into your memories without all the hate.

True freedom only comes with forgiveness. You cannot change what happened in the past; you can only change your relationship to it. When you forgive, you essentially take away the enemy's power over you. Try to view your former spouse as a person, separate from what he or she did to you. Try to think of your ex in terms of the universal human struggle, as a fellow victim, and as someone who was also hurt and in pain. Try to understand why your former spouse did the things that were hurtful to you. Remember, you transform yourself when you forgive. A choice to forgive is a choice to heal yourself.

18

Difficult Spouses/Difficult Ex's

Be Part of the Solution Instead of the Problem

> Negative events don't have to be responded to negatively.
>
> VIRGINIA SATIR

> He started his usual harangue, but this time I stood my ground. I kept saying that I wouldn't talk about the past. I didn't want to hear how it was all my fault. He went on and one about how I had done this or that, but I didn't react. I kept repeating that all I wanted was to get on with the settlement as reasonable and fairly as possible. I realized his approval doesn't matter anymore. He is more like something you just have to deal with, like the car breaking down or a bad day at work.
>
> RUTH, *separated 6 months*

Everyone thinks he is the reasonable one and that the other person is demanding, stubborn, and difficult to work with. Sometimes this is true and sometimes it is not. While we all feel justified in the actions we take, some spouses are truly obstructionistic and difficult. Not everyone is fortunate enough to have a spouse who can be reasonable about handling the divorce. Some people are too angry, immature, irresponsible, or untrustworthy.

On the basis of a study of couples who were referred to

mediation by the court, Kenneth Kressel and his associates developed a profile of the difficult spouse.[1] The study describes these individuals as preoccupied with their own needs and unable to understand the needs of the other parent or of the children. They have an irresponsible attitude toward their spouse, particularly in regard to child care arrangements, including being late, not showing up, or changing plans at the last minute. They undermine the other parent's authority by overtly or covertly encouraging the children to be disrespectful. And perhaps what makes them especially poor mediation candidates is their inability to acknowledge responsibility for their role in the conflicts even though they often take extreme and untenable positions.

If you feel that your spouse has been difficult to deal with, it would be easy to say, "Yes, my spouse fits this profile, so I am off the hook." But that would be an oversimplification. While you may be the more reasonable one, undoubtedly you've exhibited a habitual response to what your spouse does, and this may make things worse. You can't change your former spouse, but what you can change is your attitude about your ex and your reaction. Even if you are not part of the problem, you can be part of the solution. Or put another way, if you are not part of the solution, you are part of the problem.

One of the traps in dealing with difficult former spouses is expecting them to behave responsibly and holding them accountable. This is an unrealistic expectation. To a certain extent, you must set limits and hold your ex responsible for things within those limits, but to hold this kind of person up to a standard of responsible, mature behavior will only increase your anger and frustration. You must lower your expectations and learn to work with your ex's limitations. Remember, difficult individuals are operating out of weakness, not strength. If they felt okay about themselves and if they didn't feel threatened or demeaned by their situation, they would not need to threaten or demean you.

It is ultimately in your interest to figure out what minimizes the "difficult" behavior and what makes it worse, even if it means you have to extend yourself in ways that are just not fair. As Ruth stated in the beginning of this chapter, hostile spouses should be handled like a car that breaks down. It's not fair that your clutch went out and you have to do things you don't want to do to take care of it, but that's the way it is.

STRATEGIES FOR DEALING WITH A DIFFICULT SPOUSE

In his book *Coping with Difficult People*, Robert Bramson outlines several steps for coping with difficult personalities in the workplace. The following steps are adaptations of some of these principles.[2]

Step 1: Give Up Wishing That Your Spouse Would Be Different

Often there is an unconscious expectation or demand that a former spouse change by becoming more reasonable, responsible, or a better parent. At some point you have to accept that your ex is like this, a person who doesn't listen, angers easily, is irresponsible, or abuses drugs and alcohol. There is no point in continuing to blame your former mate for who he or she is. Try to let go. It's like getting angry at red lights. Stop reacting to something you can't change.

This doesn't mean that you shouldn't protect yourself against the consequences of your ex's irresponsibility or do what you can to ensure compliance with legal agreements. But once you accept something you can't change, you can anticipate the problems that arise rather than emotionally reacting to them. For example, if your spouse sabotages your time with the children by "forgetting" to pack some of the things they will need, keep duplicates of the important items at your house rather than continuing to get angry.

Step 2: Get Some Distance Between You and the Difficult Behavior

In order to change your reaction, you have to be able to step back and look at the other person's behavior instead of just reacting to it blindly. You need to become more detached, more of an observer rather than a participant. There are several ways you can create some emotional distance. One technique I have found useful in helping clients deal with angry, provocative people is to imagine that you are surrounded by a clear plastic shield, like the one in the old Colgate toothpaste TV commercial. If you remember, objects struck the shield and bounced off while the person stood on the other side with a broad smile and glistening teeth. Before an encounter with your former spouse that you expect might be difficult or antagonistic, close your eyes, take a deep breath, and visualize this shield all around you. See it unfolding and place yourself in the center. Observe what your former spouse says or does from the inside, as if you are looking out through a window. This kind of mental imagery can provide the distance and detachment that gives you more time to consider your response. This technique can be helpful whenever you are dealing with someone's anger.

A technique that Bramson suggests in his book is to imagine looking at difficult people through the wrong end of a pair of binoculars, so that they appear small and far away. Or try thinking of them in terms of their weaknesses, that is, as a big baby or as a lost soul. These visualizations give you a different perspective on the difficult person and slow down your automatic reaction, which would otherwise become part of the game. You change the game simply by not getting caught up in it.

Step 3: Try to Gain Some Insight into the Other Person's Behavior

List your spouse's or ex's behaviors that drive you crazy or that you find difficult. Briefly write down your understanding of these behaviors. Try putting yourself in your ex's shoes to figure out why he or she acts this way. Any little bit of understanding will give you a new vantage point that can help you alter your response.

Step 4: Formulate a Coping Strategy

You need to develop a strategy for how you are going to cope with your spouse when he or she becomes abusive, abrasive, or difficult. When you can anticipate this behavior, you will have more control.

Using the list you just made about what your spouse does that drives you crazy, review your own reactions in the situations in which these behaviors occur. Take a clean sheet of paper and make two columns. Head one with responses in the past that have helped. Head the other column with responses that have not worked. Choose three from the "have helped" column that seem most promising. Think about how you can use these responses in the future. Rehearse what you are going to say the next time you encounter these difficult behaviors. Visualize an encounter with your former spouse in which you lose it but then regain control.

In doing this exercise, one client discovered that when his ex wouldn't allow extra visitation, the least effective response was to threaten her with withholding child support. His ex would tell him to go to hell and threaten to take him to court. The more effective response was when he offered her something in exchange (for example, when he allowed her to have the children on his turn for Thanksgiving or the time he paid for their new winter jackets). They got along well for several months after each such negotiation.

UNDERSTAND HOW YOU GET HOOKED

Even though you are getting a divorce, it is sometimes hard to disengage yourself from the destructive games with your spouse if you don't understand how you get hooked. Powerful beliefs about who you are and what you need to do to be loved, which stem from your role in your own family of origin, prompt you to react to your spouse's "craziness." The hook comes from feelings of guilt or inadequacy, from beliefs that it is your job to rescue or save other people, from fears that you will not be loved if you are not needed, from anxiety that you will be abandoned if you assert yourself—from your deepest longings, which can blind you to current realities. *Codependency* is the term that has been used to describe many of these patterns.

> I know my stubbornness is my worst enemy. I can't let her say these outrageous things and not refute them. I regress to her level. She's like poison to me . . . this angel–devil pull. One minute she is sweet and loving and vulnerable and makes me feel like there can be this wonderful future. I get seduced into her fantasy. The next minute she is screaming obscenities about how awful I am and what I have done to her, threatening to take the kids and move back to South Dakota.
>
> Russ, *divorced 2 years*

Russ couldn't set limits because his ex-wife hooked all of his self-doubts. When she started her harangues about how he was a poor this and a bad that, he'd lose his self-confidence and begin to think that maybe he really was the flake she accused him of being. When she was sweet, his deepest wishes for a family and the perfect home were stirred. He'd lose sight of the fact that in 10 years of being together, they could not create a calm, stable relationship. Despite all of the evidence that this woman was unstable and had real psychological problems, she touched his deepest hopes and worst fears and he couldn't easily break away even 2 years after the divorce.

Try to think about what hooks you and why you continue to react or engage with your former spouse when he or she is difficult or abusive. You need to learn to understand what you get from these interactions so that you won't get pulled into them. Even though it is hard work, try to be more detached and businesslike.

TYPES OF DIFFICULT SPOUSES

You can't make lemonade out of these lemons, but you can keep them from squirting in your eye. Here are some types of spouses that require special care.

Controller

Controlling ex-spouses don't trust other people to handle things as well as they can. There is only one way—their way. In a marriage controllers tend to run the show and are usually the ones who take charge of all plans and arrangements. In a divorce they may be uncomfortable being away from the children, since they may not trust the other parent to care for the children as well as they can. They are anxious when they can't control the things that are important to them, especially as this relates to the children. They create problems by trying to exert influence in the other parent's home. Effective ways to deal with controllers include: (1) try to address some of their anxieties and concerns; (2) help them see where you share similar goals regarding the children's well-being, even though your methods for achieving these goals are different; (3) offer reassurance about your sensitivity to their concerns; (4) share, rather than keep, information about how you handle things that affect the children; and (5) gently enforce the new boundaries around your autonomy as parents.

The key to dealing with this type of ex is setting limits while at the same time being open with information. Giving more information has a better chance of relaxing the anxieties underlying the controlling behavior than giving less information or confronting your ex about his or her meddling ways. Provide details about your talk with your child's teacher, your research about swimming programs, and so on. Try to see your ex's behavior as a way of controlling his or her own anxieties and fears rather than as an attempt to control you, even though it ultimately has this effect.

Sam's ex-wife, Sandra, had a laundry list of directions whenever he came to pick up their 3-year-old son. Sam had developed a deaf ear after 10 years of marriage to a woman who always had to run the show. Sandra's anxiety mounted because she couldn't control what happened at Sam's house and Sam was uncommunicative. She intensified her efforts to get him to do what she wanted and began accusing him of being an irresponsible parent: he didn't supervise carefully enough, he didn't maintain the child's routine, he let him play too roughly with the dog, he didn't make him wear a bicycle helmet. Sam's response was to tell her to get off his back. This made things worse, however justified Sam felt. Sandra trusted him less and her fears and need for control only intensified. The arguments eventually deadlocked with threats of a custody case. What finally helped end this spiral was when Sam asked Sandra in a letter to tell him what her main concerns and fears were when their son was with him and promised that he would try to address them one by one in a letter. He also reminded her that although they were divorced and he didn't have to do things her way, he did want her to be more comfortable with the time their son spent with him. Sam was so incensed by Sandra's behavior that he felt he couldn't control himself well enough to do this in person. But ignoring her concerns didn't help either. He'd felt so justified in his anger that he hadn't understood how his reaction had only made the situation much worse. He wrote the letter, following the model of the strategic letter outlined in chapter 10, and actually got a favorable response. As it turned out, Sandra felt so lost and upset being away from her son that she developed exaggerated worries, which Sam's eventual reassurance helped ease.

Raging Retaliator

Some individuals experience divorce as a betrayal so profound that their rage, panic, and fear threaten to engulf them. Their coping mechanisms are taxed to the hilt, and the ability to control their impulses and act rationally is severely impaired. Externalizing or acting out is the only way they can drain off their intolerable pain. These are the harassers, the screamers, the verbal abusers, and the slash-your-tire types. Their primary goal is revenge. They deflect their own pain at all costs, feel justified in their actions, and don't care about repercussions. They are out of control. One difficulty dealing with this type of person during and even after divorce is not recognizing the severity of their impairment. Often these behaviors represent more serious psychological problems. The mistake is to engage with them the way you did when you were married, that is, by over- or underreacting. The spouses of this type of person tend to be fighters themselves or peacemakers who allow themselves to be walked on in an effort to avoid further conflict.

I had a client whose ex-wife would call at all hours of the night and harass him about the woman he was dating. When he unplugged the phone, she just pushed the redial button and called his answering machine, sometimes 30 times in an hour. When he finally got an unlisted phone number, she started to call his office and the office of the woman he was dating. As I listened each week to his accounts of new incidents, often involving unprovoked yelling and screaming in front of the children, I was puzzled at how long he was letting things go on and how little he was doing to try to curb her behavior or protect himself. He described her as always having had a volatile personality and admitted that he typically tried to appease her to keep things from blowing up. Now that he was divorced, he was doing the same thing, not recognizing the abusive elements of her behavior.

If you are dealing with a raging retaliator, recognize that to a certain degree you are dealing with "craziness." You need to develop a strategy to deal with the problems such an individual creates. The key is to set limits, stand your ground, not respond to accusations or outrageous statements, and remove yourself from abusive situations. Don't try to interact with this type of person when he or she is out of control. Say that you are unwilling to engage in conversation under these circumstances. Don't retaliate but communicate what you will do to protect yourself. Arrange things so as to minimize the amount of contact you have, and take appropriate measures to protect yourself: get a restraining order, change your phone number, garage your car. Talk to you lawyer, a mental health professional, or the police if you fear for your safety.

Appeaser

Appeasers want to avoid arguments at any price. It is easier for them to say yes and do what they want later than to face disagreement. They may not return children at the agreed-upon time, cancel plans to care for children, or not pay for something they said they would. They create havoc by default, by omission rather than direct confrontation. One way to deal with them is to formulate concrete plans and give the appeaser plenty of opportunity to raise objections. Ask if your former spouse has any reservations or foresees any problems about a plan. Restate the agreement or put it in writing. Reconfirm. In some sense you have to work around people who do not hold up their end of the bargain. In addition, try to reduce your interdependence. What doesn't work is lecturing and criticizing. It may be easier in the long run, for example, to pay for the soccer camp yourself or have a back-up babysitting plan than to count on the other for something you really need.

Restricting Spouse

By the time the divorce is final, blatantly hostile acts are not so common. The anger and bitterness usually go underground and are frequently expressed in an attitude of, "I don't have to help her after what she has done to me" or "I don't have to adjust my life for him." This type of spouse is not directly confrontational or volatile. A thin veil of civility often hides the underlying tension which is frequently manifest in the restriction of visitation by a custodial parent. In its worst form, visits are changed or denied capriciously or activities are scheduled during visits. It is as if the other parent just doesn't matter, except when it is convenient for the custodial parent. This can be an extremely frustrating situation for the noncustodial parent, who often has little recourse. The problem frequently escalates because the outrage and increased demands of the noncustodial parent are used as justification by the uncooperative spouse to continue to restrict visits with the children. Rational or not, these custodial parents feel justified in their actions.

Sometimes time heals the underlying anger. Sometimes restricting spouses begin to have good things happen in their own lives and become more cooperative. Sometimes new spouses come into the picture and act as buffers.

Patience is the key word. These can be very trying situations. You may not be able to do much, even through court, although legal action may be the only hope you do have. Put your energy into making the best of the time you do have with the children. Get plenty of support from friends. Follow the principles outlined in chapter 2 about being unconditionally constructive; go out of your way to think of ways to extend cooperation. Try reaching out by writing a "strategic letter," described in chapter 10. Consider consulting a psychologist to help you assess the situation. Sometimes the restricting parent has underlying psychological problems or severe anxiety in separating even temporarily from the children. Powerful fears, rather than anger, may be underlying the restriction of access to the children. Above all, make easing the tension one of your goals. Sometimes mediation can help.

I recently received a call from a client whose divorce I had mediated 6 years before. I recalled that her husband was very angry and uncooperative at the time. She said his anger seemed to have festered over the years, even though the children live with him during the school year and he has remarried. She told me how arranging time with the children was like pulling teeth. Since she and her ex had been having so many continuing problems, she had hoped he would come back into mediation, but he refused. She felt that she had tried everything to get him to be more cooperative.

> I have to let go of the wish that he will let go. He might never. I can't continue to ask him to try to work together to coparent. He has already indicated that he is not interested. He is still angry that I left him. I was the adoring student and he was the professor. When I took him off that pedestal and left, he never forgave me. Last year I wrote a loving letting-go letter saying how I had worked on forgive-

ness. He sent it back with something nasty scrawled on the envelope.

JOYCE, *divorced 5 years*

Undermining Parent

Let's say that you suspect your former spouse is telling the children negative things about you, involving them in your disagreements or painting an inaccurate picture of what you have said or done. The parent may have told the children, for example, that you refused to pay for summer camp or orthodontia or that you are not using the child support money for them. The first thing I would ask is whether you have tried to talk to your spouse about keeping the children out of your disagreements. If you have, did you approach it according to the principles of being nonaccusatory and unconditionally constructive, as described throughout this book? The way you approach an issue like this makes a big difference in whether you will get your spouse to listen. If you haven't been able to agree not to put the children in the middle of your conflicts, consider giving it another try now. The timing may be better. Make a plea on behalf of the children rather than attacking your ex for poor behavior. Try approaching the topic by following the mediation principles summarized here:

1. Describe how the children are affected and what their reactions are to being caught in the middle, not whose fault the disagreement is.
2. Compliment your ex on his or her concern and effort as a parent, and emphasize your mutual concerns for the children's well-being.
3. Emphasize how you would like to move forward and ask if the past can be put to rest. Admit that you have both made mistakes.
4. Offer a suggestion for future solutions; for example: "Regardless of fault, can't we please both make a pact not to talk negatively about each other to the children or put them in the middle of our disagreements?"

These undermining behaviors are so destructive to children that you might even want to make a written pact. Here is an example of what you could write:

> We, Mike and Jill Smith, agree in good faith to protect our children from our disagreements and disputes. They feel confused, don't know whom to believe, feel they have to take sides, and don't feel free to love us both. We therefore agree not to say negative things about each other to the children or to discuss our disagreements with them. Specifically, we will make an effort not to say or discussing the following things in front of or with the children:
>
> 1.
>
> 2.
>
> 3.
>
> Signed: _____ Mother _____ Father
>
> Date:_____

If you don't have good enough communication or goodwill to get agreement on this issue, concentrate your efforts on protecting the children and getting them out of the middle. Explain to them that you and their other parent have many disagreements and different perceptions of what happens. Tell them that it is not their job to carry messages and that they have a right to ask their parents to call each other directly. Help the children learn how to protect themselves from listening to things that upset them by stating their discomfort when the other parent says negative things about you. Help them say that they don't want to be involved or hear this kind of talk. Don't degrade the other parent for degrading you. Talk to your children about the problem in terms of misunderstandings and different perceptions.

Competitive Parent

Competitive feelings between divorced parents are quite common. To some extent they are generated by situations that are inherent in divorce itself. Competition can range from subtle, often unconscious, words or deeds to calculated activities in order to be the favored parent. For one thing, with daily contact and collaboration gone, you don't know what goes on in the other household or what the other parent discusses with the children. The other parent's relationship to the children is now a private matter. This is bound to feel threatening if there is not an atmosphere of mutual acceptance and support. Also, real differences frequently exist in lifestyle and economic status, which can be very threatening to the parent with less.

Competition becomes a serious problem when it is expressed through put-downs of the other parent, condemnation of his or her values, manipulation to limit the other parent's time with the children, or an out-and-out material battle for their affections. Even if it is subtle, the children will sense the competition, and it will make them uncomfortable. They may begin to feel that it is their responsibility to take care of your feelings and make sure that neither of you feels slighted. The burden for being fair to both parents and making everyone happy begins to fall on them. If competition is blatant, children will figure this out and will soon take advantage of you both, playing each of you off against the other to get what they want.

Rather than compete with or undermine the other parent, strengthen your own relationship with the children. Spend more quality time with your children, talk with them more, listen better, and spend more time together doing things that they like to do. Concentrate on what is good about your relationship with the children. Write down its strengths, and think about the memories of things you all enjoyed in the past. Make a plan for your relationship to be special in some new way. Invent new family traditions even if the financial resources are different.

Born-Again Parent or Super Dad

In many divorcing families the less involved parent, usually the father, has a sudden turnabout and becomes the great parent the other had always wished for. This new level of parental interest can be confusing, troubling, and even threatening to a mother whose life revolves around the children. The phenomenon occurs more frequently than you might suspect. During marriage, many men let their wives take over all parenting responsibilities or feel somewhat shut out by a wife's involvement with the children. After divorce, as they take on new responsibilities for the children apart from the influence of their wives, their relationship with their children takes on a character of its own. These fathers become more emotionally involved and more confident in themselves as parents. They find out how much they enjoy the children and start pressing for more time and responsibility.

While there are obvious benefits for the children in having more quality time with their dad, a mother is likely to be resentful of this Johnny-come-lately to the parenting scene and resist the father's requests for more time with the children. As difficult as it is to be a mother in this situation, try not to deny your former mate's requests. This can be a great act of generosity on your part. To help with your anger, concentrate on the benefits to the children. Think about how you might have liked more attention from your father as a child, and think about how the other parent's increased participation might be a benefit for you. Will you now have more time to enroll in that class you have always thought about, pursue your career, or take a trip?

Try to find creative ways for your former spouse to increase his or her participation. This does not always mean that the children should live with that parent more of the time. Extra participation can take the form of coaching, becoming more involved in the children's hobbies and interests, or providing transportation to these activities.

Uninvolved Parent

The parent who withdraws, drops out, or fails to show up for visits isn't always an uninterested parent but may be a parent discouraged and in pain. Try to understand why the involvement has dropped off. Many noncustodial parents withdraw from their children because of the pain of saying good-bye and seeing the children infrequently. They may not feel that they really have a role, or they may feel rejected if the visits are awkward and don't go smoothly.

Even though you may be angry, attacking your ex's irresponsibility doesn't solve the problem. Many of these parents are caught up in their own distress and don't really see how painful and disappointing their absence is to their children. Still others may not have the maturity or capacity to be responsible or deal with their children's stress and reactions to the visits.

If a spouse was a caring, though perhaps not very involved parent, it is better to try to be supportive and encourage participation rather than lecture about how all the responsibility is falling on you. Without overtones of blame, explain how disappointed the children feel when a visit is canceled and how they ask about the absent parent. *Let the other parent know how much he or she is valued and missed by the children.* For the sake of the children, try to be supportive of a fragile parent.

Sometimes you may be unable to reinvolve a parent who has dropped out, and you will have to face the fact that you do not have a coparent. You will need to help your children cope with their feelings of loss and rejection. Help them understand that it is not their fault, and allow them to express their sadness and anger. Explain that right now the other parent has problems that prevent him or her from giving the love and attention they need. Help them to feel valued and lovable even though the absent parent isn't giving that love. Children who have lost a parent can benefit from seeing a therapist.

Sometimes a parent drops out of the picture because of the other parent's animosity. If noncustodial parents try to maintain a relationship with their children but are continually harassed about money or other things whenever they come to pick up the children, they may eventually give up:

> My father left my mother with four kids when I was nine. Then he married his secretary. She never forgave him. Whenever he tried to

call or see us she'd scream at him about money and threaten to see him in court. Many times, she made me call him on the phone and coached me to tell him he was a son of a bitch because we had no food in the house. Pretty soon he stopped visiting and moved away. I didn't see my father again until I was eighteen. I now know it wasn't the way he wanted it to be. The things my mother said about him weren't true. She was cruel. I don't know if I can forgive her.

ELLEN, *age 30*

Carnival Parent

We are all familiar with the stereotypical weekend-dad (or mom) syndrome. These parents try to compensate for being away and attempt to "buy" the children's affections. They overdo activities and indulge the children whenever they are together. This, in turn, puts the custodial parent in the position of the bad guy or the disciplinarian who compensates for the other parent's extravagances. If you are confrontational or try to compete with the out-of-home parent, the children will learn to play you off against each other. Try to discuss with the other parent how this affects the children—their fatigue, the inflated demands they start to place on you, and so on. Let the other parent know how much he or she is valued and appreciated by the children for the love and companionship given to them, not the material objects. Be willing to consider a schedule change that might help the other parent feel more involved in the children's lives.

If you are the out-of-home parent, try to relax and think about the *quality* of your relationship with the children. Concentrate on how you relate, not just what you do. Try to stop compensating for not being there all the time. Many divorced parents feel guilty and indulge the children. Weekend parents are particularly prone to this. They say yes when they should say no, they give money when they should set limits. Children need limits and time for ordinary activities with each parent. Even though they like all the activities and treats, they will sense that you are overdoing it.

STEPPARENTS: HELP OR HINDRANCE?

The addition of a stepparent changes the dynamics of the postdivorce family. A stepparent can ease a tense situation by being a positive influence on the biological parent. Frequently stepparents help the parent take a more reasonable position toward a former mate. Sometimes they even become directly involved with logistical arrangements, thereby putting some distance between antagonistic ex-spouses.

Then again, a stepparent can create new problems and antagonisms that weren't there before. A stepparent who is eager to develop a relationship with the children and strengthen the bonds of the new marriage may come on too strong and take too active a role, which may unintentionally threaten the biological parent. A stepparent may actively compete with the biological parent out of insecurity and jealousy. Instead of taking a more neutral stand toward the hostility between the ex-spouses, a stepparent may side with the new spouse and even encourage a stronger position against the former mate: "You mean you let her get away with this? You're crazy. Look what she is doing to you!" The stepparent, accepting the new mate's one-sided view of the ex, sometimes becomes even more outraged at the ex than the spouse is. By the same token, a stepparent may give a passive parent the support needed to stand up to a difficult ex.

Competition can develop between a stepparent and the biological parent, particularly if a stepparent comes into the picture prematurely or when one parent already feels worried about losing the children's affections. It takes time to adjust to the ways in which being a parent changes after divorce. If there hasn't been time for everyone in the family to become comfortable with two parental households, the entry of a stepparent can add a new level of threat to the biological parent.

Remarriage presents many challenges when there are children from previous relationships. It can affect the dynamics between former mates in positive or negative ways. Stepfamilies are very complex, and I have highlighted only a few of the issues that relate to the changing relationship between the biological parents. Books and resources are listed in the appendix.

In sum, one of the questions you need to clarify in dealing with a difficult former spouse is whether the problematic behavior creates a hardship for you—or for the children. In many instances the behaviors are designed to hurt and frustrate you, and your ex might be quite responsible with the children out of your presence. Many irritations are best tolerated and not made into an issue. As I have suggested, when the other parent's lack of responsibility hurts your children, try to help them depersonalize the other parent's behavior. Help them understand and accept that parent's limitations in a supportive way. Unfortunately, with these difficult ex-spouses there are going to be some frustrating situations that you will have very little ability to affect.

Moving Toward the Light

The past is but a beginning of a beginning, and all that
is and has been is but the twilight of the dawn.

H. G. WELLS

There is a Sufi tale about a group of people who have to walk
through a room of demons. The room is dark save for a streak of
light under the door at the other end. The demons all have heads
representing a person's worst fears, and they scream out what
each person is afraid of most: "You will fail . . . no one will
love you . . . you will lose all your money." Only a few people
make their way through the darkness to safety. Later, they tell their
secret: "There are two things you must do—keep on moving and
never lose sight of the light."

Throughout this book I have spoken about moving toward the
light by trying to handle your pain in a healthy way, act constructively, and make decisions for the greater good of the whole
family. Walking through a courtroom door or signing legal papers
is not the end of the journey if you are a parent; you must persevere
on this path and be prepared for the bends in the road.

In giving you an overview of the divorce process, I have tried
to help you become aware of the future you create by the decisions
and choices you make now. I have urged you to strive for healing
rather than blame, understanding rather than injury, and coopera-

tion rather than competition. I have tried to help you develop skills to resolve your conflicts and work together as parents.

Being civilized is a choice that we all must make if we care about future generations. Divorce has dramatically altered the family as we once knew it, and family relationships today exist in many forms. Children create enduring ties within and between families, even when the legal bonds are broken. Right now you are focused on being separate and getting as far away from your mate as you can. You don't want to and can't even begin to think about the ways in which your lives will remain interconnected.

But what you have created through your marriage shifts to your children. Over time, these ties transcend the personal drama of your divorce. Fourteen years ago, when I divorced and was angry and hurting, I couldn't begin to grasp this concept. Recently, I had an experience that brought it home to me, when I attended my former father-in-law's funeral.

It was a hard decision whether to go back east for the funeral. I knew I would be welcome. But did I belong? It had been 14 years since I had seen most of my ex's family, other than his parents. During the service I thought back on what my father-in-law had meant to me. I thought about how he bought us our first car as a graduation present. We drove across the country in that car to a place that was to become home. When my mother died, my former in-laws helped me bury her: they were the ones who stayed with me in the small Florida apartment for 5 days as, piece by piece, we sorted through her belongings. Dave Gold was my daughter's grandpa, but he was also part of my past, part of my history. And I saw that divorce didn't change that.

Even more striking was watching my daughter during the eulogy as her father described the man who was her grandfather. I could not help but see the bloodlines and the family to which my daughter was undeniably connected. These were her roots. I don't think I really understood this before, or even wanted to. It is one thing to know a child has a family apart from you, it is another thing to see it and experience it. And I guess through her I also remain part of that family.

I don't know how you will look back on this traumatic period of your life or how time will heal the wounds in your families. Someday you will make peace with your marriage. In the meantime, just remember, the pain of this crisis is not all that this is about. One of my clients put it in perspective this way:

> My grandmother died of Alzheimer's. For the last two years of her life she was just awful. Her personality had completely changed. But that is not the way I want to remember her. I feel the same way about my marriage.

Notes

1. A New Way

1. Divorce ceremonies are beginning to be developed. Check with the churches or synagogues in your community. See Lori H. Gordon and Morris Gordon, "A Format for an Ethical and Emotional Divorce," *Journal of Pastoral Care* 38, no. 4 (1984), and Florence Kaslow, "The Divorce Ceremony: A Healing Strategy," in *101 Favorite Family Therapy Interventions*, eds. T. Nelson and T. Trepper (New York: Haworth Press, 1992).
2. Joan B. Kelly, "Is Mediation Less Expensive? Comparison of Mediated and Adversarial Divorce Costs," *Mediation Quarterly* 8, no. 1 (1991).

3. Timing: The Emotions of Ending a Marriage

1. Many authorities have defined the progression through divorce. This is an adaptation of the seven-stage model of Sheila Kessler from *The American Way of Divorce* (New York: Nelson Hall, 1975). Kessler's stages were Disillusionment, Erosion, Detachment, Physical Separation, Mourning, Second Adolescence, Exploration, and Hard Work. Anthropologist Paul Bohannan describes the emotional, legal, economic, coparental, community and psychic divorce in "The Six Stations of Divorce," in *Divorce and After: An Analysis of the Emotional and Social Problems of Divorce*, ed. P. Bohannan (New York: Doubleday, 1970).
2. K. Kressel, N. Jafee, M. Weinglass, and M. Deutsch, "A Typology of Divorcing Couples: Implications for Mediation and the Divorce Process," *Family Process* 19 (1980).

4. The Seven Keys to a Constructive Divorce

1. When one speaks of a constructive divorce, it is important to make the distinction between the process of divorce and the outcome. I describe the elements of a constructive process that would logically lead to constructive outcomes. Kenneth Kressel, *The Process of Divorce* (New York: Basic Books, 1985) identifies the eight criteria for a constructive outcome in a divorce settlement negotiation as (1) resolution of all relevant issues, (2) tolerable financial and emotional costs, (3) agreements that are fair and equitable, (4) agreements that protect the rights and welfare of children, (5) satisfaction with the overall results, (6) the couple experiences a sense of "ownership" of the agreement, (7) compliance with the terms of the agreement, and (8) spouses are better able to cooperate.

5. Healing

1. Ann Kaiser Stearns, *Living through Personal Crisis* (Chicago: Thomas Moore Press, 1984).
2. Bernie S. Siegal, *Peace, Love and Healing* (New York: Harper & Row, 1989); Norman Cousins, *The Healing Heart* (New York: Avon, 1984).
3. Shakti Gawain, *Visualization* (New York: Bantam, 1982).

6. Helping Children

1. Judith Wallerstein and Sandra Blakeslee, *Second Chances: Men, Women, and Children a Decade After Divorce* (New York: Ticknor & Fields, 1989).
2. Judith Wallerstein and Joan B. Kelly, *Surviving the Break-Up: How Children and Parents Cope with Divorce* (New York: Basic Books, 1980).
3. Joan B. Kelly, "Longer-Term Adjustment in Children of Divorce," *Journal of Family Psychology* 2 (2 December 1988).
4. Judith Wallerstein, Keynote Address for the Association of Family Conciliation Courts 1988 Spring Conference, *Conciliation Court Review*, 27, no. 1 (1989).
5. Judith Wallerstein, "Children of Divorce: The Psychological Tasks of the Child," *American Journal of Orthopsychiatry* 53, no. 2 (1983); this also appears in a different form in *Second Chances*.

7. Parenting Plans: The Transition to an Unmarried Family

1. Joan B. Kelly, "Longer-Term Adjustment in Children of Divorce," *Journal of Family Psychology* 2, no. 2 (1988), p. 137.
2. Constance R. Ahrons, "Redefining the Divorced Family: A Conceptual Framework," *Social Work* 25 (1980).
3. Susan Steinman, "Joint Custody: What We Know, What We Have Yet to Learn, and the Judicial and Legislative Implications," in *Joint Custody and Shared Parenting*, ed. Jay Folberg (Washington, DC: Bureau of National Affairs, 1984). Sandra Vogly and Craig Everett, "Joint Custody Reconsidered: Systemic Criteria for Mediation," *Journal of Divorce* 8, no. 3/4 (1985).
4. Constance R. Ahrons and Roy H. Rogers, *Divorcing Families* (New York: Norton, 1987).
5. Joan B. Kelly, "Mediated and Adversarial Divorce Resolution Processes: An Analysis of Post Divorce Outcomes," final report prepared for the Fund for Research in Dispute Resolution (December 1990). In this study of approximately 400 divorcing men and women, Kelly found that 2 years after divorce, the differences in the level of conflict between the adversarial and mediation group disappeared as the conflict subsided in the adversarial group and cooperation increased in both groups.
6. Kelly, "Longer-Term Adjustment in Children"; W. Glenn Clingempeel and N. Dicken Rappucci, "Joint Custody After Divorce: Major Issues and Goals for Research," *Psychological Bulletin* 91, no. 1 (1984); Deborah Leupnitz, "A Comparison of Maternal, Paternal, and Joint Custody: Understanding the Varieties of Post-Divorce Family Life," *Journal of Divorce* 9 (1986).
7. Kelly, "Longer-Term Adjustment in Children."
8. M. Zaslow, "Differences in Children's Responses to Parental Divorce," *American Journal of Orthopsychiatry* 59, no. 1 (1989).
9. Joan Kelly, invited address 1987 American Psychological Association; New York, reported in the *APA Monitor* (Jan. 1988).
10. Joan Kelly, "Examining Resistance to Joint Custody," in *Joint Custody and Shared Parenting*, ed. Jay Folberg (Washington, DC: Bureau of National Affairs, 1984).
11. R. McKinnon and J. Wallerstein, "Joint Custody and the Preschool Child," *Conciliation Courts Review* 25, no. 2 (1987).
12. M. Brotsky, S. Steinmann, and S. Zemmelman, "Joint Custody

Through Mediation Reviewed: Parents Assess Their Situation 18 Months Later," *Conciliation Court Review* 26, no. 2 (1988).

13. Judith Wallerstein and Sandra Blakeslee, *Second Chances* (New York: Ticknor & Fields, 1989).

14. D. A. Leupnitz, *Child Custody: A Study of Children After Divorce* (Lexington, MA: Lexington Books, 1982); Leupnitz, "Comparison of Material, Paternal, and Joint Custody" (1986); S. Steinman, "The Experiences of Children in a Joint Custody Arrangement: A Report of a Study," *American Journal of Orthopsychiatry* 51, no. 3 (1981).

15. Janet Johnston and Linda Campbell, *The Impasses of Divorce* (New York: Free Press, 1988).

16. Steinman, "Joint Custody: What We Know."

8. Parenting as a Partnership: The Working Relationship

1. The ideas in this chapter about parenting relationships as working business partnerships are based on the work of Isolina Ricci in the book *Mom's House, Dad's House: Making Shared Custody Work* (New York: Macmillan, 1981).

9. Border Skirmishes Don't Have to Turn into Nuclear War: How to Handle Conflict

1. Thomas Crum, *The Magic of Conflict* (New York: Simon & Schuster, 1987); Donald Saposnek, "Aikido: A Systems Model for Maneuvering in Mediation," *Mediation Quarterly* 14/15, 1986–1987.

2. Morton Deutsch, *The Resolution of Conflict: Constructive and Destructive Processes* (New Haven, CT: Yale University Press, 1973).

11. Diagnose the Dispute: What Is This Fight Really About?

1. "Getting present" is a technique developed by Jim Melamed in which he asks parties in mediation to clarify whether they are, in fact, arguing over past issues or trying to create future agreements.

12. Getting Ready to Negotiate

1. This questionnaire is based on the ideas about readiness to do parenting "business" with your spouse that appear in Isolina Ricci, *Mom's*

House, Dad's House: Making Shared Custody Work (New York: Macmillan, 1981). See chapter 3 of that book for additional self-surveys to assess where you stand.

2. William O'Hanlon, "Solution Oriented Therapy: A Megatrend in Psychotherapy," in *Developing Ericksonian Therapy: State of the Art*, ed. J. Zeig and S. Lankton (New York: Brunner/Mazel, 1988).

3. There are many variations on this two-dimension model of conflict-handling behavior. Fisher and Ury in *Getting to Yes* (New York: Houghton Mifflin, 1981) describe the differences between a hard and soft negotiator.

4. This analysis is adapted from the work of Jay Hall appearing in Joseph P. Folger and Marshall S. Poole, *Working Through Conflict: A Communication Perspective* (Glenview, IL: Scott, Foresman, 1984); and Alan Filey, *Interpersonal Conflict Resolution* (Glenview, IL: Scott, Foresman, 1975). The two-dimensional model also appears in *Conflict and Conflict Management* by Kenneth Thomas in *Handbook of Industrial Psychology*, ed. Marvin Dunnette (Chicago: Rand McNally, 1976).

5. These sources of power are adapted from Joan Kelly, "Empowerment and Power Imbalance," a presentation to the Academy of Family Mediators Annual Conference, San Rafael, Ca, 1984.

6. Some of these ideas were adapted from Herb Cohen, *You Can Negotiate Anything* (Secavcus, NJ: Lyle Stuart, 1980) and Chester Karass, *Give and Take: The Complete Guide to Negotiating Strategies* (New York: Thomas Cromwell, 1974).

13. The Fundamentals of Win–Win Negotiation

1. Roger Fisher and William Ury, *Getting to Yes* (New York: Houghton Mifflin, 1981).

2. John Haynes and Gretchen Haynes, *Mediating Divorce* (San Francisco: Jossey-Bass, 1989).

14. Working Toward a Settlement

1. Morton Deutsch, *The Resolution of Conflict: Constructive and Destructive Processes* (New Haven: Yale University Press, 1973).

2. These bargaining strategies are adapted from Roger Fisher and William Ury, *Getting to Yes* (New York: Houghton Mifflin, 1981).

15. Mediation

1. Christine Leick, "Guidelines for Mediation/Attorney Cooperation," *Mediation Quarterly* 23 (Spring 1989).
2. Jessica Pearson and Nancy Thoennes, "Divorce Mediation: Reflections on a Decade of Research"; Joan Kelly and Lynn Gigy, "Divorce Mediation: Characteristics of Clients and Outcomes," in *Mediation Research: The Process and Effectiveness of Third Party Interventions*, ed. K. Kressel and D. Pruitt (San Francisco: Jossey-Bass, 1987).
3. Joan B. Kelly, "Mediated and Adversarial Divorce Resolution Process: An Analysis of Post Divorce Outcomes," Final Report prepared for the Fund for Research in Dispute Resolution (Dec. 1990).
4. Joan B. Kelly, "Mediated and Adversarial Divorce Resolution Process"; Jessica Pearson, "Equity of Mediated Divorce Agreements," *Mediation Quarterly* 9 (Winter 1992).
5. Joan B. Kelly, "Mediated and Adversarial Divorce Resolution Process."
6. It is beyond the scope of this chapter to deal with this complex and difficult issue. I refer you to Steve Erickson and Marilyn McKnight, "Mediating Spousal Abuse Cases," *Mediation Quarterly* 7, no. 4 (Summer 1990) to see under what circumstances it would be appropriate to mediate when there has been abuse and how the abuse issues would be handled. This entire issue of *Mediation Quarterly* is on the topic of mediation and family violence.

16. Lawyers and the Legal Process: What to Expect and How to Reduce the Escalation of Conflict

1. I wish to thank Robert Benjamin, Herb Trubo, and Josh Kadish for their help with this chapter. They all bring the special perspective of being both family law attorneys and mediators.
2. Kenenth Kressel, *The Process of Divorce* (New York: Basic Books, 1985). Undue competitiveness was the chief complaint about opposing counsel.
3. Ibid.
4. Kressel (1985) cites a study by G. R. Williams, *Legal Negotiation and Settlement* (St. Paul: West, 1983), which indicates that 58 percent of the "cooperation"-oriented attorneys were rated effective as compared to 25 percent of the "competition"-oriented attorneys.

17. Conflicts After Divorce: Are You Emotionally Divorced?

1. Janet Johnston and Linda Campbell, *Impasses of Divorce: The Dynamics and Resolution of Family Conflict* (New York: Free Press, 1988).
2. The ritual for welcoming the new and letting go of the old was developed by Stephen Gilligan, Ph.D. It is used with his permission.
3. Sun Bear, *Walk in Balance: The Path to Healthy, Happy, Harmonious Living* (New York: Prentice Hall, 1989).
4. Lewis Smedes, *Forgive and Forget: Healing the Hurts We Don't Deserve* (San Francisco: Harper and Row, 1984).

18. Difficult Spouses/Difficult Ex's: Be Part of the Solution Instead of the Problem

1. Kenneth Kressel, Frances Butler-DeFreitas, Samuel G. Forlenza, Cynthia Wilcox, "Research in Contested Custody Mediation: An Illustration of the Case Study Method," *Mediation Quarterly* 24 (1989).
2. Robert Bramson, *Coping with Difficult People* (New York: Dell, 1981).

Resources

Academy of Family Mediators
P.O. Box 10501
Eugene, Oregon 97440
(503) 345-1205

Association of Family Conciliation Courts
329 West Wilson Street
Madison, Wisconsin 53703
(608) 251-4001

Child Find
P.O. Box 277
New Paltz, New York 12561
(800) I Am Lost

StepFamily Association of America
602 E. Joppa Road
Baltimore, Maryland 21204
(301) 823-7570

Parents without Partners
8807 Colesville Road
Silver Spring, Maryland 20910
(301) 588-9354

General References and Bibliography

Melvin Belli, and Mel Krantzler, *Divorcing*. New York: St. Martin's Press, 1988.

Robert Bramson, *Coping with Difficult People*. New York: Dell, 1981.

Herb Cohen, *You Can Negotiate Anything*. Secaucus, NJ: Lyle Stuart, 1980.

Thomas Crum, *The Magic of Conflict*. New York: Simon & Schuster, 1987.

Morton Deutsch, *The Resolution of Conflict: Constructive and Destructive Processes*. New Haven: Yale University Press, 1973.

Richard Emery, *Marriage, Divorce, and Children's Adjustment*. Newbury Park, CA: Sage, 1988.

Steve Erickson and Marilyn Erickson, *Family Mediation Casebook*. New York: Brunner/Mazel, 1988.

Alan Filey, *Interpersonal Conflict Resolution*. Glenview, IL: Scott, Foresman, 1975.

Roger Fisher and Scott Brown, *Getting Together: Building a Relationship That Gets to Yes*. Boston: Houghton Mifflin, 1988.

Roger Fisher and William Ury, *Getting to Yes*. Boston: Houghton Mifflin, 1981.

Jay Folberg, ed., *Joint Custody and Shared Parenting*, 2nd ed. New York: Guilford (in press).

Jay Folberg and Ann Milne, eds., *Divorce Mediation: Theory and Practice*. New York: Guilford, 1988.

Joseph P. Folger and Marshall S. Poole, *Working Through Conflict: A Communication Perspective*. Glenview, IL: Scott, Foresman, 1984.

Frank Furstenberg and Andrew Cherlin, *Divided Families: What Happens to Children When Parents Part*. Cambridge: Harvard University Press, 1991.

Stephen Gilligan, *Therapeutic Trances: The Cooperation Principle in Ericksonian Hypnotherapy*. New York: Brunner/Mazel, 1987.

Lois Gold, "Interdisciplinary Team Mediation," *Mediation Quarterly* 6 (1984).

Lois Gold, "Reflections on the Transition from Therapist to Mediator," *Mediation Quarterly* 9 (1985).

John Haynes and Gretchen Haynes, *Mediating Divorce*. San Francisco: Jossey-Bass, 1989.

Marla Isaacs, *The Difficult Divorce*. New York: Basic Books, 1986.

Gerald Jamplosky, *Teach Only Love: The Seven Principles of Attitudinal Healing*. New York: Bantam Books, 1983.

Janet Johnston and Linda Campbell, *The Impasses of Divorce: The Dynamics and Resolution of Family Conflict*. New York: Free Press, 1988.

Neil Kalter, *Growing Up with Divorce: Helping Your Child Avoid Immediate and Later Problems*. New York: Free Press, 1990.

Chester Karass, *Give and Take: The Complete Guide to Negotiating Strategies*. New York: Thomas Y. Crowell, 1974.

F. W. Kaslow and L. L. Schwartz, *Dynamics of Divorce: A Life Cycle Perspective*. New York: Brunner/Mazel, 1987.

Kenneth Kressel, *The Process of Divorce: How Professionals and Couples Negotiate Settlements*. New York: Basic Books, 1985.

K. Kressel, D. Pruitt, and associates, eds., *Mediation Effectiveness: The Process and Effectiveness of Third Party Intervention*. San Francisco: Jossey-Bass, 1989.

Deborah A. Leupnitz, *Child Custody: A Study of Children After Divorce*. Lexington, MA: Lexington Books, 1982.

Ann Milne, "Model Standard of Practice for Family and Divorce Mediation," *Mediation Quarterly* 8 (1985).

Isolina Ricci, *Mom's House, Dad's House: Making Shared Custody Work*. New York: Macmillan, 1981.

David Rice and Joy Rice, *Living Through Divorce*. New York: Guilford, 1986.

Donald Saposnek, *Mediating Child Custody Disputes*. San Francisco: Jossey-Bass, 1983.

Sidney Simon and Suzanne Simon, *Forgiveness: How to Make Peace with Your Past and Get On with Your Life*. New York: Warner, 1990.

Marsha Sinetar, *Elegant Choices, Healing Choices*. New York: Paulist Press, 1988.

Lewis Smedes, *Forgive and Forget: Healing the Hurts We Don't Deserve*. San Francisco: Harper & Row, 1984.

Graham Spanier, *Parting*. Beverly Hills, CA: Sage, 1987.

Ann Kaiser Stearns, *Living through Personal Crisis*. Chicago: Thomas Moore Press, 1984.

Timothy Stephen, "Post-Break Up Distress: A Reformation of the Attachment Construct," *Journal of Divorce* 8, no. 1 (1985).

Diane Vaughan, *Uncoupling: Turning Points in Intimate Relationships*. New York: Oxford University Press, 1986.

Judith Wallerstein and Sandra Blakeslee, *Second Chances: Men, Women, and Children a Decade After Divorce*. New York: Ticknor & Fields, 1989.

Judith Wallerstein and Joan B. Kelly, *Surviving the Break-Up: How Children and Parents Cope with Divorce*. New York: Basic Books, 1980.

Robert Weiss, *Marital Separation: Coping with the End of a Marriage and the Transition to Being Single Again*. New York: Basic Books, 1975.

Lenore Weitzman, *The Divorce Revolution*. New York: Free Press, 1985.

Jeffrey Zeig and Stephen Lankton, ed., *Developing Ericksonian Therapy*. New York: Brunner/Mazel, 1988.

Suggested Readings

Coping with Divorce

Melvin Belli and Mel Krantzler, *Divorcing*. New York: St. Martin's Press, 1988.

M. Colgrove, W. Bloomfield, and P. McWilliams, *How to Survive the Loss of Love*. New York: Bantam, 1977.

Diane Fassel, *Growing Up Divorced: A Road to Healing for Adult Children of Divorce*. New York: Simon & Schuster, 1991.

Bruce Fisher, *Rebuilding: When Your Relationship Ends*. San Luis Obispo, CA: Impact Publishers, 1981.

Phyliss Gillis, *Days Like This*. New York: Penguin, 1987.

Marcia Hootman and Patt Perkins, *How to Forgive Your Ex-Husband and Get On with Your Life*. New York: Warner, 1985.

Sandra Kahn, *The Ex-Wife Syndrome*. New York: Random House, 1991.

Daphne Rose Kingma, *Coming Apart: Why Relationships End and How to Live Through the Ending of Yours*. New York: Fawcett Ballantine, 1987.

Barry Lubetkin and Elena Oumano, *Bailing Out: The Healthy Way to Get Out of a Bad Relationship and Survive*. New York: Prentice-Hall, 1991.

Scott Nelson, *Lost Lovers, Found Friends: Getting Over a Romance Without Losing a Friend*. New York: Fireside, 1991.

Abagail Trafford, *Crazy Time*. New York: Harper & Row, 1982.

Anne N. Walther, *Divorce Hangover: A Step-by-Step Prescription for Creating a Bright Future After Your Marriage Ends*. New York: Pocket Books, 1991.

Children and Parenting

Edward Beal and Gloria Hochman, *Adult Children of Divorce: Breaking the Cycle and Finding Fulfillment in Love, Marriage, and Family.* New York: Delacorte Press, 1991.

Claire Berman, *Adult Children of Divorce Speak Out About Growing Up with and Moving Beyond Parental Divorce.* New York: Simon & Schuster, 1991.

Linda Bird Francke, *Growing Up Divorced: How to Help Your Children Cope with Every Stage from Infancy through Teens.* New York: Fawcett Crest, 1983.

Mirium Galper, *Joint Custody and Shared Parenting: Sharing Your Child Equally.* Philadelphia: Running Press, 1980.

Mirium Galper (Cohen), *Long Distance Parenting: A Guide for Divorced Parents.* New York: Signet, 1989.

Richard Gardner, *Parents' Book About Divorce.* New York: Bantam, 1979.

Neil Kalter, *Growing Up with Divorce: Helping Your Child Avoid Immediate and Later Problems.* New York: Free Press, 1990.

Vicki Lansky, *Divorcing Book for Parents.* New York: New American Library, 1989.

Eda LeShan, *What's Going to Happen to Me? When Parents Separate or Divorce.* New York: Aladdin Books, 1986.

Isolina Ricci, *Mom's House, Dad's House: Making Shared Custody Work.* New York: Macmillan, 1981.

Robert Shapiro, *Sharing the Children: How to Resolve Custody Problems and Get On with Your Life.* Bethesda, MD: Adler & Adler, 1988.

Doreen Virtue, *My Kids Don't Live with Me Anymore: Coping with the Custody Crisis.* Minneapolis: Compcare, 1988.

Judith Wallerstein and Sandra Blakeslee, *Second Chances, Men, Women, and Children a Decade After Divorce.* New York: Ticknor & Fields, 1989.

Mediation and Legal Matters

Judith Briles, *The Dollar and Sense of Divorce: Take Control of Your Financial Life Before, During, and After Divorce.* New York: Ballantine, 1991.

B. Clair and A. Daniele, *The Ex-Factor: The Complete Do It Yourself Post Divorce Handbook.* New York: Warner, 1987.

Roger Fisher and William Ury, *Getting to Yes.* Boston: Houghton Mifflin, 1981.

James Friedman, *The Divorce Handbook: Your Basic Guide to Divorce.* New York: Random House, 1982.

Martin Kranitz, *Getting Apart Together: The Couple's Guide to a Fair Divorce or Separation.* San Luis Obispo, CA: Impact Publishers, 1987.

Diane Neumann, *Divorce Mediation: How to Cut the Costs and Stress of Divorce.* New York: Henry Holt, 1989.

Karen Schneider and Myles Schneider, *Divorce Mediation: The Constructive New Way to End a Marriage without Big Legal Bills.* Washington, DC: Acropolis, 1984.

Daniel Sitarz, *Divorce Yourself: The National No-Fault, No Lawyer Divorce Handbook.* Carbondale, IL: Nova Publishing, 1990.

Alan B. Ungar, *Financial Self-Confidence: A Woman's Guide for the Suddenly Single.* Los Angeles: Lowell House, 1991.

Stepfamilies

Clare Berman, *Making It as a Step Parent: New Roles, New Rules* (updated edition). New York: Harper & Row, 1986.

Anne C. Berstein, *Yours Mine and Ours: How Families Change When Remarried Parents Have a Child Together.* New York: Norton, 1989.

Emily and John Vishner, *How to Win as a Stepfamily.* New York: Dembner Books, 1982.

Mark B. Rosin, *Step-fathers' Advice on Creating a New Family.* New York: Ballantine, 1987.

Karen Savage and Patricia Adams, *The Good Step Mother: A Practical Guide.* New York: Crown, 1988.

Index